AFFECTIONATELY YOURS:

The Civil War Home-Front Letters of the Ovid Butler Family

To Jim,
I wrote something
on your favorite topic!
Love
Barbara
October 2004

AFFECTIONATELY YOURS:

The Civil War Home-Front Letters of the Ovid Butler Family

Edited by
Barbara Butler Davis

With a Foreword by Alan T. Nolan

Indiana Historical Society Press
Indianapolis 2004

Printed in the United States of America

This book is a publication of the
Indiana Historical Society Press
450 West Ohio Street
Indianapolis, Indiana 46202-3269 USA
www.indianahistory.org
Telephone orders 1-800-447-1830
Fax orders 317-234-0562
Orders by e-mail shop.indianahistory.org

The paper in this publication meets the minimum requirements of American National Standard for Information Sciences—Permanence of Paper for Printed Library Materials, ANSI Z39.48-1984. ∞

Library of Congress Cataloging-in-Publication Data

Affectionately yours : the Civil War home front : letters of the Ovid Butler family / edited by Barbara Butler Davis.
   p. cm.
  Mostly letters written from 1863 to 1865 by Butler family members to Scot Butler while he served in the 33rd Indiana Infantry and the U.S. Signal Corps.
  Includes bibliographical references (p.) and index.
  ISBN 0-87195-175-4 (alk. paper)
   1. Butler, Ovid, 1801-1881—Correspondence. 2. Butler, Elizabeth Anne, 1818-1882—Correspondence. 3. Indiana—History—Civil War, 1861-1865—Personal narratives. 4. Indianapolis (Ind.)—Biography. 5. United States—History—Civil War, 1861-1865—Personal narratives. 6. Indianapolis (Ind.)— Social conditions—19th century. 7. Butler, Scot—Correspondence. 8. Butler family—Correspondence. 9. Butler family. I. Davis, Barbara Butler. II. Butler, Scot.

E601.A325 2004
973.7′092′277252—dc22

2004047401

For Rob
and for Dad
Capt. Ovid M. "Mack" Butler, USN, Ret.

Scot Butler was not a prolific writer, but in his unpublished "Recollections" he wrote of his experiences in the American Civil War and how they influenced him. As his family's letters show, Scot was more interested in his comrades' lives than in the war's battles and outcomes. His passionate story of a young soldier dying without the fulfillment of his last wish—a simple taste of clear spring water from home—reflects how Scot viewed the nature of a cruel and unforgiving war that, in his father Ovid's opinion, was being prosecuted by politicians unconcerned for the laws of God and man alike. The war divided God's brotherhood of man, which Ovid sought to foster as seen in this, Ovid's vision for his beloved Butler University, which he had largely created and to which, he hoped, Scot would safely return from the war to carry forth into the postwar era:

> My desire is that the Institution of the North Western Christian University occupy a position in the front ranks of human progress and Christian civilization as the Experiment and Advocate of the common rights of humanity without distinction on account of sex, race or color. [This] position recognizes the absolute equity before God and before the Law of the individual members of the human family.
>
> —Holograph draft note,
Women's Rights: a brief, undated.

Contents

Foreword xi

Preface xiii

Acknowledgments xv

Editorial Notes xvii

Introduction 1

Indiana Supports the War Effort 7

Family Photographs 15

The Civil War Letters 25

Postscript 145

Appendix 151

Name-Place Glossary 163

Bibliography 187

Genealogical Charts 195

Index 201

Foreword

Barbara Davis has presented us with an unusual book. The typical Civil War soldier's letter book is a collection of letters *from* the soldier in the field *to* his family back at home. This book is composed of a family's letters *to* the soldier. The soldier is young Scot Butler, the son of Ovid Butler and his wife Elizabeth Anne McOuat. These letters *from* the soldier's family contain the thoughts and activities of a committed Indiana Union family while Scot was at war.

The Indiana Butler family was no ordinary family. The family members—Scot's correspondents—were generally well educated, socially responsible, and civically concerned people. The soldier's father, Ovid, a member of a family native to New York State, had been an excellent practicing lawyer, and he was an educator and publisher. Very active in the Campbellite Disciples of Christ, he was a committed abolitionist and Republican. His wife's people, the McOuats, were originally Kentuckians and had actually owned slaves in that slave state and disposed of them on moving to free state Indiana in 1830.

Scot Butler did not share his father's zealous antislavery attitude, but he surely shared his family's ardent patriotism. Thus, he volunteered for federal service in the Civil War, enlisting in the Thirty-third Regiment, Indiana Volunteer Infantry on February 1, 1862, in Lexington, Kentucky. This regiment was originally raised in Indianapolis and mustered into federal service there on September 16, 1861. It promptly left Indiana for Kentucky and was garrisoned at Lexington, where the young man enlisted under the command of John C. Coburn. Although Scot's regiment was intended for infantry service, Gen. G. W. Morgan promptly ordered the regiment's colonel to select a group of soldiers from the regiment to serve as signalmen for his command, and Scot was one of those chosen. Detached from the Indiana regiment, Scot was mustered in as a signalman in the Army of the Cumberland, which was later to be commended by the distinguished Gen. George H. Thomas, the "Rock of Chickamauga." As a signalman, Scot participated in the battles of Murfreesboro, Chickamauga, Chattanooga, Franklin, and Nashville. His Signal Corps unit also marched with Sherman to the sea.

The Signal Corps was essentially the communications center of military service. Its soldiers forwarded orders and communications. They also interpreted enemy communications, decoded messages, defined fire direction, and kept track of troop movements.

In the mid-nineteenth century, the Disciples of Christ decided to establish a new university in what was then considered the Northwest. Ovid Butler became the chairman of the committee to carry out this plan. He was the author of the charter for the school, which was ultimately to be named Butler University, located in Indianapolis. The charter was legislated by the Indiana General Assembly and was premised on equality of education for men and women and white and African-American students. Chartered by the General Assembly in 1855, the Northwestern Christian University, now Butler University, stands as a memorial to the Butler family. It was the first private, nonsectarian college in the country to allow men and women and whites and blacks to pursue the same degrees together in the same four-year curriculum. After the war Scot became active in Butler University affairs, serving as president of the university from 1891 to 1904 and again in 1906 and 1907.

Barbara Butler Davis and the Indiana Historical Society deserve thanks for disseminating the history of the activities and accomplishments of the Butlers.

Alan T. Nolan
Indianapolis

Preface

In the great migration of the early 1800s, families of humble beginnings traveled westward to make a new life in the unsettled Northwest Territory. Among them were people of vision who wanted to create a new society that would be better than the one they left behind. They felt stifled by overcrowding in growing industrial cities, particularly in the New England states, where competition in the job market and an increasingly rigid class structure dampened the dreams of their immigrant fathers and forefathers. These pioneers were excited by the challenge of developing out of raw land a network of towns, cities, and farms based on a new concept of society. What they were doing was important, and they knew it. Among them were a number of intellectually bright men and women who were characterized not by wealth, but rather by fortitude, commitment, and a sense of God-given duty.

What began as the Indiana Territory in 1800, with a population of 5,641, became in 1816 the state of Indiana, population 64,000. By 1820 the population had grown to an astounding 147,178. These early Hoosier pioneers became the complex fabric of the new state of Indiana during the rending of this nation from Fort Sumter through Gettysburg to Appomattox. The Civil War left them behind to carry on the duties of their sons and grandsons, to support the war effort from their hometowns, to maintain the social structure to which the young veterans would return, and as we see in this case study, to create the vision needed to lead their communities and the country into a prosperous future.

This volume contains transcriptions of sixty-five holograph letters written from 1863 to 1865 by members of the Ovid Butler family of Indianapolis to their son Scot while he was serving, first, in the Thirty-third Regiment, Indiana Volunteer Infantry and, then, in the United States Signal Corps. For various reasons, few letters sent to the front from families back home survived the war. Even fewer survived the intervening postwar years to the present. Soldiers had little room in their knapsacks to keep letters received from loved ones at home, and since Indiana regiments often consisted of entire hometown neighborhoods, soldiers passed their letters containing local news around camp until the letters were destroyed or so worn as to be illegible. Sometimes young soldiers passed on letters from home to brothers or other relatives serving in different units in order that they, too, might enjoy a bit more news from home. Rarely, however, were such letters saved.

Thus social historians, for the most part, have relied on political data and the diaries, journals, and letters of soldiers in the field to reconstruct the wartime experiences of the families and communities these soldiers left behind. In this volume, however, the letters written by the people who experienced the war from the home front itself document the personal attitudes and concerns of the families and community presented here.

Why and how some collections did survive remains a mystery; but these particular letters were passed down in my family from Elizabeth Anne Butler (Scot's mother) to my great aunt,[1] who deposited them with the Irvington Historical Society, Indianapolis, in 1964. While the letters have rested undisturbed these many years, their value to social history is inestimable. The letters chronicle the sparsely studied hometown culture of the Civil War and tell the story of the families left behind. Combined with the history of the family who wrote them, the letters illuminate such issues as social class, religion, gender roles, humor, economic conditions, and political alignments on the home front. I am pleased to present them now as an example of an American-bred pioneering family that helped others of like mind and vision promote a developing society, endure the devastating effects of the Civil War, and provide for the future needs of the nation.[2]

1. Elizabeth Anne (Butler) Recker (1887–1973), daughter of Scot and Julia (Dunn) Butler.

2. The American line of the Ovid Butler family originated in New England ca. 1660 with James Butler I. From 1660 to 1860 six generations of Butler men and women traveled westward in the adventurous spirit of American pioneers, building churches, supporting human rights, participating in government reform, promoting education, and establishing free schools and a major university. A detailed history of the Butler family appears in the appendix. That account shows how the Butlers' values and dedication, so strongly reflected in this collection, developed over the course of two centuries. It is a valuable resource in understanding Ovid's, Elizabeth Anne's, and Scot's social, political, and religious motivations. It also reflects the times and the culture of Indianapolis during the Civil War.

Acknowledgments

Many people have helped this project come alive. The Irvington Historical Society, with the gracious help of William Clarke, historian, gave me ready access to the Scot Butler letters and permission to print them. Editors Paula Corpuz, Doug Clanin, Kathy Breen, and Judy McMullen of the Indiana Historical Society Press offered guidance in standardized editing. Butler University archivist Sally Childs-Helton and former Butler University archivist Erin Davis located student and staff records and histories of the university, and the late Newberry librarian David Thackery of Chicago provided Civil War records and census materials. Professors Steven Rosswurm, Carol Gayle, Rosemary Cowler, and Arthur Zilversmit of Lake Forest College encouraged me with their enthusiasm, skilled guidance, and confidence. Proofreader extraordinaire Sam Jones of Lake Forest College was untiring in his efforts. "Typist" Robert Davis provided computer skills, hot meals, fresh laundry, and a great deal of loving patience without which this work would not exist.

I am most grateful to members of my family for their assistance. First, my father, Ovid M. Butler, lent me his contagious excitement and many of the original materials I have used in this project. His memories of his grandparents, Scot and Julia Butler, their home in Irvington, Indiana, and his oral history of family stories were invaluable. Dad gave me a sense of awareness and awe of this personal story and its place in Indianapolis history. My uncle, Scot Butler 2nd, has trusted me with many materials and original records. He has been a constant source of reference and inspiration to me. His research suggestions led me to the Irvington Historical Society, where I found the holograph letters here transcribed.

Above all, it is Elizabeth Anne (McOuat) Butler who is responsible for this work. She lovingly saved and protected these letters after Scot's Civil War service. I am forever in her debt.

Editorial Notes

Below are notes on the transcription of the enclosed sixty-three holograph letters received by Scot Butler from his family during his service in the Union army. The letters are dated from July 22, 1863, to January 26, 1865. In addition to these home-front letters, the present collection includes two letters from Pvt. Scot Butler to Julia Dunn, dated May 10, 1863, and April 10, 1864. They are included to convey some idea of the personality of this young man who was the object of his family's great concern.

This is the entire collection as it is known to exist. All letters included here are signed original documents. No drafts or copies, transcribed or otherwise, have been used. The paper on which they are written is of the following sizes: Ovid Butler's stationery measures 8 by 11.75 inches, Elizabeth Anne's, 8 by 10 inches, and the size of Scot's two letters varied, depending on whatever writing paper was available to him. Each letter was folded in a pocket-size manner, once vertically and twice horizontally. Most of the letters are addressed on the back of each folded packet. A few have addressed envelopes, but their stamps were removed at some undetermined time.

The aim of this transcription is to retain the essence of the letters, making only minor editorial changes where necessary. Syntax errors, elements of style, spelling, and punctuation have been left undisturbed to the maximum extent possible so that the reader might better identify with the educational background, personality, and specific qualities of each writer. Underlined words have been rendered as italic.

The letters, which are arranged in chronological order, include two undated letters. These have been placed where they might logically have occurred, with assumed dates shown in brackets. If any other material has been added or deleted it is indicated by brackets or ellipses. In rare cases, a misplaced comma or a misspelling has been corrected when needed to clarify the context. Word order has been retained except in a few instances where a change was necessary for clarity. Repeated words, such as "and and" or "was was," have been reduced to a single "and" or "was." In some cases it was difficult to determine whether Ovid and Elizabeth Anne intended to write a capital or a lower-case letter. Their general practice was followed in such cases. For example, Elizabeth Anne rarely capitalized the days of the week, while Ovid typically did. In the holograph letters, the closing lines are often crammed into available space, but in transcription they are conventionally spaced. The endings of letters were often written across the sides of the page, perpendicular to and sometimes over preceding lines. These have been put into traditional format. The position of date and salutation lines is as appears in the holograph letters. What the transcriptions cannot show, however, is the handwriting itself that so strongly profiles each personality. Ovid Butler wrote with a strong, deliberate hand, reflecting his austere and forthright manner. Elizabeth Anne, on the other hand, wrote with a scrawled penmanship, in a spontaneous and hurried manner, suiting her nature.

Ovid Butler was basically a self-educated man, but his broad reading and law practice gave him a strong command of the English language. His writing was straightforward and direct. His vocabulary was precise and clear. He wrote quickly and forcefully with a strong, decisive slant. He rarely changed a word. His ideas were clearly developed and well thought out. Limited decisions regarding paragraph separation were necessarily arbitrary.[1]

Elizabeth Anne's letters required more active intervention. She often wrote hurriedly while sitting at a sick child's bedside, and perhaps for this reason her periods, commas, and pen pauses often resemble one another. She used dashes of varying lengths to indicate a comma, colon, semicolon, or period, and occasionally to indicate a new sentence or paragraph. Although Elizabeth Anne's use of capitalization was also erratic, her capitalization has been retained. Elizabeth Anne typically used capitalization to indicate a new sentence, but did not use periods between sentences. The editor has used triple spacing to indicate a new sentence in such cases. Elizabeth Anne's sporadic use of the apostrophe has also been maintained.

As the war years passed, Elizabeth Anne's calligraphy, grammar, and spelling noticeably deteriorated, and she increasingly ignored proper sentence structure. Her letters, though lacking in complete clauses and punctuation, have not been altered in transcription except where necessary for comprehension. Paragraph formatting has been employed to improve readability.

Both Ovid and Elizabeth Anne occasionally replaced a word by scratching through it and inserting a different word. The replacement word has been used in the transcription, and the crossed out word has been ignored. Both of them frequently used the "&" and "&c" commonly to denote "and" and "et cetera," respectively. This shorthand has been retained in transcribing the letters.

Since, as was the custom, periods were not often used at the end of abbreviations, abbreviations such as "Gov," "Doct," and "Lieut" have not been corrected. Other abbreviations that constitute a personal shorthand into which

Elizabeth Anne lapsed when writing rapidly, such as "G" for Greencastle or "J" for Janett, have been left undisturbed and footnoted so that the flow of the letter is not interrupted. Once such an abbreviation is identified no further notation is made.

Because the letters contain many references to persons and places associated with the Butler family, every effort has been made to identify them in that context. The first time such a person or place is mentioned in a letter it is identified in a footnote, but not repeated subsequently. More complete information on persons and places is provided following the letters in the Name-Place Glossary.

1. Steven J. Schmidt, "Brief Biography of Ovid Butler," and "Letters of Ovid Butler," personal collection.

Introduction

In the first gray light of a cold February morning in 1862, Scot Butler left his friends and family to enlist in the Thirty-third Regiment, Indiana Volunteer Infantry.[1] Earlier that morning his warm, openly affectionate Scottish mother served him breakfast, while his usually austere father shed tears but spoke few words at Scot's parting. The boy left behind the comfortable home of his wealthy abolitionist father and a community of visionary Union liberals, many of whom saw the war as an opportunity to enhance political reform and social welfare.

As he later detailed in his "Recollections," Scot was blind to their ideals. He saw himself, a lad of eighteen, going forth with the youthful spirit of a boy to seek adventure and manhood. He was excited by the idea of soldiering. In Indianapolis, as throughout the country, the times were full of stirring events. Troops came and went, greeted by great throngs of patriotic flag-wavers; people cheered, drums beat, and newspapers reported the progress of the war at the front.

For Scot such patriotism was an element of citizenship, and he loved his country because it was *his* country; its blood ran through his veins. Scot felt no cause, as did his father, to wipe out the sin of slavery. He was, perhaps, too young and not fully mature enough to understand or to appreciate his father's concept of the moral and holy war Scot was about to enter. Scot did believe, however, that it was his duty to serve his country, which was in danger of being irrevocably split apart.

To his radical Unionist father patriotism ran in the line of a higher duty: that of God's eternal purpose. Ovid Butler had become interested in the Stone-Campbell movement as a young man and had converted from his Baptist upbringing to the Christian Church (Disciples of Christ), becoming a leader of the movement in Indiana.[2] He believed in the Bible as the inerrant word of God and raised his family with that belief. Ovid professed that slavery was a mortal sin, staining all society and any future greatness his country might attain according to God's purpose. To this end he preached active participation to halt the spread of slavery. "Our National sin," he wrote, "will die out if limited to its current confines."[3] In Ovid's mind, there was no harmony between slavery and God's eternal purpose of universal brotherhood.[4]

Scot grew up under the tutelage of a philanthropic and humanitarian family that surrounded itself with a circle of friends and families of similar beliefs. Politically influential and religiously committed to the Campbellite movement, Ovid Butler had achieved more before the war than most men could hope to accomplish in a lifetime. He was a man of vision who saw what the country needed and strove to provide it. Ovid was an eminent educational leader, noted lawyer, respected publisher, political activist, and an influential religious leader. His personal friends included current and future governors, presidents and vice presidents, educators, and Disciple leaders.

Despite his youthful patriotism, Scot's trip to Lexington, Kentucky, where his regiment was encamped, was lonely and depressing. A three-year enlistment seemed a long time to a boy, and the war had already been in progress long enough for Scot to be aware of its danger. The thought that he might never return caused him mentally to engrave the familiar scenes about him. The fear of the unknown haunted him.

Lexington had been his mother's homestead since 1810. Thomas and Janette Smith (Lockerbie) McOuat, Scottish immigrants, raised their daughter Elizabeth Anne[5] and her nine siblings there. Janette's father, George Lockerbie, owned a small cotton gin and five slaves to work it; but by 1821 the slavery issue caused him to question his political beliefs. After all, the Scottish government had imprisoned George, the family's immigrant ancestor, for his pro-freedom writings, and he had fled his native country to seek greater political freedom in America. Here, George hoped, society would more readily accept his writings against the order of imposed social class. His own writings contradicted the very institution of slavery that he supported with his cotton gin. Son-in-law Thomas McOuat attended the first sale of city property in Indianapolis in 1821 and purchased three lots there. In 1830 George sold his slaves, and the family moved to the free state of Indiana.

Indiana's 1816 constitution prohibited slavery in the state in the strongest possible language. The 1820 Supreme Court case of *Lasselle v State* upheld the constitution's position, stating "The framers of our constitution intended a total and entire prohibition of slavery in this State."[6] While remaining faithful to the state's constitution, a society of Northern Democrats developed that opposed slavery yet sympathized with the South. Many of these "doughfaces," influenced by their southern heritage, traveled through Kentucky and settled in Indiana.

Although the McOuat and Butler families maintained a correspondence with friends and relatives still in Kentucky, Lexington was a strange place to Scot. At the time of his induction into the army in 1862, the sympathies of longtime friends and family in Kentucky remained decidedly with the South, so Scot did not care to make himself known to them.

The morning after his arrival in Lexington Scot walked out to camp, located some three miles from town. He vividly describes the scene that day. The air was raw and chilling and the road muddy. The colonel of the regiment was John Coburn, commander of the Thirty-third Indiana Volunteer Infantry, Department of the Cumberland. Coburn was a longtime friend of Scot's father and a fellow radical antislavery moralist. In fact, Ovid agreed to his son's enlistment only if Scot were to serve under the wing of his close friend, who might be able to protect Scot from danger and disease. Scot had never been a strong boy; illness and lack of strength plagued his youth. By war's outbreak, he had retired from his studies due to poor health.

Coburn wanted to give the lad a chance to return home before Scot signed his papers to participate in the horrors of war. The colonel had hoped that after a week's drilling perhaps the boy would have had enough soldiering. Such was not the case. "It is sometimes easier to do a disagreeable thing than not," Scot wrote. "All the discomforts of camp life in the most uncomfortable season of the year did not suggest to me that I reconsider enlisting."[7] Young, naive, and idealistic, he took the irrevocable oath to serve his nation and was inducted three days after his arrival.

This was not Scot's first attempt to enlist. At the calling for troops by Indiana governor Oliver P. Morton in 1861, Scot began agitating to join up. His continued ill health, however, had left him puny and weak. At 5′8″ and lean in build, his hazel eyes and blond hair set against his fair complexion, Scot appeared even younger than his eighteen years. Early in the war, recruiting officers sought young lads of fine physique who could shoulder the musket and knapsack. Scot was rejected by each recruiter he approached.[8]

Elizabeth Anne feared Scot's participation in the war would result in his physical and moral undoing, if not his death. Ovid, however, was a man of strong principles. When faced with any issue, he decided the course of his duty to it and committed himself to that course whatever the cost. Ovid was also a radical Republican. To him, the war waged by the North was a holy war supporting God's will to eradicate slavery. Ovid saw God's hand in it and therefore gave his entire soul to it. Although he must have felt an inner conflict in seeing his oldest son enlist in the war, Ovid also felt that the eradication of slavery was the work of man through God's desire. He allowed Scot to enlist, but with a concern that carried beyond ordinary parental anxiety.

In 1847, following a life-threatening illness, Ovid decided that God had spared him in order that he might achieve God's purposes, as yet unveiled. In 1849 that purpose was revealed to him. The Disciples of Christ Church was exploring the idea of establishing a university in what was then the northwest, based on Alexander Campbell's Bethany College in southern Virginia. Ovid was chosen chairman of the committee to organize such a plan. The conflict that arose over slavery and women's rights issues caused Ovid and his fellow bene-factors to take their proposal for universal advanced education to the Indiana General Assembly. Ovid wrote the charter, shepherded the bill through the leg-islature, and procured the necessary financial backing. Breaking with Campbell, he and other members of the original charter committee succeeded in seeing North Western Christian University become the first private, nonsectarian Christian college in the country to allow men and women, regardless of race, to pursue the same degree in the same four-year study of the classics.[9] In 1855 North Western Christian University (now Butler University) opened its doors. Scot was to inherit the project and assure its success; therefore, it was necessary he return from the war morally and physically healthy in order to fulfill God's, and thus Ovid's, purposes for him.

While his faith in Coburn's ability to find a safe haven for Scot seemed well founded, Ovid's concern for Scot's safe return increased as the war intensified. Gen. George W. Morgan's General Order No. 22, requesting that Coburn organize and send forth a detachment of recruits to serve as signalmen, served both Ovid's and Coburn's purpose.[10] In reality Scot was a perfect selec-tion; he was bright, quick to learn, and lithe enough to scale the signal towers with ease. In inclement weather or when his services were not needed, Scot, as did many signalmen, would serve as Morgan's aide or would be stationed at gen-eral headquarters. Coburn thought that the assignment would take Scot off the front lines and keep him relatively safe. Coburn transferred Scot to the Signal Corps on detached duty on December 1, 1862.[11]

Coburn could hardly have predicted that as the war progressed the value of the once fledgling Signal Corps increased, and the danger under which it operated intensified. With the increasing need for signal soldiers in the front lines to speed along messages of enemy troop movements, signalmen became increasingly vulnerable to sniper fire. Their red and white flags visibly waved high above the tree tops, sending along orders of advance, relaying warnings of coming danger, and sending out news of defeat. Signalmen decoded messages, interrupted enemy communications, defined fire direction, determined the location of armies and troop movements, and served as geographic topogra-phers. Scot's unit in the Army of the Cumberland participated in the battles of Crab Orchard, Murfreesboro, Chickamauga, Nashville, Franklin, and Chattanooga and played a major part in Gen. William T. Sherman's Atlanta campaign and the "March to the Sea."[12]

Never before had a noncombat corps suffered such disproportionate casualties as did the Signal Corps. Signalmen's sense of duty, necessary exposure to fire, and the remote and isolated locations of their stations were conditions that contradicted personal safety. Many were captured and suffered the inhospitality of Confederate prisons. Still others were wounded, killed, or maimed. By the end of the war the Signal Corps reported that 35 percent of its signalmen were wounded or died at their outpost stations.[13]

      Scot wrote his "Recollections" fifteen years after the war ended. In hindsight, he tells how he learned that in war, as in life, the trial came not on the battlefields of Tennessee and Georgia. There boys, in the rush of battle, became heroes as they faced the cannon thunder and the flash of artillery. "While the world looks on," he wrote, "the soldier is incited to noble deed; *mean* is he that is *not* a hero. It is toil and privation and hunger of body and of soul, and disappointment and defeat and bondage, and mans injustice, and cold and loneliness, that crush and grind."

      From a mountain's peak or a makeshift tower high above the battlefield, Scot's view was a macrocosmic experience of the war's brutality. He saw the world differently from most other soldiers. It was the signalman's duty to "get the message through"; but for Scot the message that came through was not restricted to troop movements and weather conditions.

---

1. The story line presented here and on the following pages is documented in Scot Butler's holograph manuscripts entitled "A Boy's Summer in the Mountains" and "Recollections, I and II," located in the Scot Butler papers of the Irvington Historical Society, Indianapolis, Ind.

2. The Stone-Campbell movement developed during the early 1800s as an offshoot of the Presbyterian Church. Today its full name is the Christian Church (Disciples of Christ). Its founders were Thomas Campbell, his son Alexander, and Barton W. Stone. Today it is a worldwide religion of approximately 900,000 members, headquartered in Indianapolis. Richard L. Hamm, general minister and president of the Christian Church (Disciples of Christ) in the United States and Canada, interview with the editor, Apr. 15, 2003.

3. Ovid Butler holograph letter draft, undated, collection M36, Indiana State Library, Indianapolis, Ind.

4. Most Christian Disciples avoided direct involvement in the slavery conflict. Alexander Campbell, leader of the Campbellite movement, wrote, "Let *political* Abolitionists and political anti-Abolitionists fight this battle themselves; let Christians do justly, love mercy, and walk humbly with our God, and then our righteousness shall flow as a river, and our peace as the waves of the sea." But Ovid broke off his relationship with Alexander Campbell, insisting that Christians had an obligation to reform society and play an active role in the march against slavery, both in battle and on the home front. He particularly rejected Campbell's practice of using the Bible as a historical and religious precedent in support of slavery. Ovid felt that Christian scripture reinforced the universal brotherhood of man. He considered brotherhood to be "the radiating point of all Christian faith and Christian duty."

5. Elizabeth Anne McOuat, widow of Kentuckian George Elgin, married Hoosier Ovid Butler in 1840. She was the daughter of Scottish immigrants who settled in Kentucky sometime between 1794 (the date of her father's birth in Scotland) and 1809 when her father first appeared in the Lexington City Directory.

6. Randall T. Shepard, "For Human Rights: Slave Cases and the Indiana Supreme Court," *Traces of Indiana and Midwestern History* 15, no. 3(summer 2003): 36.

7. Butler, "Recollections."

8. Scot Butler Service Records, U.S. Signal Corps, National Archives, Washington, D.C.

9. "Ovid Butler and Northwestern Christian University," *The Christian Record* (Apr. 7, 1850); "Dispute within Christian Church," *The Christian Standard* (June 19, 1897); *Indianapolis News*, Dec. 14, 1960; Henry K. Shaw, "The Founding of Butler University, 1847–1855," *Indiana Magazine of History* 58 (Sept. 1962).

10. Butler Service Records.

11. Scot Butler Service Records, Thirty-third Regiment, Indiana Volunteer Infantry. National Archives; Rebecca Robbins Raines, *Getting the Message Through: A Branch History of the U.S. Army Signal Corps* ([Washington, D.C.: Center of Military History, United States Army], 1996).

12. Scot was assigned to the Department of the Cumberland under Gen. George W. Morgan's division, Capt. Samuel Bachtell, commanding, in Atlanta, Georgia, September and October 1864.

13. Larry Holden, telephone interview with the editor, Oct. 10, 1998. Two months prior to Scot's transfer, a disorganized unit of raw recruits, under the direction of 1st Lt. Jesse Merrill (soon to be Scot's commanding officer), received Maj. A. J. Myer's Special Order No. 27 to establish a Signal Corps camp of instruction in Louisville, Kentucky. Merrill's unit, one of three ordered to instruction camp, consisted of two officers and ten privates. The Signal Corps of 1862 was rudimentary, at best. Most of the men assigned as signalmen, including Scot Butler, were detailed or "loaned" to signal units for a brief time. Although the corps remained disorganized until the war's end, in 1863 the army succeeded in receiving both financial and legislative approval for a federal signal commission, known as the United States Signal Corps. Today it is the United States Communication Corps. The men assigned to this unit became "signal soldiers." Raines, *Getting the Message Through*, 23–39.

Indiana Supports the War Effort

For the Northern Civil War community left behind, letters were the only direct contact families had with sons and daughters serving away from home. So family members took pen in hand to provide their absent loved ones insight into how the home front felt about and reacted to social, political, and military events. What they wrote about reflected hope, fear, and worry, not only for their own children and community but also for their state and country. This section provides the reader specific insight into Indiana's participation in the war, particularly focusing on those issues addressed by the family letters in this collection.

Although Indiana fought for the Union, its extensive population of Southerners and Southern sympathizers endangered its position as an antislavery state. Its southern neighbor, Kentucky, separated only by the Ohio River, was one of four border states undeclared in support of either North or South, but which did not secede. Kentucky's political and physical relationship to Indiana caused President Abraham Lincoln great concern because he could not afford to lose what Union support remained there.

Indiana's Democratic party had grown in popularity throughout the fifties. Its support of federal legislation to extend slave territory, however, was so flagrant that many, such as Ovid Butler, left the party. The political realignments that resulted from these party desertions gave birth to splinter parties such as the Free Soilers, the Abolitionists, the Free Democracy, the Libertarians, and the People's party. For the most part, these splinter parties ultimately merged into the Republican party.

Ovid was particularly active in the campaigns of 1848 and 1852. First a Democrat and then a Whig, he was instrumental in organizing antislavery Democrats and Whigs into the Free Soil party, establishing and financing in Indianapolis the *Free Soil Banner*, which not only opposed the extension of slavery but also took up the cause of antislavery. In 1852 Ovid aided in establishing and financing another paper, the *Indiana Free Soil Democrat*. In the same year he established an antislavery paper in Cincinnati, the *Herald and Philanthropist*.

In both the 1848 and 1852 campaigns Ovid served on important committees and as a stump speaker for the Free Soil party; but he clearly saw that the splinter parties could accomplish very little as separate entities. In 1854, when Congress repealed the Missouri Compromise, Ovid worked with other antislavery leaders to combine all opponents of slavery into one political party. In order to promote this goal, Ovid purchased a controlling interest in the *Indiana State Journal* (hereafter, the *Journal*).[1] In it, he called for a statewide meeting to discuss the political ideals and goals of all antislavery interests in the state, and on June 15, 1854, more than ten thousand men assembled to initiate the formation of the Indiana Republican party. The *Journal*, with Ovid as its publisher and principal financier, became the mouthpiece of the party. For his action in solidifying antislavery supporters, Ovid was named cofounder of the Republican party of Indiana.[2]

The Republican party was officially established at the state convention of February 22, 1856, in Pittsburg, Indiana. Four years later Oliver P. Morton, with Ovid's active support, was elected governor with a Republican majority in the General Assembly.[3] Morton's ascendancy was deemed a blessing for Indiana. The state needed strong leadership in order to maintain good relations with Kentucky since border state settlers, many actively proslave or at least Peace Democrats, continued to cause great turmoil within the state. Originally organized by those pioneers headed north through Kentucky, southern Indiana was equally divided in its support of the South and of the North, while northern Indiana, mostly settled by early New England Whigs, generally supported the Republican party. The irreconcilable antagonism between supporters of free and slave labor grew more and more bitter as the issue was forced upon them.

Two unique factions developed among Indiana's Southern sympathizers: those who were simply not in sympathy with the war or with the North's policy toward secession and the "doughfaces" who were distinctly pro-Southern in their sentiments. In the first year of the war, when a Southern victory seemed likely, Indiana's Southern patriots became more confident and expressed themselves more defiantly in rallies and Democratic newspapers such as the *Indianapolis Sentinel*. Public hostilities and periodic violence in the form of localized, spontaneous fighting became common, particularly in the southern portions of the state where the Kentucky boundary was a prevalent issue.[4] Peace Democrats blamed violent acts of Southern raiders on the hatred Unionists felt toward those disloyal to the Union. Although Kentucky did not secede, its Southern sympathies provided fuel for Indiana's disaffected southern population. Indiana Southern sympathizers, strongly influenced by Kentucky's Copperhead movement, became more rebellious as time passed, making a home militia necessary. The "Indiana Legion" was established as an active home militia whose duty was to provide for the state's internal defense.

Three raids into Indiana called the Legion into service. The most invasive raid was that of John Hunt Morgan that, had it succeeded, would have put Indiana's safety at great risk. Initially sent by Braxton Bragg to interrupt federal communications with the forces in the rear of the U.S. Army of the Cumberland, the high-strung Morgan disobeyed Bragg, believing he could enhance his reputation as a dashing model of J. E. B. Stuart by creating a diversion to aid the southern army of Tennessee. Morgan was one of many who believed that the pressure being endured by the Southern forces could be relieved by bringing the war into the North and by encouraging Southern sympathizers to rise in support of the South. This would, he hoped, direct the nation's attention to the western conflict and relieve the pressure being put on eastern states.

In the North, Morgan's reputation was that of a reckless cavalier whose troops showed no mercy for the people whose towns he invaded. On July 8, 1863, Morgan and his cavalry crossed the Ohio River into Indiana at Brandenburg, Kentucky. The Indiana militia retreated in the face of Morgan's brutality, and Morgan continued northward to Corydon (the initial capital city of Indiana), where he easily defeated the 450 Indiana Home Guard there, too, holding most of the local militia for ransom. Morgan's men killed townspeople, looted stores, robbed the county treasury, burned most of the town, and appropriated food, supplies, cattle, and horses as spoils of war. They kidnapped women and forced them into Morgan's ranks to serve his troops as cooks while his raid continued through Indiana and Ohio.

Morgan continued northward, splitting his unit to cover more territory. They reunited at Salem, Indiana, where they continued their pillage. Basil W. Duke, a member of Morgan's raiding party, wrote:

> This disposition to wholesale plunder exceeded anything that any of us had ever seen before. They did not pillage with any sort of method or reason. It seemed to be a mania, senseless and purposeless. They pillaged like boys robbing an orchard. I would not have believed that such a passion could have been developed so ludicrously among any body of civilized men.[5]

The state was, in Elizabeth Anne Butler's words, "in excitement."

Morton responded immediately, putting out another call for troops. Within two days Morton mustered in 20,000 recruits at Indianapolis, and another 45,000 troops volunteered ready for service. "Young and old alike all swarmed in constantly thickening throngs to the capital . . . as if there were no duty or interest of that hour but the safety of the State."[6]

Alert to the strength of the Indiana troops he would be facing, Morgan crossed into Scott County, Kentucky, for reinforcements and reentered Indiana at Vernon in Jennings County, the homestead of Ovid Butler's family. Morgan's erratic course was finally cut short by a strong and unexpected defense at Vernon. He fled eastward to avoid capture, but federal troops captured Morgan in Ohio, where he was imprisoned in the Ohio State Penitentiary until he escaped November 27, 1863. Morgan was shot and killed by a Union private on September 4, 1864. During the six-days' raid into Indiana, Morgan's 2,500 troops demolished some $419,000 in property and took several hundred lives.[7]

Charges of disloyalty spread throughout the state. Opposition to Morton's Republican legislature became so bitter that the Democrats took control of the general assembly in the fall of 1862. Two attempts were made on the governor's life, rancor marked the legislative sessions, and Democrats refused the governor the right to speak at his annual address to the state. Democrats denied Morton new appropriation bills for the funding of the militia and attempted to remove him as its commander in chief. Morton funded the troops by credit and took military control of Indiana. In 1864 the Republicans rallied, electing a legislature supporting the governor's platform and his pro-Union policy.

Disaffection, nationally as well as locally, continued to grow in the formation of secret societies, known for their plots to form a Northwestern Confederacy and hurry secession. Rumors spread that treasonous organizations such as the Knights of the Golden Circle had infiltrated the army in order to encourage desertions and weaken Union forces. Other Copperhead organizations, such as the Order for Treason, the American Knights, and the Sons of Liberty, became promoters of the Southern cause,[8] numbering some 15,000 members in Indiana alone. Their defense was that such societies were necessary "to fight to preserve constitutional liberty against the 'despotism' of the Lincoln and Morton administrations."[9]

In retaliation, Morton encouraged the statewide development of Union secret orders. They included the Union Clubs and the Union Leagues that were armed and stood ready for internal defense. Their purpose was to expose the "disloyal" societies and be alert to suppress armed uprisings. The existence of such groups served to ignite the already explosive situation.[10]

An example of the conflict resulting from these Orders and Societies is the Indiana Treason Trials of 1864. The Grand Jury of the United States Circuit Court called for an investigation of criminal acts committed by those known to belong to such societies. The "undesirables" were charged with interferring with enlistments, encouraging desertion, protecting deserters, resisting the draft of 1862, and other acts of violence that caused agitation for the Unionists.

After a lengthy trial Harrison H. Dodd, commander of the Sons of Liberty in Indiana, and his supporters were found guilty of treason. The implicated members were sentenced to death, although all were later paroled as a conciliatory measure toward the South. Ovid's account in his letters supports the general opinion that the "Sons" was sinister and dangerous, and that "it aimed at nothing less than an organized insurrection throughout several states, including Indiana."[11] Although this attitude may seem radical, it was typical of the leading abolitionists of the day.

The treason trials fueled Southern support and affected the recruitment efforts in certain counties where quotas were not met. Consequently, these areas were targeted by the draft. Nearly 18,000 men were drawn into service by the drafts of 1862, 1864, and 1865. Names of eligible men were placed in a rotating drum from which the military drew its required number of draftees. These men were required to report to the nearest point of rendezvous within five days. Those who did not report were classed as deserters.

Most young men were embarrassed to relinquish themselves to the draft rather than enlist. The names of those who were eligible, but failed to support the state's military efforts, were published in newspapers throughout the state as being disloyal to the Union.[12] Many feared that Copperhead draft dodgers would riot, carrying out their threats in resisting the draft.

Three elements of the draft emphasized an imbalance between the haves and the have-nots. First, any man could buy himself out of service for a three hundred-dollar fee. In this way the rich were virtually exempt from serving. Secondly, a drafted man could purchase a "substitute" for his place in the service. Finally, for those not sufficiently affluent to escape by such means and who dodged the draft, the state paid bounties of ten dollars to five hundred dollars for their return. Thus, bounty hunters could earn their own exemption by returning "jumpers" to the state.

The shame of this process was meant to stimulate volunteers and solidify patriotism in addition to filling quota numbers; but it was not unusual for scams to occur when men would accept three hundred dollars script, enlist, desert, and repeat the plan in other counties. This practice of bounty jumping became so profitable that a business developed around it. In order to control the practice, those caught were taken to Indianapolis and shot. The sum of these bounties cost the state $15,492,876 during the three periods of draft enforcement.

Scot's letters from home included just such political and military news items. Absentee soldiers also received news of their family's involvement in hometown support of the war. Elizabeth Anne, for example, wrote regularly about the sanitary fairs, the soldiers aid societies, and aid to soldiers' families that covered the country. Volunteers for those organizations worked locally and nationally selling homemade trinkets, magazine subscriptions, and pictures; picking and collecting lint, which was used to pack into wounds; rolling bandages; and putting on small sanitary fairs of their own to demonstrate that they, too, were fighting for the cause.[13]

In order to provide badly needed fresh foods to supplement inadequate army rations, friends and family at home shipped supplies to the front. But a more organized system of home-front care was necessary. Many local communities and neighborhoods organized to provide additional aid. These societies included the Patriotic Women of Indiana, the Sanitary Commission, the Sanitary Fairs, and the Sailors' and Soldiers' Homes Society. Although these societies were not limited to women only, through them women found a way to support the war effort. Women doubled their already extensive workload and turned themselves into bakers, farmers, seamstresses, wagon drivers, and more.

In 1861, with Morton's support, a group of women founded The Patriotic Women of Indiana. This organization called for contributions of extra blankets, warm, strong socks, woolen gloves and shirts, and underwear as discussed in the letters below in the humorous fiasco of "the box." Another relief organization was the Indiana Sanitary Commission. Its duty was to canvas the state for needed clothing, food not provided by government rations, delicacies, bedding, books, and bits of home life (needles, thimbles, stamps, books, and magazines) that would comfort and aid sons away from home. Scot Butler even received a subscription to the *Journal* so that he could read of local news and reports of the war. The organization was centrally located in Indianapolis with auxiliaries in the county seats. These local societies were then broken down into neighborhood collection sites. To encourage donations of goods as well as cash, the commission hired soliciting agents to travel throughout the state overseeing the project.

The third means of providing relief was the organization of sanitary fairs that were held throughout the state. In cooperation with the state agricultural fair, or State Fair, the Indianapolis Sanitary Fair of 1863 raised approximately $40,000. During the course of the war, the amount raised by counties, townships, cities, towns, and neighborhoods totaled $5 million in cash and goods for the relief of soldiers and their families.[14]

Certainly such a sum indicated the generous and dedicated support of both the state and individuals for their sons at war. It also reflected the home-front dedication to aid their families, enabling sons and husbands to enlist. By volunteering for the ranks, men were forced to leave their businesses and homes unattended and unpaid for. This also left their families to suffer the hardships incurred by living on the pay of an army soldier. A thirty-day or hundred-day enlistee may have suffered hardship, but a three-year volunteer placed his family in dire straits.

In November 1862 Morton, recognizing that a soldier's needs could not be met by the sum of a private's $156 annual income, organized a fourth statewide system of aid societies and solicited, particularly, all ministers of the gospel, township trustees, and town councilmen. The resulting organization became the Soldiers' Aid Society and rivaled the success of the Sanitary Commission. Households provided clothing and wares, while farmers donated wagonloads of wood and barrels of flour, apples, and potatoes. Flags and bunting decorated wagons as the farmers drove through the streets of Indianapolis welcomed by a parade of dedicated townspeople cheering for the safe return of their boys at war. The community rallied behind organized contests between neighborhoods to see which could demonstrate the grandest display of patriotism.

The state established temporary and permanent soldiers' homes in Indianapolis as early as 1862. Sometimes soldiers, returning home or rejoining units after sick leave, sought a stopover along the way. The Soldiers' and Sailors' Home, for example, served as a refuge for traveling soldiers and for ill soldiers who could not be cared for in military camps or overcrowded field hospitals. The building was erected, furnished, and managed by the Sanitary Commission. The facility offered soldiers a "taste of home" during their journeys, free of cost. Later in the war the Ladies' Home was established for a similar purpose. Families trying to visit their sons or husbands often passed through the capital city and needed a place to stay. Here men on furlough could meet with family members and visit expense free. By war's end, many permanently disabled patriots needed lifelong care. The commission raised subscription funds to buy a hotel with village cottages surrounding it in the outlying village of Knightstown, Indiana, to provide a permanent residence for those who had suffered permanent injuries.

The commission's work is just a sample of how the Indianapolis community rallied behind the war effort. The city's population rallied to support its soldiers, its state, and the nation at large. The following letters reveal how one family, unique in its political and religious influences, participated in activities to support the war effort, carried out ordinary daily tasks, supported maimed family members, harvested crops while enduring labor shortages, dealt with wartime economic conditions, redirected female roles and networks, expressed concern for illnesses and injuries, and relied on their faith for assurance that their absent son would return and their nation would be healed. The collection also illustrates how this same family maintained the ideals of its heritage, born of six generations of American pioneers, and how, in particular, its members looked to the future of a burgeoning, new era and sought ways to promote and guarantee its betterment.

---

1. The *Indiana State Journal* changed names throughout this era. It was known as the *Indiana Journal* and the *Indianapolis Daily Journal*. The *Indiana Journal* was established in 1853 to represent the views of the Whig party. By 1854 the paper was owned by Ovid Butler, its publisher and principal financier. In 1858 Butler sold his interest to Berry Sulgrove, but the paper continued to represent the opinions of the Republican party and Butler.

2. Russel M. Seeds, *History of the Republican Party of Indiana* (Indianapolis: The Indiana History Company, 1899); Kenneth M. Stampp, *Indiana Politics during the Civil War*, Indiana Historical Collections, vol. 31 (Indianapolis: Indiana Historical Bureau, 1949).

3. Henry S. Lane was elected to the position, but by a prearranged deal Lane was appointed to the United States Senate the day following the election, and the lieutenant governor, Oliver P. Morton, ascended to Lane's position as governor. Emma Lou Thornbrough, *Indiana in the Civil War Era, 1850–1880,* The History of Indiana, vol. 3 (Indianapolis: Indiana Historical Bureau and Indiana Historical Society, 1965), 86–87.

4. George S. Cottman, *Centennial History and Handbook of Indiana* (Indianapolis: Max R. Hyman, 1915), 140, 143.

5. Basil W. Duke, *A History of Morgan's Cavalry* (1867; reprint, Bloomington: Indiana University Press, 1969), 436, 437.

6. W. H. H. Terrell, *Report of the Adjutant General of the State of Indiana*, 8 vols. (Indianapolis: Alexander H. Conner, State Printer, 1865–69), 1:178.

7. Cottman, *Centennial History and Handbook of Indiana*, 141–42.

8. Ibid., 143.

9. *Indianapolis Daily Journal*, July 8, 13, 1864; Thornbrough, *Indiana in the Civil War Era*, 180–217; Mayo Fesler, "Secret Political Societies in the North during the Civil War," *Indiana Magazine of History* 14 (Sept. 1918): 278–86.

10. Cottman, *Centennial History and Handbook of Indiana*, 143.

11. Ibid., 144.

12. Ovid Butler letter, Sept. 4, 1864.

13. The United States Sanitary Commission was originally established to care for the unsanitary camp conditions and disease in front-line camps. Although it had earlier, humble beginnings, the expanded commission referred to here was organized in April 1861. Jan P. Romanowich, "United States Sanitary Commission," www.netwalk.com/~jpr (accessed Feb. 22, 2004).

14. Cottman, *Centennial History and Handbook of Indiana*, 148.

Family Photographs

FOREST HOME
The Ovid Butler Homestead
Indianapolis

Daughters of Thomas and Janette "Grandma" Smith (Lockerbie) McOuat (left to right):
Jean "Jennie" Maitland McOuat; Elizabeth Anne (E. Anne) McOuat; Mary Gray McOuat;
and Martha J. "Mattie" McOuat. Photo taken in 1845 in Indianapolis.

OVID BUTLER
(1801–1881)

ELIZABETH ANNE McOUAT
(Mrs. Ovid Butler)
(1818–1882)

SCOT BUTLER
(1844–1931)

JULIA WESLEY DUNN
(Mrs. Scot Butler)
(1845–1937)

JANETT BUTLER
(Mrs. Marion T. Anderson)
(1846–1868)

CAPT. MARION T. ANDERSON
(1839–1904)

THOMAS BUTLER ANDERSON
(son of Marion T. and Janett Butler)
(1864–1919)

DEMIA BUTLER
(Mrs. George Ellis Townley)
(1842–1867)

DR. PATRICK HENRY JAMESON
(1824–1910)

MARIA BUTLER
(Mrs. Patrick Henry Jameson)
(1831–1911)

CHAUNCEY BUTLER
(Ovid Butler's brother)
(1807–1875)

ANNA WAITE SCOVEL
(Mrs. Chauncey Butler)
(1832–1894)

ROBERT LOCKERBIE McOUAT
(1827–1883)

ELLEN C. WALLACE
(Mrs. Robert Lockerbie McOuat)
(1832–1863)

GEN. DAVID REYNOLDS

JEAN MAITLAND McOUAT
(Mrs. David Reynolds)
(1838–1864)

ANDREW W. McOUAT
(1830–1895)

ELLEN MORTON MCCROSSON
(Mrs. Andrew W. McOuat)
(1832–1863)

GEORGE LOCKERBIE McOUAT
(1821–1872)

MARTHA JEANETTE McOUAT
(Mrs. Samuel Edgar/Mrs. Robert N. Todd)
(b. ca. 1835)

THOMAS McOUAT BUTLER
(1854–1872)

ANNE ELIZABETH BUTLER
(1857–1937)

WILLIAM WALLACE
(married Scot Butler's
half sister, Cordelia)

GEORGE MURRAY LOCKERBIE
(1771–1856)

THOMAS McOUAT
(1794–1838)

JANETTE SMITH LOCKERBIE
(Mrs. Thomas McOuat)
(1800–1870)

ELIZABETH ANNE McOUAT
(Mrs. Ovid Butler)
(1818–1882)

OVID BUTLER
(1801–1881)

SCOT BUTLER
(1844–1931) in later life

{ THE LETTERS }

{ M A Y   1 0 ,   1 8 6 3 }

SCOT BUTLER TO JULIA DUNN

Franklin Ten.
May 10th

Miss Julia:[1]

    I must beg pardon for taking the liberty of writing you without first obtaining your consent to do so. I will trust however to your good nature and forgiving spirit for entire forgiveness, when I shall have stated the circumstances under which I am placed. If you will permit a correspondence, it will afford me great pleasure.

    Often when wearied by the dull unchanging monotony of camp life[2] I have longed to hear from you. But fearing that a correspondence, however pleasing to the one party, might prove just the contrary to the other, and not wishing to incur your displeasure by intruding myself upon your notice I have very reluctantly refrained from writing.

    When I visited home in november I had intend to ask your consent to a correspondence. Unfortunaty for me I received orders to report to the regiment sooner than I had expected, for this reason I was compelled to leave sudenly and my intentions were thus frustrated. And now after long resistanc I yield to my inclinations, trusting that you will not misunderstand me or deem me impertinent. Probably we may become better acquainted by a correspondence: My foolish bashfulness, I suppose has often excited dislike, perhaps disgust where I have been the most anxious to make a good impression.

    I am well aware how wearisome letterwriting is under certain circumstances. The most pleasing entertainment becomes dull and insipid, when we take no interest in it. But as I suppose that all young ladies take an interest in the army (ladies generally have a weakness that way) I hope that I may not prove all together a profitless correspondent.

    No one can truly appreciate what a Godsend a good letter is untill they have tried "sogering." A letter from home or from some old friend that brings to mind a happy scene in the "bright long ago," will drive the shadows from the darkest brow and cast a roseate hue over the whole mental horizon. The greatest punishment that could be inflicted on us, would be to deprive us of the mail.

Its arrival is *the* event of the day. An event which we all look forward to from day and allmost count the intervening hours. Dont think from this that we are all 'home sick,' and have forgotten what we came into the service for. Far from it. There are more light hearts in the army than can be found elsewhere. A soldiere is not half a soldier that cannot accommodate himself to circumstances.

I received a very disconsolate letter from Net[3] the other day. She predicts a very lonely time, as you were going home, Demia[4] going East and her Captain was *her* Captain no longer.[5] She say she is trying very hard to capture another beau. I can only wish her success.

In the late telegraph dispaches there is much cause for disappointment among us. What we were led to believe would eventuate in a glorious triumph of our arms has proved a failure to say the least of it. The other day we heard that Hooker had crossed the 'Rubicon' and was driving the enemy before him. Anon we heard of glourious victories. Then came dark rumors of disaster and defeat.[6]

Yesterdays paper distroys all hope and realizes all our fears. Surely Fredricksburg[7] will live in history. Nearly twenty four thousand lives have been sacrificed in this and previous battles. I suppose the result of this battle has elevated Indiana Butternuts[8] a great deal. Never mind, their punishment will only be the more severe for having been defered so long. 'Roseys' army is anxiously awaiting their share in the fight.

We are well prepared to give the 'rebs' a warm reception, should they see fit to change their base "and roll the tide of war["] against us.

Anything is preferable to this endless inactivity. It stagnates the liveliest mind and worst still; leaves us without an item for our letters.

The Signal Corps[9] holds communication from one wing to the other of Rosecrans army. The station which I am on is situated on a hill near Franklin, several hundred feet above the surrounding country and its warlike occupants. From here we command one of the most beautiful landscape views I ever beheld. This is called the "Garden spot" of America. Away of[f] to the north stretches a valley of unrivaled beauty. Alternate paches of meadow and woodland, its dashing streams, shining through the mist of morning like threads of silver, and the hills, ranged on each side, clothed with towering trees and stand like eternal sentinels over this scene of (seeming) quiet beauty and content. What a beautiful place was Franklin & its surroundings of elegant country mansions and extensive plantations before the hearts of the people were corrupted by political leaders, in their lust for power. Franklin is war worn. The shattered glass in her churches and school houses, her lonely streets and the closed shutters of her store houses, the battered doors and ruined machinery of her manufactories, and above all that deathlike, breathless silence, that absence of all sound, that can be felt no where but at the desolate hearthstone, here reins supreme. Here & there a lounger attired in the butternut garb of chivalry, with hate gleaming in his eyes. But enough of Franklin. We hear today that Richmond is taken. So note it be but "I cant see it."

Truly
Scot Butler

[Side note] Please address—Signal Corps. Maj. Gen Grangers Hquarters.

1. Julia Wesley Dunn (1845–1937), daughter of John Wesley and Evelina (Mitchell) Dunn, married Scot Butler on November 3, 1868, in Bloomington, Indiana.

2. Restlessness and boredom between engagements were common elements of the war. Scot had not seen action since March 4 at the Battle of Thompson's Station, Franklin, Tennessee, where Union troops were defeated. Scot Butler, Military Records, United States National Archives, Washington, D.C.

3. Janett/Net/Nettie Butler, Scot's younger sister.

4. Demia Butler, Scot's older sister. At this time Demia and a friend, Mary Beaty, were traveling to Philadelphia.

5. Marion Thomas Anderson of Kokomo, Indiana, also called Capt./Captain Anderson. He served in Company C, Fifty-first Regiment, Indiana Volunteer Infantry under Abel D. Streight and received the Congressional Medal of Honor for bravery in the Battle of Nashville, 1864.

6. Scot's reference is to the Rubicon River of ancient Rome. If a Roman general or his army crossed the river, it was considered an act of war and an indicator that he was intent on felling Rome. Crossing the Rubicon commits an individual irrevocably. Here Scot's allusion is to Gen. Joseph Hooker, commander of the Army of the Potomac, who reorganized and strengthened his command to an unprecedented Union force. His aim in April 1863 was to cross the Rappahannock River, threaten Gen. Robert E. Lee's presence, and develop an offense to take Richmond. Lee, meanwhile, developed a brilliant battle plan to split his army and surround Hooker, who mysteriously lost his nerve. He and his army retreated into the Wilderness, where that battle ended in the "defeat and disaster" Scot mentions. Patricia L. Faust, ed., *Historical Times Illustrated Encyclopedia of the Civil War* (New York: Harper and Row, 1986), 126–29; Philip Katcher, *The Civil War Source Book* (New York: Facts on File, 1995), 275–76; James M. McPherson, ed., *The American Heritage New History of the Civil War* (New York: Viking Press, 1996), 274–80; E. B. Long, with Barbara Long, *The Civil War Day by Day: An Almanac, 1861–1865* (Garden City, N.Y.: Doubleday and Co., 1971), 344–48.

7. Scot's reference here is to the Second Battle of Fredericksburg, Virginia (May 3–4, 1863), where Hooker split his army into a second branch under the command of John Sedgwick in order to attack Lee's rear. Hooker, however, never moved to help or reenforce Sedgwick's line, and Sedgwick was defeated. Long, *Civil War Day by Day*, 344–46.

8. Scot refers to Confederate soldiers or partisans whose uniforms were dyed yellowish-brown with an extract from butternuts, copperas, and walnut hulls. His use of the derogatory term to identify Southern sympathizers, "traitors" to the Union, reflects Scot's Unionist beliefs that the seceded states were rebels to their country. McPherson, ed., *American Heritage New History of the Civil War*, 476–79.

9. Scot was transferred from the Indiana Thirty-third to the U.S. Signal Corps, Army of the Cumberland, in 1862.

{ J U L Y   2 2 ,   1 8 6 3 }

OVID BUTLER TO SON SCOT BUTLER

Forest Home[1] *near Indianapolis Ind.*
July 22d 1863

Son Scot

You have been advised by your Ma's[2] letters (if you have received them) of the receipt of sundry letters from you among which was yours to me of the 3d inst.   Yours to Demia of the 15th has also been received. I might perhaps complain that you write me so seldom not that it matters much if I get the information from you in your other letters but that it indicates something of a disposition to write only when you are written to. This principle if it be right at all is not right in its application to me for you know that I have but poor health generally and am heavily taxed by an extensive correspondance on behalf of the University and other matters   But this is intended not as a complaint but as an intimation to prompt you to write me more frequently.

I have recently sent you the papers containing accounts of the battles at Gettysburgh, the repulse of the rebels at Halena, the fall of Vicksburgh and Port Hudson, the New York riots—the Morgan raid into this State and Ohio   and other matters which will be of interest to you. I hope that you have recd them

The Morgan raid will especially interest you as its operations were near home and gave us even here considerable of a scare   It was thought that Morgans object in crossing the river was the destruction of the Arsanel and public property here and I have little doubt that that was what he intended and at the same time to inaugurate insurrection and revolution in this State by [encouraging?] the Copperheads[3] and rebel sympthisers to rise. But he was speedily headed and so pent in as to make it his paramount object to escape. His flight up the river was simply an effort to find a place to cross into Kentucky. But you will perceive that he was finally headed near Portland Ohio and compelled to surrender   But when looked for among his captive forces it was found that he himself had slipped away. So ends I trust the career of John Morgan.

In one of your recent letters you express a wish that I would write you and give you my opinion of the present situation in reference I suppose to the probability of the speedy termination of the war. The defeat of Lee's army at the battle at Gettysburgh, the rebel repulse at Helena, the fall of Vicksburgh and Port Hudson, the Advance of the Army of the Cumberland and I may add the suppression of the riots in New York and the destruction and capture of the Morgan army of raiders have produced a pretty general impression that the rebellion has received its death blow and a hope and confidence that it will speedily be crushed out and peace be restored to an undivided Union   I participate in that hope and confidence   I trust that the present advantages may be improved and pressed earnestly until no vintage of the rebel army or the Confederate government shall remain

But it may not do to be too sanguine in this matter. We are all too ready to believe what we most earnestly desire   Lee's army has escaped to Virginia. Braggs retreating army although at present concealed in the folds of the great rebellion will probably turn up some day united with Johnsons army formidable in its numbers and its strength. With those and with the aid of small bands of guerrillas the rebels may hope to protract the struggle until the expiration of this term of service of most of our soldiers believing that when that time comes our armies will be disbanded and our government measurably defenseless. That term of service you know will expire next year. The rebels too may rely with some confidence upon the chances that in the excitement of a Presidential canvas which must come off next year bitter [strifes?] and animosities will be engendered and developed in the loyal states which will weaken the government and strengthen the rebellion

But perhaps the greatest and most immediate danger to the Union is to be apprehended from Foreign intervention: England and France have thus far been content with the position of professed Neutrality. In that position they have found means of aiding the rebellion without the hazzards of an open war with the United States   There can be little doubt that they much desire the success of the rebellion Not that they love the rebels or their cause   But they much fear the future power and grandeur of the American Republic should the integrity of the Union be preserved—Our existence and prosperity as a Nation is a perpetual argument in favor of free Institutions and a perpetual rebuke of the Monarchial system of the Old world and soon all too soon for the Autocrats of Europe should our national integrity be preserved, the Mastery of the world will have passed from Europe to America. Without an effort to attain the position, the American Republic will be the Worlds Arbiter. The European Cabinets see this very clearly and they may have determined to make the present rebellion the excuse and occasion for breaking up the Union. Hitherto, in the expectation that the Confederacy would maintain itself and fight its own way to recognized Nationality the European Cabinets may have been content to give it only such aid as they could cover under their hollow pretenses of Neutrality   But now they must perceive that their aid to be efficient must involve the attitude of open war, avowed hostility to the Union   It may possibly be that the final response which shall come to us from beyond the waters to the news of our recent successes may be to us the Godsend of a foreign war or it may be the presence of a foreign and hostile fleet in our waters and upon our coasts.

All this is possible and it is well therefore that it should be contemplated   But although I have little faith in the honesty and fair dealing of the European Cabinets, I will not believe without further evidence that they could be guilty of so great a crime and I may add so great a blunder. I will not now speculate upon the consequences of such an event further than to say that it would by no means be the harbinger of a speedy termination of the war   It would rather indicate a severe trial a more terrible conflict than we have yet had   The next arivals from Europe may dispel all these apprehensions. Till then hope on. And in any event and under all circumstances Trust in God. He will defend the right and will work out the great problems of human rights by the inflexible rule of human efforts human endurance and human suffering   God reigns—Let the Earth rejoice—None but the guilty need tremble

Lieut Flook[4] some time since wrote me in reference to getting permission from Gov Morton for himself, Mr Harrison & You to engage in the Artillery recruiting service   Gov Morton was absent but I was told by Col Fryberger that no batteries of Artillery were now being raised in the State. I however spoke to Col Coburn and Wm Wallace[5] to see Gov Morton upon the subject on his return   They did so before I had an opportunity to see him myself. I spoke to him myself about it so soon as I had the opportunity   He stated that it was not contemplated to raise more batteries for U.S. service though some might perhaps be raised for the State   But he said he could not with [propensity?] give permission or suggest a wish for any person in the field to engage in the recruiting services   That for such service they should be detailed by their Commanding Officer   But that if you could get furloughs and come home he could accept the service and would be willing to do so with the understanding that if successful you should have Commissions. Whether you should engage in the service or not we would like to see you home for a while if a furlough could be got honorably and if the chase of Bragg is over   I do not see why it might not But of course I do not understand the situation there

Col Coburn at his own request was relieved of his command here and started for his post in the Army of the Cumberland   This was just at the commencement of the Morgan raid   He had got no farther than Louisville when Morgans army crossed the river below   He was stopped there and put in command at New Albany   I have not heard but suppose he has been relieved of that command and is probably by this time with the 33d regt   You will of course see him   We sent you some papers by him among which was a Potograph of the Family gathering on the 18th June   This we supposed you would like to see   We much desired that the *Absent One*[6] should appear in the picture but that could not be. I spoke to Col Coburn of you & your situation and prospects and of my wishes in regard to you. He is interested in your behalf and will do what he can to advance your interest. He will I think have it in his power to do something for you should an opportunity occur.

You suggested in a recent letter that you might conclude to return to your regiment should the Signal Corps be reorganized. If you can stand the drill and the duties which would thus devolve on you I should prefer your doing so to reenlisting in the Corps for a longer time or for an indefinite period   I suppose if you return to the regiment you will be discharged when its time expires and it is disbanded but am not certain as to this. You would do well I think before taking any step in the matter to consult with Col Coburn

I conclude this long letter with the admonishion Hope and Trust both for your Country and yourself

Your affectionate Father
Ovid Butler

1. Ovid Butler's home at what is now Park and Thirteenth Streets, Indianapolis, is located in the Historic Northside District. The Greek Revival house, built in 1848, still stands and is being renovated to preserve much of its original design.

2. Elizabeth Anne (McOuat) Elgin married Ovid Butler in 1840 and raised a family of ten children, including her daughter by first husband George Elgin, Ovid's three surviving children by his first wife, Cordelia Cole, and six children by her marriage to Ovid.

3. Democrats in the North who were more conciliatory toward the South than were Republicans.

4. Lt. Henry R. Flook of the Indiana Thirty-third was transferred to the Signal Corps along with Scot.

5. William Wallace, son of former Indiana governor David Wallace and brother of author Lew Wallace, was Scot's brother-in-law.

6. Scot.

{ JULY 26, 1863 }

E. ANNE BUTLER TO SON SCOT BUTLER

Forest Home
July 26th 1863

My Dear Son Scot

Yours of 19th inst I received on thursday of last week. You have doubtless learned by this time by mine of the 21st inst—that your letters sent home have not be lost but some of them were somewhat halted on the way. Your letters Scot are more gladly welcomed than you are likely to imagine. What would

we do in your long absence without this means of communication, hope would
die out leaving in its place despondency and sad forbodings. There are times that
I grow more anxious about you than at other times. I think from some unac-
countable depression of spirits that I feel, that All is not well with my absent boy,
when here comes a letter written some four or five days, to be sure, ago but *then*
he was *well* and the cloud is lifted from my spirits for the time—

You named in your last that you were in expectation of making still
another move but did not know in what direction it would be   Rosecrans
advance is said by some of the papers to be at Rome Georgia. Will not that division to which you belong be likly sent forward too. I hope not for this advanc-
ing into the enemy's country always suggests to my mind bushwhacking and all
kinds of unmilitary warfare.

In yesterday's paper is an account of Capt. Dille's murder near Guys
Gap[1]   His wife makes her home in the city with a sister   I am some little
acquainted with her having come up last winter from Louisville[2] at the same
time and was thrown for a while in her company   I since met her at Col.
Coburn's the evening he entertained the officers of his regiment & thier wives
She is left with several young children, her trial is hard but hers alas is not by
thousands the only one. How many have within a very few weeks had to mourn
the death of their nearest friends by the hands of rebels. Rebels alike to the Laws
of God and Man—

You inquired how the butternuts turned out against Morgan, well the
younger men turned out almost I think to a man, but some of the older ones
did not seem moved at all   They professed to think that the Capital[3] was in no
danger.

There is a young fellow by the name of Jackson,[4] a graduate of last
year of the University   The same that called at Julia Dunn's and reclined himself on the sofa and received such a rebuke in the Sigournean Casket[5] for so
doing. He is now studing law with Tom. Hendricks[6] in this city & had the
temerity to offer his name, that is the traitor Tom. Hendricks name as the
speaker before the joint literary societies of the University   At the meeting
which was appointed for the societies to make thier selection for a speaker and
at which time Jackson proposed Hendricks, the boys had quite an exciting
time. Our girls were over at the University that night and Demia said for a
while she almost trembled for fear that it would end in violence but the butternuts were so far in the minority that when the vote was called and they
found how unsupported they stood they rose and left the hall in disgust and
I believe they have been from that time relieved of Jacksons presence & his
secesh argumentations. Well who should shoulder his musket first fellow but
Jackson, and he really seemed proud of himself and I have no doubt he was a
better man for even showing that amount of loyalty—

I believe I must tell you the revenge that Jackson took of Nettie for putting him in the Sigournean Casket—but I must name here that Demia too had given him umbrage by expressing to a fellow graduate and special friend of his, her dislike of him generally and specially for his seseh [secesh] proclivities which information was conveyed with all dispatch to Jackson. One evening when the Mathesian's had open doors and all the girls were invited over, Jackson read for his essay an article written in the style of the book of Chronicles, Commencing with "Two-Maidens journeyed to a far country (meaning—Mary Beaty[7] & Demia) and one maiden said to the other Maiden let us get unto ourselves head gear" I cannot go on with the yarn in this style but will give the heads of it as I can. Mary Beaty & Demia bought themselves bonnets while in Philidelphia These bonnets were somewhat peculiar in being bent down in front and the indenture filled up in flowers. This smash down on the bonnet front Jackson showed up in a very [ludicrous?] manner describing the horror of "The Maidens" when they first met thier gaze, but when assured that they were brought from a far country and cost many pieces of silver, they were at once pronounced exquisite—But his *rub* on Nettie was the *cruelest* of all being there considerable truth at the bottom of it It run in this wise Once upon a time a young maiden said come let us have a fishing party and she called together all the young men and maidens in all that country and when each young man had taken the maiden of his choice there was none no not one to take this Maiden who had gotten up this great fishing party—

Nettie has written to you to day but as I never see what she writes you, I cannot tell how much news she has given you but do not think that we have written on the same topics I can not tell what Grandma[8] and the family have to say about the raid of Morgan   they did not however fall into rank and drill any of them   Even Jim Wallace[9] did not make any move in that way I have not seen any [of] them but Grandma since and then there was little or no allusion made to the matter

Rob Duncan[10] has just called on his way from night meeting to tell us that a telegram was just recieved that Morgan and the last of his forces are captured

Affectionately your Mother
E Anne Butler

1. Capt. Israel C. Dille served with Company G, Indiana Thirty-third. He was killed in action at Guy's Gap, located in southwest Tennessee on the Mississippi border, twelve miles southwest of Shiloh, on July 17, 1863. www.itd/nps.gov/cwss/regiments.html: Soldiers and Sailors, sponsored by the National Park Service and maintained by the National Archives and Records Administration.
2. Louisville, Kentucky.
3. Indianapolis.

4. John T. Jackson of Indianapolis. Jackson graduated from Butler University, where he received his A.B. and A.M. degrees. He died in 1866, one year before Demia Butler.

5. Publication of the Sigournean Literary Society, the first literary society for women at Butler University. This Society, founded in 1859, was originally called the Young Ladies' Literary Society. In April 1860 it took on the name of The Sigournean Society, named for Lydia Sigourney (1791–1865), a prominent author of the day.

6. Thomas Andrews Hendricks, future Indiana governor. Here Elizabeth Anne refers to Hendricks's and Ovid Butler's acquaintance through their mutual practice of the law from 1825 to 1835 in Shelbyville, Indiana.

7. Members of the Beaty family, Davey, John, and Mary, were close personal friends of the Butlers.

8. Janette Smith (Lockerbie) McOuat, Scot's grandmother.

9. Scot's cousin and member of the David Wallace family.

10. Robert P. Duncan, Scot's classmate and distant cousin.

———⊰∘⊱———

{ JULY 31, 1863 }

E. ANNE BUTLER TO SON SCOT BUTLER

Keithsburg Illinois [1]
Friday July 31st/63

My Dear Son Scot

You will no doubt be surprized to recieve a letter from me dated so far away from home, but if you remember of having heard that your Pa has been of late making some purchases of farming lands in this locality, our being here will be explained. Your Pa Nettie & I left home last tuesday on the night train for Chicago, we stopped there but an hour or so & then came on by rail to within about twenty miles of this place where we left the rail road and came across to this by stage coach   This is quite a nice little town on the Missisippi river   a boat has just passed up to St. Paul which is the regular packet plying between St Louis

& St Paul. Your Pa had expected to visit Minnesota this summer but will I think now extend his travels no farther than this place. Your Pa will have a good deal to see to here in the way of fixing up his fences and having his share of the crops stored away. I think if he is likely to be detained here beyond the middle of next week Nettie and I will start back home the first of next week. Tomorrow I expect to go out to look at your Pa's *brag* farms for your Pa has a great fancy for this kind of country for farming And it is a pretty sight, great field after field of grain as far [as] the eye can reach Oceanlike, unbroken even by the division lines of fences. I have never thought very well of Illinois as compared with Indiana, but after seeing Chicago and these great, almost boundless grain fields I will have to acklowledge that Indiana can be beaten in some respects—

There were on the cars quite a number of Illinois soldiers from Vicksburgh Gen. Grants order giving them thirty days furlough was to them very unexpected and to thier friends at home their visit will be a great surprize

I wrote you about the excursion to Niagara and of Lon[2] & Mrs Burns having gone. The party returned Monday, but Mrs "B.["] & Lon stopped at Cleveland where Mrs Burns father lives They will be back to our house by saturday. George Spurior, a gentleman of Demia's acquaintance from Hanover who went on this excursion to the falls, was out to call on his return, was telling us that Lon's devotion to Mrs B. during the trip, was the most untiring he ever witnessed He thought it would be a match in short order, but I do not think so as said of friendships some times "It is too thick to last"

I believe there has been but little said of late about Nettie's captain in our letters to you, poor fellow he is now *suffering* the hospitalities of Libby prison,[3] and I sometimes think that Nettie['s] preferance is but a slight affair, for if it has caused any depression of spirits with her I can't see it. His long confinement and risk he run at the time the captians drew lots who were to be hung in retaliation by the rebels, for those spies hung in Ky by Burnsides[4] All this does not seem to affect her spirits in any way perceptible indeed I *guess* she has given up that fancy for another or may be two or three others—

I was sorry Scot that I did not think until too late of the possibility of you wanting money when we sent by Col. Coburn You ought to let us know what you want so when oppertunities occur for sending to you we will know what you need. I expect Lon will be going south now before a great while and if he goes in your direction I wish I knew what you most need Write and let us know I thought before this time that I would have Annie's[5] likeness ready to send you. Demia expected to take her down to the rooms this week and get her photographs taken and if good to send you one Annie's is quite a *book worm* and great on spelling she commences with spelling a word and then goes on with every thing that can be made to rhyme with it spelling the whole rigma role through. Annie is in disposition very *sun shiny* and loves her brother Scot she says "so good bless his heart"   I will miss seeing your letter home this week will have to wait till we hear from Demia or maybe until we get home   Write often and let us know how it is with you I remain My Dear Scot

Your affectionate Mother
E Anne Butler

1. Keithsburg, Mercer County, Illinois, site of Ovid's Illinois farm, "Butler's Grove."
2. Alonzo/Lon M. Atkinson of Wabash, Indiana, Scot's classmate. Lon married Nancy Elizabeth Burns, the first woman to graduate from Butler University (1856).
3. Confederate prison just outside Richmond, Virginia, second only to Andersonville in notoriety.
4. Union general Ambrose Everett Burnside, noted for his lackluster career as Commander, Army of the Republic.
5. Anne Elizabeth/Annie Butler, Scot's youngest sister.

{ A U G U S T   2 ,   1 8 6 3 }

DEMIA BUTLER TO BROTHER SCOT BUTLER

Forest Home
Aug 2/63

My Dear Brother;

Since I wrote you last I have received two letters from you, both of which were warmly welcomed and anxiously read. The first one was so splendidly long that it was a real treat to look at it such letters are so rare. I am glad you see the joke in your long hard marches. It is very amusing to read your descriptions but I could imagine it not quite so funny to realize them. It may not be very pleasant to you to live a "listless do-nothing kind of life" but there is a great satisfaction to me in knowing and feeling that you are under shelter and comparatively safe. How did you get back to Murfresboro or is that farther south than Guys Gap. In fact Scot I have hardly known where to place you since you left Franklin.[1]

I have been expecting to hear of your return to Nashville as you wrote to that effect some time ago. There is a real pleasant young girl living in

Nashville whom I want you to get acquainted with—if you return there. I suppose you have heard Janett speak of her. She attended school here this winter. Her name is Scovel[2] She is a splendid union girl and quite a beautiful performer on the piano. Such an acquaintance I should think would be pleasant as it was rare in your case. Now Scot don't think because I am anxious to have you form the acquaintance of certain ladies that I am entertaining any matrimonial plans for you. I am so very ambitious for you that I have never seen the girl yet that I thought would suit you. As you are so young of course I have not been "looking out" for *the one* yet. I expect you to have fancies preferences and perhaps fall in love with a half dozen or more girls which you would never dream of marrying but Janett you know has always thought if you or I or any other one look side wise at a lady or gentleman of course we were thinking of marrying that one. Now seriously Scot Janett has laid her plans completely for a match between you and Julia. I have often laughed at her for being so absurd as to think you dreamed of such a thing. I am glad Janett has had delicacy enough not to intimate such a thing to Julia for it would certainly be very embarrassing to you and Julia both for her to talk that way to you.

I am glad to hear that Janett has not abused Mollie for she is certainly very unreasonably preduiced against her and I was afraid she would yield too much to her dislike to speak truthfully of Mollie.[3] Mollie is pretty and she knows it. She has been petted and spoiled at home and she expects every one to caress her and treat her kindly. Charley Davidge[4] gave her great attention for a little while but I believe she was not smart enough for that brilliant youth. I send you her photograph. You can dispose of it as you like. It is not so pretty as she is for her eyes are blue and her complexion clear white and pink cheeks   To these of course a photograph cannot do justice.

Wm Wallace and Dr Jameson[5] have been to see Gov Morton. Sister Delia[6] is writing you today the effects of their efforts. I believe that Gov has promised to give you an appointment. Scot make every effort to come home for then you will surely get a position. Try very very hard and you will surely succeed. Get Col Colburn to ask for a furlough for you. I am afraid the Gov can not do anything for you until you leave the Signal Corps. But you know more than I do about this. Do try and get a leave of absence and there will be no further trouble about a position. Ma Pa & Janett started to Keithsburg last Tuesday night. If they can go they will keep on to Minnesota. I am rather lonely at home but get along very well. Hoping to hear from you soon I am your loving sister

Demia

Don't tell Mollie you never heard of Connersville. She thinks there never was such another place. It is a very pretty village.

1. Nashville, Murfreesboro, and Franklin form a triangle in north-central Tennessee, with Nashville serving as the northern axis. Franklin, to the south, and Murfreesboro, to the southeast, are each located fifty miles from Nashville. Guy's Gap is located in southwest Tennessee on the Mississippi border, twelve miles southwest of Shiloh. It is significantly south of Murfreesboro.

2. Anna Scovel. Although Scot's sisters first write of Anna as a likely match for Scot, Anna married Chauncey Butler, Scot's brother, in 1870.

3. Margaret/Mollie Elgin, Scot's cousin through his mother's first marriage in 1836 to George Elgin.

4. Charley Davidge, Scot's classmate.

5. Dr. Patrick Henry/P. H. Jameson, Scot's brother-in-law.

6. Cordelia (Butler) Wallace, Scot's half sister, married William Wallace.

———⋙∘⋘———

{ SEPTEMBER 13, 1863 }

E. ANNE BUTLER TO SON SCOT BUTLER

Forest Home
September 13th/63

My Dear S. Scot

We have all remained at home to day having had no preaching among our brethren. The pastor of the fourth Presbyterean church having returned we will no longer have services by our preachers there. We will however, until our chapel is ready for occupancy, still attend at the 4th church and return the courtesy shown our preachers by them, in attending our meetings—[1]

Mrs Col. Coburn has returned within a few days from quite a long visit at her fathers in White county   While there she was engaged in nursing a brother, Thad. Test,[2] through a long sickness, which resulted in his death. On her arrival at home, she found the Coburn family in great distress on account of the loss of Col. Coburn's brother Augustus of Ontanogan, who was drowned, together with all aboard save one, (the Pilot of the boat) of the Steamer "Sunbeam" which went down in a heavy gale on Lake Superior. This to Col. Coburn will be a severe shock and a very sad bereavement. The brothers were here together in July and seemed to enjoy being together so much. They had had for years some business copartnership that Col. Coburn had been very anxious to arrange in referance to the uncertainties connected with his own life   But how limited is human foresight. He that seemed the least exposed, was thus so suddenly cut off—

If you have received the last letter or two I have written you, you will know of William's[3] visiting Nashville and that we sent you a package by him   He has returned and we feel much disappointed that he did not see you nor get the package conveyed to you . . . we may have an oppertunity before long to send it as doubtless there will be some going in that direction   John Beaty was ordered to his regiment the other day suddenly, as all military orders and movements generally are. John kept very close at home   I did not see him at all he was ailing with chills most of the time while home   We took Anne down at last to have her picture taken, we have not got them home yet and do not know how good they will be—

Dont you think the war news is very encouraging. Are not events marching grandly to the music of the Union. A few more months will surely wind up our national conflict, and see our worn battered soldiers resting from all thier toils and hardships in thier dear old homes. Sometimes Scot I feel that I can hardly wait for the time to come when we can have you with us all the while now if you were but ready to go in to college when it opens next week. This session was the expected time when you were again to reenter college, after an interval of three years. One half of that time has been spent by you in a way that none of us dreamed of at the time you quit school. Obeying as you did, what you considered the call alike of duty and patriotism. I fondly hope to receive you my dear boy home to my heart unbroken in health and strengthened in every principal that constitutes the true man, and in this we will find ample reward for all the trials of the past—be they physical or mental

William and Cordelia are out this afternoon, they have now gone over to look at their lot   Your Pa has made sale of the remainder of that field, to a German, who is very well off, for a family residence. He will put up a fine residence and fix up the grounds about it tastefully   As I wrote you of Mati Brown[4] being in great danger of losing her eyesight I must not fail to tell you that she is much improved in that respect   Is now able to see to go about and can read some I think her father thinks her improvement is permanent.

Your Pa received yours of last week   It came through quite expeditiously beyond our expectation for we did not think but that your letters would be delayed on the way

Affectionately Your Mother
E Anne Butler

1. The Christian Chapel at the corner of Delaware and Ohio Streets was established in 1836. At this time it was undergoing renovation.

2. Thaddeus Test, Scot's distant cousin and brother of Mrs. John (Caroline Test) Coburn.

3. William Wallace.

4. Members of the Brown family, close friends of the Butlers.

<hr />

{ SEPTEMBER 27, 1863 }

OVID BUTLER TO SON SCOT BUTLER

Forest Home near Indianapolis
Sept 27th 1863

Son Scot

The papers tell us of the great battle of Chickamauga[1] fought by the forces of Rosecrans and Bragg on the 19th and 21st insts. They tell us that the fight was fierce and desperate and that the Union Army was largely outnumbered and repulsed   We know that you were there and although we believe that your position in the Signal Corps exposed you to less danger than a position in the ranks yet we can but feel some solicitude on your account and some impatience to hear from you   The last we have from you is your letter to your Ma dated at Chattanooga the 14th inst with a postscript dated at Crawfish Spring the 18th inst   The last date is the day before the battle   We do not know where Crawfish Spring is but suppose it not far from the battle field   Notwithstanding we have not yet heard from you we have confidence that you have passed the terrible ordeal with honor and with safety—that God who has hitherto protected you has done so still. We much desire to learn that fact from you and to hear from you a full statement of what you experienced and what you saw of this, what by some is called the greatest battle of the war.

Most of the accounts which we have received are rather vague and indefinite and somewhat conflicting. The correspondent of the Cincinnati Gazette has given a very graphic description of the two days fight. It is fuller and clearer than any other I have seen   Apprehensions are still entertained for the fate of Rosecrans Army but it is thought if he can maintain his position a few days till reinforcements can reach him   His army will not only be safe but will be able to drive the rebels south or annihilate them. I need not however speculate upon the position for before this reaches you all our doubts in reference to it will be solved

Well Scot you probably now know something of the horrors of the battle field. The heart sickens in the contemplation and grows sad, Oh how sad at the thought that the sacrifice of so much of human suffering and human life is required to atone for our great national sin   May God accept it as a complete atonement and may the National heart be purged of its great transgression

Your Aunt Ellen (your Uncle Roberts wife)[2] is quite sick. She has been sick some two weeks & for several days it was thought she would not recover. She is now regarded as a little better. Your Ma has gone to stay with her tonight On this account or on account of our heavy company during the day your Ma has not written to you today according to her almost uniform practice of writing Sundays   But of course she will supply the omission soon

Your Ma has heretofore written you that Chancy[3] had gone to Illinois with your Uncle Chancy[4] to try farming this fall. He is there yet and your Uncle writes [he] is working well   He will probably return about the 10th or 15th of next month   He seems reluctant to go to College when he returns and much desires to go into the Army   I think him too young but if I thought the necessities of the service required such recruits I should have the less objection to it

The frosts in August & this month have done immense damage to the corn crops in the North West   Your Uncle Chancy and I have suffered much by them on our Illinois farm

The present session of the University has opened finaly and the prospect is very fair   I feel that it is not in vain that I have labored to build up that Institution   I wish it to be present in your thought constantly—not only in memory but in expectation and I trust you will mark out no path way in future life which does not lead you through it.

But I must close. Remember that there are anxious hearts at home desiring to hear from you and to know that you are safe and well

Your Affectionate Father
Ovid Butler

1. Scot was actively involved in the battle of Chickamauga under Capt. Jesse Merrill's detachment of the Signal Corps.

2. Ellen C. (Wallace) McOuat, Scot's aunt and wife of Robert Lockerbie McOuat.

3. Chauncey Butler, Scot's younger brother (variant spelling: Chauncey, Chauncy, Chancy).

4. Chauncey Butler, Scot's and Chauncey's uncle and Ovid Butler's brother (variant spellings: Chauncey, Chauncy, Chancy).

{ O C T O B E R 1 1 , 1 8 6 3 }

OVID BUTLER TO SON SCOT BUTLER

Forest Home near Indianapolis Ind.
Oct 11th 1863

Son Scot

Your letter to your Ma of the 26th ult relieved us of much anxiety on your account   The papers told us of the battles of Chickamauga of the 19 and 20th ult and believing from previous advices that you were in those battles   We could but feel much apprehension for your safety. That you escaped your letter gives us the assurance and for that we feel truly thankful   We conclude too that you escaped unhurt although you do not say so   Indeed you say far too little about yourself   You must be fully aware that however deeply interested we may be in the incidents of those terrible conflicts the points of greatest interest to us are where you were what you saw and what you did. Around these points our deepest warmest sympathies would concentrate   Will you tell us of these that we may be with you and go with you through these conflicts. The battles of Chickamauga rank among the great battles of the war and although the Union forces were pushed back by overwhelming numbers yet the honor of the National Arms was not tarnished

The indications are that another and a greater battle is pending near the same place   Treason is gathering all her forces and seems disposed to stake the fate and destiny of the rebellion upon the result of a single battle   If I mistake not the government is preparing to meet the terrible [. . .] and the conflict when it comes will probably be the greatest ever fought upon the American Continent— perhaps the greatest of Modern time. The soldiers of the Union when they shall see the united Armies of the rebellion in battle array before them will feel that they have then the opportunity to strike a blow which shall extinguish treason and wipe out the rebellion forever   And May God crown their effort with full and complete success. The soldiers of the Army of the Cumberland who shall have passed safely and honorably through the campaign to its closing victory and triumph will be regarded as Fortunes Favorites. But suffering and death are along the path way and how many—Oh how many must still be the victims

Yet Death is not limited to the Battle field and the Camp. His attentions are not confined to the soldiery. He visits the peaceful habitations and selects his victims from among those who know nothing of wars alarms   He has just stricken down one near us. Your Aunt Ellen—Your Uncle Roberts wife died last night. I wrote you some time since that she was very sick. When Your Ma wrote you last she was thought to be better but she took a relapse and she has gone whither we all whether soldier or citizen are hastening

Other names might be added to the list of the departed but they are more remote and you would not probably recollect them. Your Ma is writing to you and will give you the "local items"

We wish to know whether you are still with Lieut Flook as formerly and whether Mr Harrison is still with you   We want indeed to know upon whom we could rely to write us in case of any accident to you   Such a contingency is possible and if from any cause you should be unable to write we want to know that some friend would truly and promptly communicate the facts to us   May God avert such a contingency and may you at all times be both able and willing to keep us advised of your safety and health

Your affectionate Father
Ovid Butler

{ OCTOBER 12, 1863 }

NETTIE BUTLER TO BROTHER SCOT BUTLER

Forest Home
Oct 12th 1863.

My Dearest Brother,

Your two letters of Sept 28th & 30th have just been received and read with much pleasure. I will first explain what I meant by your trusting Demia more than you did me. I asked her to let me read your letter but she would not I saw at the close though these words "remember this letter is strictly confidential." Now Scot you know you never wrote me such a letter in your life.

The photographs you speak of were some of Ma's   I will send you one in this letter. We think them very good.

You ask if Julia has returned, no she will not come until Christmas   she has a free school in Greencastle. Mollie is back at our house. We are real good friends *now* [that we] have made a bargain to *try* not to quarrel any this three months. Speaking of you the other day she said she had not answered your last letter, that soon after she got it you moved and she did not know where to direct to and now it was so late she was ashamed to write.

Oh! Scot if you could only spend Christmas & New Years with us! do try and get a furlough about that time or Thanksgiving. You told me about writing to some girl in Ohio did you ever recieve any answer? Why did you think I would scold you for writing to Julia when I've been trying to persuade you to take that step ever since you went into the Army? She told her Aunt in confidence and Mrs Hoss[1] supposing that you had told me spoke of it to me. When I expressed surprise she told me not to say anything about it to you. I wanted you to tell me *so much* for I wanted to tell you how glad I was. Demia says that you never said anything to her about it. Julia did, when I wrote to her about not telling me anything, told me that you and she were corresponding but said for me not to mention it to you for if you were writing to me all the while and did not tell me she ought not to be the one to tell it   It's real amusing how *very* consciencious you both are getting to be.

I wrote to J—[2] asking about her engagement she says there is not a word of truth in it that she has a perfect contempt for the Lieut; these are very strong words *from her* and mean a good deal she says he is *so* concieted struts about the streets of G[3] as if the ground wasn't good enough for him to walk on.

Scot do you know any of the clerks at Maj Gen. Crittenden's[4] Head Quarters? I have an anonomous correspondent there. I wish you'd have him pointed out to you and tell me what kind of a looking fellow he is. His name is Serg't John E. Gardner. Writes a splendid letter.

I suppose Ma told you of Aunt Ellen's death, poor Uncle Robert[5]   I feel so sorry for him. Demia is Secretary of the University and I've stopped school to keep the house clean   I do enjoy staying at home, so much, although I have to work real hard.

My Capt is still in Libby Prison has been there over five months. Mr. Frenyear[6] chaplain of the 51st died a few weeks ago do you remember him? he used to come to school, a very promising young preacher   The College is remarkable full this year. We have four young lady boarders. Duncan's have five *chaps* from Kentucky. One is Demia's devoted another is *trying* to be Molls but she dont like him. I'm in love with two of them but they wont look at *me*   One is lame, has red hair, colors it black except a tuft of red on top   Oh! I tell you he looks divine.

Aint I a good girl for answering your letters so soon? Write very very soon.

Your loving sister
Nettie Butler

1. Mrs. George W. Hoss, wife of Butler University professor George Washington Hoss.
2. Julia Wesley Dunn.
3. Greencastle, Indiana.
4. Union general Thomas Leonidas Crittenden saw action at Chickamauga where Scot was assigned to signal duty.
5. Robert Lockerbie McOuat, Scot's uncle, brother of Elizabeth Anne (McOuat) Elign, and husband of Ellen C. (Wallace) McOuat.
6. George J. Frenyear (Frenyer), hospital steward and chaplain in Company A, Fifty-first Indiana Infantry Regiment.

{ O C T O B E R [1 8 6 3] }

DEMIA BUTLER TO BROTHER SCOT BUTLER

Office NWC University
Oct [1863]

My Dear Brother:

I wrote you about a week ago but it is very doubtful whether it or the many other letters sent from home have yet or ever will reach you. Communication is so uncertain that it is very discouraging to write not knowing whether the letter will ever be received. We get your letters about 10 days after they leave you and right glad are we all when they arrive. I often laugh and tell Ma she need not laugh at young girls looking for letters from their lovers for they surely could not watch the mail more closely, seize more gladly and devour more eagerly their most endearing "billet doux" than Ma does a letter from her dear son Scot.

Did Ma ever tell you about a joke Bob Duncan tells on a poor old woman who came into the Clerk's Office to have a letter written for her to her son in the Army. The poor creature was too full for utterance and could only give him short commonplace sentences to write but between every few words she would say now put down "My dear son Stephen" This one epithet repeated so often of course had a very ridiculous effect and to hear Bob repeat the letter word for word is quite amusing. Ma says the joke has just spoiled her favorite address to you for she never writes My dear son Scot without thinking of the poor old woman and her son Stephen.

Bob and John Duncan have both started to School. They have five Kentucky boys boarding with them and of course so many boys together have very gay times. They have been having a great time gallanting the girls but Pres. Benton[1] has made rules prohibiting the young ladies receiving calls from the Students and I don't know what they will do now.

Scot in a letter you wrote sometime ago you said something about the ladies of Nashville not associating with the officers or soldiers and at the same time you advised that some other young ladies should emulate their example. Since that letter you have slyly hinted the same matter which makes me think you wish to be understood on that topic. Now I did not take any of this to myself for I knew you were not aware that I had my *Military beaux* but even if you intended it for Janett who is always talking about some Lieut. Capt. &c what did you mean by it. Dont you think it were better to select our gentleman friends from those who at least appear to love their country and are trying to defend it rather than from those staying at home who have brains too weak and souls too narrow ever to feel a lofty sentiment of patriotism and those whose principles and actions have branded upon their characters the hateful odium of "butternut" I vastly prefer the blue coat and brass buttons though I know they often button over a black heart and base nature I've heard young ladies say that soldiers should not visit them There needed nothing more to tell me whether that girl stood for or against her country. I know we ought to be careful whom we associate with whether among soldiers or civilians but I cannot believe you have so poor an opinion of your "brothers in the cause" as to wish them discarded from genteel society Write to me soon and tell me your opinion on this subject.

Your Aff. Sister
Demia

1. Allen R. Benton, Butler University president of the faculty.

{ O C T O B E R   2 6 ,   1 8 6 3 }

DEMIA BUTLER TO BROTHER SCOT BUTLER

Office NWC University[1]
October 26th 1863

My Dear Brother:

Yesterday Ma re'cd two letters from you of the 11th & 16th insts. It seems to take letters a long while to make this trip. I am waiting very patiently for a reply from some of mine but perhaps they have not reached you. You ought to be thankful however that communication is not entirely cut off for every thing seemed to threaten this for a while.

Well Scot if you expect me to tell you any news in this letter I fear you will be disappointed for every thing for the past week has been moving on with extreme dullness and monotony. I am at the University where I come every morning to do my duty as Secretary which office I presumed you have heard I have now the honor of holding I find it rather pleasant as it only keeps me busy during the morning. I am taking a Commercial course which I think rather tiresome however profitable   Perhaps you will think me rather masculine in my choice of pursuits but I have always had an ambition to do something for myself and I would much prefer keeping books to anything else that is placed in womans reach. If I had my choice between teaching and taking in washing and sewing I think I should not hesitate to take the latter alternative. My Franklin[2] experience though comparatively light easy and pleasant still did not leave me altogether insensible of some of the sacrifice of a teachers life. I made a visit to Franklin this Fall and of course had quite a pleasant time. They offered me great inducements to come back and take up another music class but I declined

While I was there there was a constant train of soldiers going through on the Jeff road to reinforce Rosecrans. I was at the depot several nights to see them pass. They would sometimes stop more than an hour and drum sing dance and eat the good things the ladies had brought them. They seemed so very merry all packed into miserable freight cars like so many cattle. Scot in speaking of Lieut Flook going to the eastern Army you seemed to like the idea of going. Now do you think it would be half as pleasant up there during the cold winter as it is south where you are now   I am sure there must be quite a difference in the climate and I have heard the eastern soldiers describe some of the cold weather to which they were exposed so I dont see how you can want to go but maybe I dont know anything about it. I am very sorry to hear the Lieut Flook still keeps in such poor health. I should think he would rest if he did not get better soon.

I am so sorry you did not get your photographs   We want to see how you look by this time. It will soon be a year since you were at home. How I wish you could [be] with us this Thanksgiving day. Our church has been for a long time undergoing repairs and it is to be finished next week and before the seats are put in we are going to have an oyster supper. Won't that be grand. I am not going into the church until it is finished   Most every one has gone to see it and say it is perfectly beautiful. The ceiling is arched & ornamented elegantly   Mary Sharpe[3] & Joe Moore were married last week. It was quite an elegant wedding. Lidi Brown is going to take Mrs Burns place next week and then we may expect the "grand Union" of Alonzo & Nancy Elizabeth. Chauncy arrived from the west on saturday. He seems to have grown every day and his hair hangs on his shoulders unoiled and uncut since he left home. He looks like a heathen even worse than if he had been in the army where he vows and declares he will be soon. Ma wants him to get a new overcoat but he thinks he would sell it as he expects to have a blue one soon. I dont know what we will do with him. Write Soon.

Demia

1. Butler University.

2. Demia spent a brief period in 1863 teaching music at Franklin College, fifteen to twenty miles south of Indianapolis.

3. Mary Ella Sharpe married first Joe Moore and, on his death, married Robert P. Duncan.

———

{ NOVEMBER 15, 1863 }

E. ANNE BUTLER TO SON SCOT BUTLER

Forest Home
Nov 15th 1863

My Dear Son Scot

Yours of Oct. 27th was handed me by Nettie at the church on last Tuesday after noon, when we were engaged making ready for the festival that was to come off at night. Although you said but little in regard to the scarcity of food, still, it confirmed the fear previously entertained that there was much privation among the troops there   The thought that that trying period was passed for the present, relieved many fears; still, the tears would come & the heart would ache—How it saddens the heart to contemplate even in imagination those feelings of terrible conflict and bloody carnage. How deep the debt of gratitude we owe our brave soldiers   I sometimes fear that we cannot half appreciate the many sacrifices they have made in leaving the joys & comforts of home nor yet the many hardships & trials they constantly endure in the field   Nothing, but the conviction that the very life of the Nation is involved in this struggle reconciles me in any degree to this protraction of the war—If it were a war of conquest or any of those minor points of differances, on which wars are predicated I would have them thrown to the winds & say give us peace. Call back to thier homes our sons our husbands & our fathers and let them study war no more—It is a homely saying though none the less true "That it is a long lane that has no turn in it," and in this matter of the termination of the war I think we are pretty near the turning point—What hope the rebels can have of gaining thier ends is hard to imagine. Thier sky is all darkness and thier surroundings all gloom—

To provide for our soldiers families is the topic and the work of the day. This week is to be given to the work of raising funds to help the families of soldiers living in the city who may need such help—The city & vicinity have responded most liberally to the call and a large amount has been contributed. Two evenings will [be] given to serving a supper the material of which is collected by contribution. On these evenings the adission [admission] ticket will be 50 cts and the supper a separate charge, as at fairs there will be oyster tables   Ice Cream tables &c each table having [to] pay for whatever sold   Interspersed will be Music vocal & instrumental & tableaux—One evening there is to be a concert made up of some of the best singers of the city and on saturday there is to be a fair at which the contributions sent in by our merchants—Mechanics, Milliners, Hatters, Bazaar-Keepers &c will [be] offered for sale and converted into cash. The feeling prevailing is very sanguine of success   I wrote you last week that we intended having a festival at the Chapel which accordingly came off on last tuesday evening   It was announced a *success*   The Chapel with its beautifully arched ceiling looked as magnificent as anyone could wish, the furnace warmed the building [to] a pleasant summer heat   The refreshments seemed satisfactory and we raised one hundred & thirty two dollars in money besides passing, apparently a very pleasant evening to all present. Our pastor announced that the chapel would be ready to hold services in on next sunday at the morning meeting at the University to day

Your cousin Chancy Wilkinson[1] was here a few days ago   The 7th Minnisota Reg. to which he belongs is doing provost duty at St. Louis   He is now

1st Lieutenant and with a guard of twenty men brought some 82 rebels from St Louis to Camp Morton—he is looking well and is in good spirits apparantly His stay was short arriving in the city one night and leaving the next evening. He was in that expedition that last summer drove the Indians across the Missouri river, a march of over a thousand miles and some three or four fights with the red skins

This large sheet of paper looks formidable, but I will not attempt to write it all over, the night is now too far spent and you are doubtless already tired out with it [what] may be to you uninteresting details already given. I want to send you as soon as I learn that it can be done a box by express All of us are anxious to get it done and wonder what of clothing you need but we will have to guess about that

Now Scot I hope you will keep in good heart. Preserve your self respect by good habits and the thought of how much you are loved at home and how justly we all feel we may be proud of you. Take good care of your health all the care you possibly can. In your life and well doing are garnered the hopes of your mother and the pride of your father. With earnest prayers that God will protect my dear boy through all dangers and in His good time return him in health & safty to our hearts & home I remain dear Scot

Your affectionate mother
E Anne Butler

1. Chancy Wilkinson, Scot's first cousin and son of Robert and Eunice (Butler) Wilkinson.

{ N O V E M B E R   2 6 ,   1 8 6 3 }

E. ANNE BUTLER TO SON SCOT BUTLER

Forest Home,
November 26th 1863

My Dear Son Scot

I wrote you on last monday before leaving Nashville which letter stated our having gone there in the hope of seeing you and also that we had forwarded through the agency of the Indiana Sanitary commission a small box of articles to your address from that city   The box contained a pair of boots pairs socks 2 do gloves 2 woolen shirts, [a] necktie some news papers a new french novel, Les Miserables, a work which I have not read but have heard very highly spoken of and some canned fruit with a few apples thrown in that were then real good ones but I fear if the box is long reaching you will not only be spoiled but may make bad work among the other things—I had gone feeling very doubtful as to our getting to see you, but felt anxious to make the effort any how as there seemed but a poor prospect of seeing you soon obtaining a leave of absence to visit home—I think surely now when Grant will have driven the rebels well back he will let furloughs be given, with this thought hopes again revive of yet this winter seeing you at home—

At Nashville we met on last monday Col. Coburn he arrived there the night before on business   He looked well and in pretty good spirits   I think when the three years are out he will let some one else, on the reenlistment of the 33d have the chance of being Col—

Your Pa and I would like to have you mustered out with the regiment when in nine months its time will have expired. Write if this is practicable. I suppose it would be necessary for you to return to the regiment a while before the term of its enlistment shall have closed in order to [be] included among its members.[1] Look the ground over and tell me your thoughts in regard to it   I do not feel willing for you to prolong your term of service and have feared that any new organization of the corps would likely involve that contingency   Your Pa and I have feared that a longer period than that of your first enlistment would break in upon any plans of your completing your education and that would be a thing we would very much regret as being to you a loss that you would always feel its disadvantages through life

We visited while at Nashville Col. Harrisons[2] encampment found it looking very comfortable and snug—In answer to my inquiry of Sam having deserted, I learned that a younger brother of his but not Sam, had indeed deserted but was brought back   He was punished by a forfeiture of pay and in some other way made to feel the error of his way but in all was but lightly dealt with considering the crime committed—

Tonite a squad of the 70th came up to get recruits to fill up the regiment they left Nashville the day before we did. We found Nashville alive with officers and men the blue coats predominated largely. The route all along the road from Louisville to Nashville is studded with tents and the soldiers numerous—

To day Scot is Thanksgiving have you in any way observed it? You remember that this time last year you were with us, while I regret not having you with us to day I still feel thankful for the preservation of your life and health and fondly hope that by this time next year you will be with us to go to the wars no more for I begin to have strong hopes that before another year rolls round the victory of our arms will be complete—I will now close praying this will find all well with you—

Affectionately your Mother
E. Anne Butler

PS

Upon looking this over your Pa thinks you would not know that he accompanied *me* on that occasion, especially would you not so understand it if the letter sent you from Nashville has not been received. In writing I am not always very clear and am apt to take it for granted that things are understood—I thought too that I would not now write much about my impressions in regard to what I saw in the south nor yet how your Pa liked the trip to Dixie but would wait and let him speak for himself—this he expects soon to do as he purposes soon to write you

    1. Scot had left the regiment for the Signal Corps. The question here was a matter of expiration of term. Had he remained a member of the Indiana Thirty-third, his term of enlistment would have expired on January 31, 1865, three years after his enlistment. With his official transfer to the Signal Corps, Scot's date of discharge might have been considered to be three years from the date of transfer. It was important to Ovid and Elizabeth Anne that Scot be mustered out at the earliest possible date along with his original regiment, the Thirty-third.
    2. Future president Benjamin Harrison.

{ NOVEMBER 27, 1863 }

OVID BUTLER TO SON SCOT BUTLER

Forest Home near Indianapolis
Nov 27th 1863

Son Scot

    Learning from your letter dated Nashville the [blank space in letter] inst that you were at that place & might be detained there several days your Ma and I concluded to make an effort to see you there   We left here on the train of Wednesday night the 18th inst but owing to obstructions on the track did not get to Louisville till 11 OClock the next day   There we were refused a pass to Nashville & telegraphed to Col Harrison to send us by telegraph a pass from Gen Granger   We got that pass but too late to leave Louisville till the morning of Saturday the 21st   We arrived at Nashville [past?] night of that day and found upon inquiry that the Signal Corps party had left for the front on the day we left home   This was a great disappointment to us as we had hoped and much desired to see you there   We found that however much we might desire it we could go no farther   We spent Sunday and Monday at Nashville [and] saw Col Harrison who is encamped in the vicinity of Fort Negly   We were also fortunate in meeting Col Coburn there. We made some acquaintances there especially with the family of Mr Scoval[1]—a Staunch Unionist who has done much for Indiana State Soldiers since the occupation of that place by the Union forces   We brought home with us his daughter Miss Mary Scoval to go to School at the University

On monday afternoon there was a report in Nashville of fighting at Chattanoga and I felt reluctant to leave until I could learn more about it. Your Ma however disappointed in [not] seeing you was very anxious to get home and thought we should get the news here as quick as at Nashville   She supposed from your position you would not be presently exposed   In this she was probably right but possibly she may have been mistaken. We left Nashville on Tuesday morning and arrived at home on wednesday morning

The fight it seems did commence on Monday and was continued through tuesday and wednesday with most brilliant results for the Union arms according to the accounts which have reached us through the papers   Of the subsequent operations we have as yet no information. In our rejoicings for the victories we remember that they have been won by the sacrifice of many valuable lives and we trust and hope that our own dear boy is not among the sacrifices

I expressed to Col Coburn the wish that you be returned to your regiment before it should be mustered out of service [and] that you might be discharged with it. There will be an effort made to reenlist the regiment and this will probably be successful with the greater number of the men   I do not think that patriotism or the exigencies of the service require that you should reenlist You may yet complete your education son if you should not be discharged till next Spring and the want of that education would be a greater sacrifice of your future than it seems to me you are called upon to make. The rebellion is I think about exhausted and in a few months probably will complete its utter overthrow. If you could be discharged with your regiment in August next it would give you the advantage of the next Session at the University which you would loose by continuing in the Service till your three years expires

I am most anxious that you complete your Education at the University. I have felt the want of a liberal education myself and to give it to others I have invested thousands and spent some 12 or 15 years of my life in efforts to build up the University Of course I am deeply anxious that my children should have the benefit of the Institution and for you to fail in this would be to me a matter of more than ordinary regret.

I would write you something of my impression about "Dixie" and of my convictions as to its future which have been deepened and strengthened by my recent trip to Nashville. But I have neither time or room now

Your Uncle Chancy is quite Sick and I propose going tomorrow to see him. I am fearful of the result of his sickness but have not heard directly from him since my return from Nashville

May Heaven bless and preserve you and permit your safe return to home and friends

Your affectionate Father
Ovid Butler

1. H. G. Scovel, father of sisters Mary and Anna Scovel. Anna married Chauncey, Scot's brother.

{ N O V E M B E R   2 8 ,   1 8 6 3 }

E. ANNE BUTLER TO SON SCOT BUTLER

Forest Home
November 28th/63—

My Dear Son Scot

Your Pa left home this morning for Hanover to visit your Uncle Chancey who is quite sick. Upon leaving he left a letter addressed to you which I will enclose with this

I wrote you from Nashville and also since our return on Thanksgiving day. We attended services on that day in town, our chapel now being completed. The improvements thereon are I believe highly satisfactory and the necessary sum is on hand to pay off all the expenses incurred which are some three or four thousand dollars   We have received no letter from you since that written at Nashville on the 13th inst   I feel anxious to hear from you especially since the engagements of last monday tuesday & wednesday   The news is very encouraging from Chattenooga   The days of rebellion seem to be fast drawing to a close   The end must surely be nigh

The series of entertainments gotton up for aid to soldiers families of which I wrote you, was pronounced a complete success. The sum of sixty two hundred dollars was realized in the eight days that they occupied   There has been great liberallity shown by the people. Our farmers here and in other parts of the state have on stated days brought in produce of all kinds and large amounts of wood which have been deposited safely for distribution among the soldiers families   In this mornings paper I notice the appointment of Wallingford[1] of this place, as adjutant of 33d Ind he has been all the while with the regiment since it left here holding the position of Lieutenant. He is brother in law of the Hunts of this place.

Your Grandma is now in much better health than when your Aunt Ellen was sick. She comes but seldom to see us. This war has made in many instances much alienation of feeling among those that heretofore were most fully united in feeling and me & mine have not altogether escaped its influence In regard to this conflict, its cause and almost everything connected with it, our convictions, our opinions, our hopes are perhaps as antagonistic as they possibly can be. When this is the case you can readily appreciate that when to gether how constantly guarded each has to be to avoid giving offence, this of course throws much of restraint upon the intercourse and mars in a great degree the pleasure of mingling with my mothers family—

I have on several occasion said to the folks at Ma's that nothing that my brothers had ever done had given me shame (though thier ways had not always been faultless) as thier blind adherence to thier party which had taken sides if not with the enemy at least against our Government—such an utterance from me no doubt stung them—but how could one consistently disclaim against all others occupying just the same position and in one's own kin wink at the whole thing Uncle Obe Foote[2] wounded my feelings quite severly the other day by suggesting that all the ladies engaged in the effort to aid the soldiers and soldiers families should don full regimentals. In thus satirizing an effort that I held sacred as my religion Obed Foote wounded my feelings most deeply besides casting upon me as I take it a personal insult knowing as he did full well that I was then on my way to a meeting connected with this same object—You must not infer that there is a breach of friendship existing from what I have written above, you might so think, it is simply a kind of offishness, no frequent seeking of each others society. This will pass away in time when the war is over or when they leave the butternut persuasion and turn war democrats which latter event—would not at all surprize me to see—

Nettie has turned her attention from John Dunn[3] and is now all taken up with Henry Long who has been quite attentive during the late entertainment She hears from Anderson through his brother who a few days ago sent her a communication that Anderson had sent for publication with the request that when published a copy would be sent to Nettie   It was an account of thier capture and treatment in Richmond. His friends thought it was not advisable to publish it as it might be to his disadvanage as he is still held a prisinor so they sent her the original manuscrip

To day is quite wintry some snow has fallen and the air is cold and damp. Your Pa's trip to Shelby will be quite unpleasant having to ride in carriage of some kind ten miles. Uncle Chauncey has not been well since his return from Illinois   He worked too hard, I fear his recovery is very doubtful as his health is quite broken

I hope you will get the box we sent you before the apples spoil   The office of the Indiana Sanitary commission is the place for you to inquire for it We would like to get up a box of eatables for you if we had any assurance that you would get it before the things would spoil. Col Coburn told us that he had shortly before recieved a box his wife had sent him in which almost every thing was spoiled by its long delay on the way. I will not now write more Hoping to soon hear again from you and learn of your health and safety I remain my son

Your affectionate Mother
E A Butler

1. Estis Wallingford, first lieutenant and adjutant to the Indiana Thirty-third.

2. Obed Foote, Sr., Scot's uncle, was a Democrat who had a strong affiliation with many Southern sympathizers in Indianapolis. He often vexed Elizabeth Anne with his insulting political comments, alienating her from her McOuat family.

3. John E. Dunn, brother of Julia Wesley Dunn.

{ D E C E M B E R   6 ,   1 8 6 3 }

E. ANNE BUTLER TO SON SCOT BUTLER

Forest Home
Dec. 6th/63

My Dear Scot

After meeting to day Ovid[1] handed me your letter of Dec 1st written at Bridgport.[2] It was nearly three weeks since we received yours of Nov 13th dated at Nashville and you can well imagine our anxiety about you especially in view of the stirring times there has been about Chattenooga—Your field of labors however seems to have been away from that point and attended by other difficulties and no doubt hardships more severe than you would have met there. The trip was I know a hard one and until I hear that you are none the worse for it, I will feel very anxious about you.

Scot I terribly fear this hard life is telling severly on your health. If this is so do not try to conceal it from us. How your constitution can bear all this exposure and hardship is a wonder to me   I want you to write me if you are still subject to camp diarhea. This disease if not checked ultimates in chronic Camp diarrhea which is almost incurable. Do not neglect using every precaution to keep off these ailments or if attacked with them to get cured as speedily as possible

We have been all the while sending you letters and if not in the mean-time misplaced at the Department Head quarters you will have quite an assort-ment upon your arrival there   I will not attempt to recapitulate what has heretofore been written you and as to what may now be on hand [I] must say that it is neither strange or very interesting news that is now afloat—

To day your Aunt Jennie[3] sent me from New York a letter she had lately received from Mollie Elgin[4] now Mrs Prescott of Louisvill, Mo. She writes that her two older brothers are in the Southern Army under Bragg that she herself is much changed has grown old looking and is a plain farmers wife—

It is reported that Col. Tailor was arrested the other day charged with being the "Capt. Tailor of John Morgan Staff"   How true this may turn out I do not Know, but he has been now some time strongly suspected of being con-nected with the rebels of Ky   To which his long absence from home at differant times would seem to give some coloring of truth as his relatives here profess to be ignorant of his whereabouts at such times

John Dunn expects in a week or two to leave for an eastern hospital he is not yet able to go into the field, he was able to walk a little on his foot but by so doing he injured it so as to have to use the crutch again. Julia has been all along expecting to come to her Aunts after the holidays and had wished to get the school of little folks that Lidi Brown had been teaching. The prospect now is that Miss M. Brown sister of Phil. Brown will get the school before Julia gets here. Lon. Atkinson and Wife are now in the City   He says that he would like to visit Chattenooga in about a month, and that he has been sending a large amount of Sanitary goods to that point lately

I hope to hear soon of your safe arrival at Chattanooga and of your getting the box we sent you from Nashville   I am fearful that the apples will rot and spoil the other things before they come to hand   The war news from Grant and Burnside is very cheering   The change since this time last year in the hopes of the Union men is very great in regard to the final success of the government in putting down the rebellion

The liberallity of the people is constantly on the increase in giving aid to soldiers families and in furnishing sanitary goods to sick & wounded soldiers

We heard from your Uncle Chancy last night he is still in a critical condition and we much fear the result. Good night my dear Son and believe me to be

Your affectionate Mother
E Anne Butler

1. Ovid Dyer Butler, Scot's half brother.
2. Bridgeport, Kentucky, located outside Frankfort, between Lexington and Louisville.
3. Jean Maitland (McOuat) Reynolds, Scot's aunt and sister of Elizabeth Anne (McOuat) Butler.
4. Scot's cousin. See Elgin letters collection held by the Indiana Historical Society, Indianapolis, for an intimate detail of the Elgin-McOuat relationship.

{ D E C E M B E R   2 0 ,   1 8 6 3 }

E. ANNE BUTLER TO SON SCOT BUTLER

Forest Home
Dec. 20th/63

My Dear Scot

It seems a long while now since your last letter was received   I have been expecting with no little anxiety to hear from you. You have been having a rough hard time of it I know and we all have been fearful that it has made you sick. The great lack of transportation is going to bear severely on the troops at Chattanooga   I learned upon inquiry at the Express Office that nothing but small packages could be forwarded by express to that place. I had intended to get up a box of eatebles for you which we hoped to get to you by Christmas, but that gratification is denied us, but so soon as we learn it to be practicable we are anxious to get it done   In the meantime if you should find that it can be done let us know and we will make the attempt

From a letter in last nights Evening Gazette written at Chattanooga Dec 7th by the Chaplain of the 100th Ind Reg. it seems that the Sanatary Agent was unable to establish an agency there owing to the impossibility of getting transportation for his goods. From these accounts there seems but little prospect of you having yet got that little box we went you from Nashville

In yesterday morning's Journal there was a telegram from Baltimore that two union escaped prisoners from Libby prison had arrived in that city on the 18th inst. One of these is Nettie's Captain so I suppose we will likely see him in these parts before long especially as his Uncle Jerry and family are now here from Missouri

We took John Dunn in the carriage with us to town yesterday to get his furlough extended. His foot is yet too tender to walk much on it he says in another month he thinks he will go back to his company but I do not think he would be able to do much at scouting this winter with such a bundled up foot. He is a corrospondant of Molly Frybarger's[1] (if writing one letter constitutes a corrospondant) already having written her although she only left here about four days since. John is rather susceptible and Mollie has I beleive been quite as devoted in her *visits* and attentions as the friend of ours I wrote you of in my last. Her army corrospondant in the meantime shows her great devotion, sending her in the past week letters music &c. She was sick a week or two before she left and indeed was sick a good part of the term and in low spirits and discontented nearly all the time and is not likely to come back to school

Nettie is expecting Henrietta Mullins to spend the Christmas hollidays with her   Demia expects to go to Franklin and Vernon during the holidays to visit the relatives. Your Pa went last Monday to Hanover to see your Uncle Chauncy who is still very sick   He is slowly getting some better but it will take him a long while to recover. Our town is getting its name up in the way of street robberies, housebreaking &c   Forest Home was the scene of some excitement the other afternoon when it was found that the purses of all the young ladies with us had been riffled to gether with a gold watch taken that one of the girls had left by a *friend* in the army with her for safe keeping   all had disappeared leaving no trace whatever of the thief or of the time when it was done. After some days the money & watch were returned by a girl who was in the habit of running in to return them *sans ceremony* who stated she took them *in sport* to give the girls a fright. She was here going to school but will not likly come back next term   As she is one of whom you have never heard it is not worth while to give her name

Grandma has invited us there Christmas Eve except that we have no arrangements for visiting in the holidays. I had been hoping all the while to have you with us but I fear there is not much prospect of that now

Affectionately Your Mother
E A. Butler

1. Molly Frybarger of Connersville, Indiana, a student in the university's preparatory school. *Catalog of Students Not Alumni, Butler College, 1855–1900* (Indianapolis, Ind.: Butler University, n.d.) (hereafter cited as *Catalog*).

{ D E C E M B E R   2 7 ,   1 8 6 3 }

E. ANNE BUTLER TO SON SCOT BUTLER

Forest Home
Dec. 27th/63

My Dear Son Scot

Yours of the 11th & 12th inst was truly welcome, bringing as it did assurances of your continued good health and safe arrival also at Chattanooga   I hardly know how to express how thankful I feel that your health is preserved and life spared through all the exposure you have experienced since you left home that I am often very anxious about you I must confess but all the while I have had a very strong abiding trust that you would be restored in safety to your home & to those who love you dearly there.

        Christmas has come & gone with out any special event to mark it with us. Demia on last wednesday went to Franklin to spend her christmas with cousin Eliza Vawter[1] and from there to go to Vernon for a few days   Romy Todd had returned here from Hanover, as your Uncle Chauncey had got better, but receiving word that his brothers Irby & Ovid had enlisted he went down to see them[2]   Mary Scovel had gone to Knightstown to visit some friends. The school girls have gone home and but for Nettie and her friend Henrietta Mullens we would be almost alone

        On christmas eve we were invited to supper at your Grandma's to a family gathering. We met an unexpected guest, a Doct. Townsend from Decotah and I expect an accepted suitor of your Aunt Mattie's. He has been in the service as surgeon for a year or so but is now tired he told me of frontier life and thinks of settling down for life in Springfield Illinois.

        On returning from your Grandma's that evening I found Capt. Anderson here. I never saw him looking so well   His escape from Libby prison made him feel glad "He was alive." His, usually, to me, dull face was so lit up and animated that he looked real handsome and then his *regimentals* were bran new from top to toe. Christmas afternoon William and Cordelia, Henry & Maria[3] were out to supper. Ovid was over to supper but Mattie[4] was afraid to venture out with her young daughter[5] now but little over a month old. On the same day I attended the funeral of James Edgar. His decline & death was much like his brother Samuel's[6] from bleeding of the lungs,   a few minutes before his death he sat eating his breakfast by the fire. It was within a few days of being three years since the demise of his brother that his own occurred

        I will get you Lala Rhook[7] and the other articles you named in your letter to Demia ready to send by Finly should he call and in case he does not will try expressing to you if practicable. As I named to you in one of my late letters the agent here refused to forward to Chattenooga any thing heavier than packages at that time. We all desire very much to send you a box of things to eat would it do to ask Finley to take any thing so cumbersome? I wonder much whether you have yet got the little box we sent you from Nashville and in what plight you will find the contents but for the apples and canned peaches that were in it a half years delay would have done no hurt   as it is I expect the clothing and reading matter will be useless to you when it arrives   We had no choice in the way of forwarding it to you, as the express agent at N.[8] positively refused to forward it. This you know was at the time that the fight was pending and indeed in progress at Chattenooga

George & Tom Brown[9] did not get home at christmas as I wrote you was expected. Several are here recruiting who have thier homes here but none I believe that you know Mrs Sanders has had a very severe surgical operation performed lately the cutting of a cancer from her breast Henry says that she is doing as well as he expected but I suppose her condition is critical

Write me the word you may get from Capt Seaton and write to us often

Affectionately your Mother
E Anne Butler

1. The Vawter family members were Scot's cousins from Vernon, Indiana, the Butler homestead in Jennings County since 1817.

2. Irby Smith, Ovid, William P., and Jerome Jillete (Romy) Todd, Scot's cousins.

3. Maria (Butler) Jameson, Scot's half sister, and Patrick Henry Jameson.

4. Ovid Dyer Butler, Scot's half brother and son of Ovid Butler and his first wife, Cordelia Dyer Cole, and his wife, Martha Meeks.

5. Maria Butler, daughter of Scot's half brother Ovid Dyer Butler and Martha Meeks.

6 Samuel A. Edgar, Scot's uncle and first husband of Martha J. McOuat.

7. Poem by Irish poet Thomas Moore.

8. Nashville, Tennessee.

9. Thomas A. Brown, Chauncey's classmate and comrade in the 132nd Regiment, Indiana Volunteer Infantry. *Catalog*.

{ J A N U A R Y   1 0 ,   1 8 6 4 }

E. ANNE BUTLER TO SON SCOT BUTLER

Forest Home
January 10th/64

My Dear Son Scot

I have just written a line to Mary Scovel's father at Nashville in reference to that said box and if it still is there it will no doubt be in a few days in the hands of the express company. There is some uncertainty about any thing in it being fit for use unless it is the boots but I want you to get it any how. The time that you named for Finley to give us a call is nearly here I hope he will not fail to come   I would like to see some one that had been with you lately, but in case he should not [come] Capt. Anderson says he will take a package to you   We have been reading a novel by Bayard Taylor[1] that I was very much pleased with which I intend sending you and will gather up some other reading for you

We do not like to give up the idea of sending you a box of eadibles and think if others can succeed in getting them through we must try too before long

We have been having intensely cold weather since New Years Eve, to day it has slightly moderated, but now at eight oclock at night it is as cold as one would care to feel. We have any number of accounts of suffering and deaths from exposure to the weather during this cold spell, among soldiers and civilians but how much they are exaggerated I hardly can tell. Many things stated in regard to our soldiers here having suffered was contradicted in the papers

Last night I received yours of 24 & 31st Dec. was very happy to learn that you had suffered no ill effects from your trip to Nashville & were in the enjoyment of such very good health—hope it will be continued you and that you will take all the care of yourself you possibly can. We want to see you as you now look and are therefore quite anxious to get your ambiotype that you spoke of sending home—You named that you had lately received some daily Journals, at your suggestion your Pa ordered the weekly to be sent you and the daily discontinued but I suppose they have been sending you all the while the daily. I wish you could get your papers regularly, it would help to wile away many a lonely hour,   we sent you a Journal the other day with Col. Goddard's, Gen. Rosecrans Chief of Staff report of the late battle at Chattenooga in which there was a very favorable report of the aid given by the Signal Corps[2]—

Ovid has left the Clerks office and is preparing to open a law and collecting office in company with Doct Wallace ex county Auditor a fine business man and well acquainted throughout the country—

College is going on this term much as the last. John Duncan and George Gist[3] are in the parlor now with the girls—Gist just got in last night being detained at home. The Ohio river was very difficult of crossing last evening owing to the floating ice

Demia got home monday from her visit to Franklin & Vernon   the friends are talking of the family Gathering of next June which is to take place there   When it was proposed to have it there by someone at the gathering here last summer, I suggested that we make a picnic of it in some nice shady place and have a basket dinner, and from what Demia tells me that will be the programme   I hope Scot that you will get leave to come this time but should you not your turn if life lasts will surely come next time—

I wrote you in my last an item of family news that I know must have surprized you very much. I have not much to say about it. I know nothing to Andersons disadvantage, but feel that Nettie is very young to enter into such a relation and had she been going from us could hardly have consented at all. The arrangement is for the marriage to take place Thursday Morning 14th inst at ten oclock. They will leave on the 12 o'clock train for Kokomo where his parents live they will return on saturday evening or monday morning. On tuesday he leaves for Chattenooga and she remains with us at home. None but the relatives are to [be] present at the wedding.

Good Night and may God in his mercy bless and protect you is the prayer of

Your affectionate Mother
E. Anne Butler

I had forgotten Scot that we had sent you the Journal with the names of those subject to the draft and was thinking that they had been sent you from the office. The word is that there will be no draft in Indiana. Indiana has furnished her quota and two Thousand and over

1. Bayard Taylor, American author whose novel *Hannah Thurston*, referred to here, dealt with social idealism.
2. The article reads: "The Signal Corps has been growing into usefulness and favor, daily, for the last four months, and now bids fair to become one of the most esteemed of the staff services. It rendered very important service from the time we reached the valley of the Tennessee. For its operations we refer to the report of Captain Jesse Merril, Chief Signal Officer." *Indianapolis Daily Journal*, Jan. 7, 1864.
3. George Washington Gist, Scot's classmate and comrade in the 132nd Indiana. *Catalog*.

{ J A N U A R Y   1 3 ,   1 8 6 4 }

OVID BUTLER TO SON SCOT BUTLER

Forest Home
Jany 13 1864

My Son Scot

Capt A Atkinson called this evening to let us know that he should leave tomorrow night for Chattanooga and would take any word to you we might send

He could not take a box even if we could get one ready in time which I suppose would be doubtful. Indeed under present circumstances I have time to waste but little that I would desire to say to you and your Ma & Sisters will probably have no time to write anything   If you have got your Ma's recent letters it will be no news to you when I tell you that Nettie is to be married tomorrow to Capt Anderson of the 51st Regt. Ind. Vol. You will recollect that he was taken prisoner with Col Streights[1] detachment near Rome Georgia. He has been 7 or 8 months in Libby prison from which he recently escaped. He got a furlough for 30 days & has improved it in persuading Nettie to marry him before his return to his regiment   The wedding will take place in the morning. About noon they will leave for Kokomo and will probably return here Saturday or Monday   Next week he will be on his way to join his regiment at Chattanooga or wherever it may be found   He thinks it is either at Chattanooga or between there and Knoxville   You will probably see him for he will be near to call on you if practicable. The new relation will give you the claim of Brotherhood upon each other and may be used by both to your mutual advantage

I am somewhat anxious that you should get a discharge in time to enter College again at the opening of Next Session but I fear that the prospect for it is not good. I do not understand clearly your position on the Signal Corps. At first you were detailed from your regiment for duty in the Corps but your connection with the regiment concluded you were held as a member of it   I understand that subsequently upon some modification or reconstruction of the Signal Corps you were retained in it and your connection with the regiment severed   You were no longer counted a member of it. Was this effected by your reenlistment or without it   In other words are you now in the service under your enlistment in the regiment or are you serving under a subsequent enlistment in the Signal Corps. I do not understand why you should have been excommissioned and a new descriptive list taken and you continued in the Signal Corps unless in some way you were regarded as having reenlisted in the Corps   You have I think in some of your letters suggested that the proposed reorganization of the Corps fell through & was never consummated   How then did you get entirely disconnected from your regiment   I have not sufficient information to answer these questions myself and submit them for your solution with such help as you can get there. You think however that you have not reenlisted but that if you take pay under your new descriptive list you will be held to service beyond the time of the regiment—that is that you would be held as upon reenlistment in the Corps   If you are now upon this point it would be well to learn definitely and certainly the length of the service to which you would thus bind yourself and if unwilling to undertake it to decline to receive pay on that descriptive list. In that case you would need some money for expenses which if I had opportunities I would be willing to send you   But be careful not to be mistaken in this matter for I doubt whether you can get your original descriptive list from Col Coburn for the purpose of receiving pay on it. While at Nashville Col Coburn told me that you had been wholly disconnected with his regiment and was no longer a member of it. I know too little of the subject to advise you how to act but make these suggestions to induce you to act cautiously and prudently in the matter   If in honor and integrity you can get an honorable discharge in time to enter College at the next Session I should much prefer it but if that cannot be done I desire you and I doubt not your wish to fulfil all the obligations of the service you have assumed

Jany 14/64 PM. I left this letter open to give you another item. This forenoon Capt Anderson and Nettie were married and they have left for Kokomo as contemplated   I will leave it to your Ma and Sisters to describe the wedding and tell the incidents so far as they think will interest you   Should the Capt go to Chattanooga as he will if his regiment is there he may be of some service to you in the matter referred to in this letter. I will probably write again by him

Your Affectionate Father
Ovid Butler

Scot By way of Postscript I will say in reference to the Box of which you have heard so much from home but cannot it seems hear anything of from any other source. I a few days since wrote to Mr H G Scovel of Nashville to inquire for it there & if found to forward it to you by the Adams Express. I have also requested Capt Atkinson to inquire for it at Nashville and on the rout to Chattanooga   If either of them find it you will probably get it. But whether you get it or not let us know & also let us know what things you need   We can probably now send by the Adams Express

Your Father
Ovid Butler

1. The occasion of Col. Abel D. Streight's capture was noteworthy. In a raid into Alabama, Streight met the forces of Gen. Nathan Forest. Forest deployed his much smaller force in a way that convinced Streight that he was severely outnumbered, causing Streight to surrender his entire command.

{ J A N U A R Y   1 7 ,   1 8 6 4 }

E. ANNE BUTLER TO SON SCOT BUTLER

Forest Home
Jan 17th/64

Dear Scot

Yours of the tenth was received yesterday   the prospect of little delay in mail communication is real pleasant for a long while the tardiness of the mails was truly provoking

The "theme" of the "Box" is well nigh exhausted but I will venture to further state that your Pa commissioned Lon Atkinson, who left here on the 14th to look it up which he will accomplish no doubt if it is at all "findable" at Nashville or on the route to Chattenooga

Lon has his wife with him   She will not likly go farther than Nashville while he will go to Chattenooga. He expected to see you. Your Pa sent by him a letter to you. I would have sent a package by him if he had not said that he could take nothing but letters, and besides I expected to send it by Capt Anderson. Your comrade Finley has not made his appearance as yet and it may be that he has not come this route—Mrs Coburn is talking of visiting Col. soon but how soon I do not know   I see by the Cincinnatti that Col Coburn's brigade and also that of Col. Harrison have been transferred to the 11th Gen. Howards Corps. We up here think that this means "fight" for them

We could send you any number of newspapers if you wish to have them by Mail   You[r] Pa sent you two or three last week   There was a while that no papers were carried through but now I suppose there would be no hindrance

Demia thinks it very strange that you took no notice of the word I sent you in mine of the 3d in referance to Nettie's contemplated marriage. I did not think it [at] all strange but rather characteristic of you—but I believe I will not pursue the topic until you let me know if you wish to hear any further particulars   I expect Scot I write you many things that interest you but little for I know you always appeared to take but little interest in the gossip of the day—You ought to let me know if it *bores* you   Now do not forget to say whether or no

Miss Mullens is still with us but expects to start home on next wednesday   Miss Sed Hamrick spent a good part of two weeks with us she left for Noblesville last friday. We have two young ladies that were with us last term and

Miss Scovel from Nashville   Romy[1] is with us this term also so you can see we have a pretty good sized family   I sometimes think I will give up having so many besides our own folks about, but some how it seems almost unavoidable. Your Pa will write you by Capt Anderson who expect to leave in a few days   I will send you some reading matter if he can make room in his valise to take it Good Night

Your affectionate Mother
E A Butler

1. Jerome Jillete Todd, Scot's first cousin. Romy was a Butler University student of the English Department and a volunteer in the Indiana 132nd. *Catalog.*

{ J A N U A R Y   2 0 ,   1 8 6 4 }

OVID BUTLER TO SON SCOT BUTLER

Forest Home near Indianapolis Ind.
Jany 20th 1864

My Son Scot

This will be handed you by Capt Anderson of the 51st Regt Ind Vol. who if you have received recent letters addressed to you you will recognize as a Brother in Law   In those letters you were advised of his recent escape from Libby prison—his brief furlough home—and his and Nettie's marriage on the 14th inst. He leaves tomorrow to join his regiment which he expects to find some where in East Tennessee   He tells me that he contemplates reenlisting but that fact should not influence you in that direction   I cannot conceive that either honor, duty or patriotism require you to make so heavy a sacrifice as to deprive yourself of the opportunity to complete your education. But were it other wise and were you desirous of continuing in the service it would be better first to serve out your present time and enter the service anew here   As you are situated on the Signal Corps you are not in the line of promotion & have little chance for it. After your time expires should you desire to reenter the service a better position might I think be had for you   The present [. . .] is a matter of no importance to you and when you have completed your present term of service you can judge better of the necessity for reenlistments

I have had some apprehension that upon being transferred from the Reg to the Signal Corps you had in some way assumed the obligation to serve for three years from the time of the transfer. I have had some talk with Capt Anderson about it & he thinks that cannot be the case but that it is probable that you will be held to service for Three years from the time of your enlistment in the 33d regt and will not be entitled to a discharge when the term of the Regt expires. He says he will probably be detained a short time at Chattanooga and will assist you in solving the question as to the time of the expiration of your term of service   I would prefer your discharge when the regimental term expires but if that is not right and practicable you must of course continue till your Term of three years expires and I trust you will do so cheerfully and serve faithfully and you must make the better use of your time after your discharge to contemplate your education

I have strong faith that before the expiration of your Term the rebellion will be crushed out and the war closed   The indications are now strongly in favor of such a result. Then the army will have done its work and it will remain for the Civil Authorities so to reconstruct the Union as to secure it for all time to come against a repetition of the terrible crime of rebellion   I think President Lincolns Amnesty Proclamation indicates a way in which such reconstruction may take place and I am expecting the speedy return to the Union under it of several of the Seceded States   But whether accepted or not the Loyal sentiment requires that the rebellion be crushed out even at the expense if necessary of a [. . .] of the South

In reference to the box we tried to send you from Nashville I have written you that I wrote to Mr H G Scovel of Nashville to inquire for it there & if found to forward it to you. I also requested Capt Atkinson to look for it at Nashville & on the rout to Chattanooga. Should they fail to find it it would be well for you to make some further inquiries for it. To enable you to do so I will give you a fuller statement in reference to it   When we went to Nashville we took some few things for you expecting to hand them to you there. Finding you gone I attempted to forward them to you. We found a small box & packed those in it which I first tried to get the Adams Express to take   But they declined to receive freight for Chattanooga or any point in that direction for the reason that they were already crowded with such freight & could get no transportation. W J Wallace of this City was then in Nashville as the Special Agent of Gov Morton He told me that Mr Thomas was appointed Sanitary Agent for Indiana at Chattanooga and was then expected at Nashville on his way to Chattanooga and advised me to leave the Box with Mr Ed Shaw[1] Indiana Sanitary Agent at Nashville to be forwarded by Mr Thomas. I accordingly left it at Mr Shaws Office

No 42 1/2 Cherry Street with a young man by the name of Carter who was offi-
ciating there. Mr Carter was from this City formerly a student in the University
and I think an acquaintance of yours. He promised to put it into Mr Thomas
hand   Mr Wallace has since told me that before he left Nashville Mr Thomas had
arrived there and taken charge of the Box understanding to take it to you   This is
the last we have heard of the Box. The contents as I now recollect were one pair
Cavalry Boots Two woolen under shirts Two pair socks. Two pair gloves—a Carvat
two Cans fruit—Some reading matter and Green apples to fill up the Box

  I wrote you a few days since by Capt A Atkinson (Lon Atkinson)   He
and his wife (formerly Mrs Burns) are on a trip south   He takes no Sanitary
Stores this time. Since he was married he and his wife have been engaged in the
Sanitary business in the Northern part of the State and they expect to work
together in that business when they return. I wrote you by him as he expected
to be at Chattanooga & said he would see you

  In your last letter to your Ma which has been received you say you have
drawn no pay since June but expect pay soon   As that may be uncertain I send
you $20 by Capt Anderson that you may have something for necessary expenses
If you should get *that* furlough next month you may need some to come home
on. I hope you will get a furlough to come home if you can get it without being
required to reenlist. That I think would be paying too high for it and I do not
desire to see you now upon these terms

  You wrote some time since for your Ma to send you a ball of [. . .].
These she sends by Capt Anderson. We also send by him Moores poems containing Lala Rook which you desired also "Hannah Thurston" by Bayard
Taylor—and a gold pen and a pair of gloves. The Gloves are some I bought for
myself a short time since & have been worn some but as it was inconvenient to
go to the City today to get you a new pair we send these   This will be all that
Capt Anderson can take unless it should be a little of the wedding cake which
your Ma will send if he has room for it

  I think I have written enough for one letter—more perhaps than you
will like to read at one sitting   Committing you to the care of the Heavenly
Father and wishing You Faith Hope & Courage I am

Your Affectionate Father
Ovid Butler

  1. Edward Shaw, Indiana Sanitary Agent and a member of the Butler University Board of
Trustees. *Catalog*; Cline & McHaffie, *The People's Guide: A Business, Political and Religious Directory
of Marion Co., Indiana* (Indianapolis: Indianapolis Printing and Publishing House, 1874), 130;
Gisela S. Terrell, comp., "Alphabetical Listing of Butler University Board Members, Board of
Directors (July 27, 1852 to February 23, 1861) and Board of Trustees (since March 2, 1861),"
Butler University Archives, Indianapolis.

{ J A N U A R Y   3 1 ,   1 8 6 4 }

CHAUNCEY BUTLER TO BROTHER SCOT BUTLER

Indianapolis Ind.
January 31st 1864

Brother Scot:

We have been having the querest weather up north of late that I ever heard of, ever since the day before Newyears it has been cold as Greenland untill the last week which has been just like summer.

I was down to the public reception of the 31st Reg. which has reenlisted. Gov. Morton received them for the State with one of the best speaches I ever heard. The Mayor, next received them for the city with a short speach, when the Col. & Leut. Col. made short speaches, tendering the thanks of the Regt. to the ladies of the city and the Gov. for the maner in which they had been received. By the way the Maner in which Indiana is receiving her reenlisted Soldiers is teaching New York a lesson.

Scot I am glad that you did not get a position in the six Month men. I met Ingram Fle[tcher] at the depot the other evening and he read me a part of a letter received from Kise[1] that day, who said that Government mules and six months men are treated about alike [and] that since the first of this month 22 men had positively died from starvation and exposure. They were fead one ear of hard corn a day and martch[ed] to death.

The battery that Tom Brown enlisted in has reenlisted and are expected to be home before long. Tom, Wm, & George, have all reenlisted. Cousins Irby and Ovid Todd have enlisted in the 122nd which is not yet organised but will be in a few days as it is all most full. The 33d, Mrs. Coburn[2] says, will not reenlist unless they can be formed into batteries.[3]

I have given up all hopes of being in the army. Pa & Ma will not let me and I cannot think of taking a French furlough.[4]

I wish you could get discharged with the Regt. so you could go to school next year. Romy thinkes he can get Willie[5] to come with him. Hoping to heare from you soon I remain your affectionate brother

Chauncey.

1. Ingram and Stephen Keyes Fletcher, sons of Calvin Fletcher, Ovid Butler's law partner.

2. Caroline (Test) Coburn, wife of Col. John Coburn.

3. Regiments that had served together formed a loyalty to their commanding officers and to each other, and it was common that veteran regiments would not reenlist unless such regiments were formed into batteries that would not be split up.

4. Chauncey did enlist in the 132nd Regiment, Indiana Volunteer Infantry. The regiment was organized on May 18, 1864, at Indianapolis, and he was mustered in that same day. The regiment was immediately ordered to Tennessee and was assigned to duty as railroad guard in Tennessee and Alabama, Department of the Cumberland, until September. Chauncey then served duty at Stevenson, Alabama, until July and at Nashville, Tennessee, until September 1864. He was mustered out with his regiment on September 7, 1864. The regiment lost twelve soldiers to disease during the war. The French furlough is a term similar to the modern AWOL (Absent without Leave), meaning, in this case, that he would not run from home to join up without permission from his parents to do so. It is similarly used to indicate a leave from the service without permission from one's commanding officer.

5. William P. Todd, brother of Jerome and Ovid and son of Dr. Robert Nathaniel and Martha/Mattie Jeanette (McOuat) Todd.

{ JANUARY 31, 1864 }

E. ANNE BUTLER TO SON SCOT BUTLER

Forest Home
January 31st/64

My Dear Son Scot

Yours of the 24th came to hand day before yesterday, as we had had no letter from you for nearly two weeks I was looking rather impatiently to hear from you and was very happy indeed when it came. I feel rather disappointed to learn that you cannot be mustered out with the regiment for I still hoped it possible that it could be done but I must submit to things as they are. Many think that next summer will finish up the war—this feeling is I think quite strong among the soldiers who are now returning on furlough after reenlisting—Mrs Coburn confirms by what she tells me the doubts you expressed as to the 33d reg. reenlisting—she says in Col Coburn's absence from the regiment the officers of the regiment remaining wrote to Gov. Morton that on conditions that they would be reorganized as a battery they would reenlist, but on no other They felt that they had done thier share of marching. Col Coburns special friends here think he ought to be made a Brigadier General but whether his services will be so recognized is a question

You have in naming that there was some prospect of you getting a furlough home raised "Great Expectations" in that direction. To night is Demia's birth-day anniversary—in nine more days is yours, now it would be just the thing if you could be with us then, but if you get here later than that we will not complain though it would be very pleasant to have you home at that time

We have been having a great time here giving the "Veterans" as the regiments reenlisting are called all kinds of "Receptions" such as the City gives through the Mayor and the State by the Governor and other state officials and last though not least a reception dinner by the ladies to each regiment as it arrives. The dinners are served at the soldiers Home where all the usual army rations are furnished all the while to all troops passing through to which the citizens of this place have for the past week   To these reception dinners [are] added such luxuries as trukies chickens pies cakes and canned peaches and other fruits—It has all gone off finely so far but I fear that it will be more expense that our city fathers will be willing to shoulder and may be more than our taxpayers will be able to bear   The ladies have entered very earnestly in the work and they seem to enjoy it very much though it is attended with much labor and fatague—When at the Home at the dinner given the 31st on last saturday, I saw some of the returned six months men from Kentucky   They were convalescents and a more pitiable looking set of poor fellows you could hardly imagine. Pale dirty and shabby and as broken down looking and dispirited as they could well be, it made me heart sick to look at them   The other troops however are looking finely rugged and hearty in looks and in fine spirits. They are here long enough before hand to get new clothes and get fixed up before their *receptions*. Your Pa is writing you so to him I will leave the fruitful theme of "The Box"   Every thing moves on in the usual way   Nothing new or very interesting "Has turned up" of which to write about—I hope it will not be long before we will see you at Home

Your affectionate Mother
E. Anne Butler

{ F E B R U A R Y 1 , 1 8 6 4 }

OVID BUTLER TO SON SCOT BUTLER

Forest Home near Indianapolis Ind
Feby 1st 1864

My Son Scot

I had just commenced a letter to you last evening when I was interrupted by company which prevented my writing   I have written you two letters latterly partly in reference to the box we attempted to send you from Nashville This last was by Capt Anderson which I suppose you have received before this The other was by Capt Lon. Atkinson who was going South and expected to be at Chattanooga   I had previously written to Mr H G Scovel at Nashville to look for the box there & if found to forward it to you by Express if practicable. I also engaged Lon Atkinson to look for the box at Nashville & on the rout to Chattanooga & if found to forward it to you. Lon did not get further than Murfreesboro and has returned here. He says that there were some barges gone near Murfreesboro which prevented his going through. He says that Mr Scovel had found your box at Nashville   He says that they opened it & threw out the apples which were spoiled cut down the box to a smaller size and repacked the things in it. The letter to you he put in the box in one of the stockings   It was left with the Sanitary Agent to be forwarded to you as subject to your order if called for before it could be forwarded.

Lon said that the Adams Express would not take it but that both Mr Scovel and the Sanitary Agent would seek an opportunity to forward it. You may perhaps have some opportunity to send for it. If so you can send an Order for it to Capt Ed Shaw Indiana Sanitary Agent no 42 1/2 Cherry Street Nashville

In your last letters to your Ma you speak of applying for a furlough to come home this month and I notice that your Ma in her letter to you of yesterday is very urgent for you to come. I need not tell you how anxious we all are to have you come but as it is the policy of the Government to encourage reenlistments and furloughs are freely offered for that purpose it is but a natural consequence that furloughs for those who do not reenlist should be almost an impracticability. We do not desire you to pay that price for a furlough and therefore I shall not be greatly disappointed if you do not come now   If however you can get a furlough fairly and without the reenlistment it would be a gratification and a joy to us to see you at home for a short time.

I would not discourage reenlistments   The fact that the old soldiers are reentering the service so cheerfully and in such large numbers is perhaps the best evidence we now have that the rebellion will speedily be crushed out. Its moral influence is encouraging to the Union and discouraging and demoralizing to the rebel cause

But in your circumstances I think you may be well excused from reenlisting at least for the present. In my letter by Capt Anderson I gave you my views upon the subject   If I understand the subject now, your time will not expire until three years from the time of your enlistment and not at the expiration of the three years term of the regiment   That leaves you another year of service which I trust you will discharge well and cheerfully and that in the soldier life you will not forget the home feelings and [. . .] that you are to be a citizen after the relations and duties of the soldier shall cease

In your last letter to your Ma you say that if you should not come home you will send us a list of what things you need   In that case we will endeavor to supply them and send them to you in some way by the Express if practicable.

Whatever may be before you I desire you to trust in God and keep a brave heart and a steady purpose a purpose looking to honor and usefulness when the rebellion shall be remembered with the crimes of the past

Your Affectionate Father
Ovid Butler

PS We sent you some papers—among them this Mornings Journal by which it seems that there is a further call for two hundred thousand more troops the draft to be the 10th March next O B

{ A P R I L 1 0 , 1 8 6 4 }

SCOT BUTLER TO JULIA WESLEY DUNN

Graysville, GA
April 10th 64

Friend Julia,

Your very welcome letter has just been received and my interest in the arrivals of the mail, which had been on the increase for several days past has—in a measure and for the time being—subsided. For the past week or two I have been doing duty on a station near Ringgold[1] and only returned to this place day before yesterday. Our situation at that place was a very pleasant one and I was sorry to leave it. Its advantages were manifold. In the first place you know, it is the extreme advance of our army—The hill which we occupied, besides enabling us to look right down on the enemies scouts and pickets—commanded one of the finest views of mountain scenery that I have ever beheld. I liked to lie out under the shade of the tall pine trees, while the soft winds whispered through the branches—gazing off toward where the clear outlines of Lookout Ridge cut the hazy atmosphere, thinking of home—*and some of the neighbors.*

Now, Julia, I appeal to your good taste to know if that isn't what you would call rather Poetic—all but the last part   But it is a well known fact that truth will very often spoil poetry. At such times—when I was lying in the shade of the pines—I was wont to call to mind and live over again my recent visit home—or I should say certain parts of it.   Could the winds speak and could you find those selfsame winds that came sweeping over White Oak Ridge—They came from the south, flying northward, bearing Spring on their wings and are no doubt ere this fanning your cheek—Ah! how I envy them—They could attest to many a long drawn sigh, breathed on their unappreciative ears an account of the fleetness and frailty of "earthly Joys." When I first came back old father Time seemed to be wearing clogs on his feet, the days dragged by so slowly. The days were very fleeting when I would have them linger—but when I returned to "the scenes of all my past glory" they were as much too slow as they had been too fast before.

Do you think that I was homesick? I suppose you will—but I am getting bravely over it now and think I can safely pronounce myself convalescent.

I am not afraid, Julia of getting such long letters as to tire in reading—I read your letters over half a dozen times and then read the address on the envelope—and as to your liking to "stay at home"—that is another common failing with young ladies—ain't it? I am sorry that the oportunity was not offered I am—to give vent to this pent up eloquence on the occasion of the presentation to Prof. Hoshour[2]—Very Truly—Scot

Please direct your letters to Chattanooga, Julia. By so doing they will reach me sooner. Did you ever discover how Miss Scovel[3] got home from Miss Tilfords[4] that night?

Scot

1. At this point Scot was assigned lookout following the 1863 Chattanooga-Chickamauga campaign but prior to Sherman's siege of Atlanta. The town of Ringgold was the forward position of Union forces after the battle of Ringgold Gap.
2. Butler University professor Samuel K. Hoshour, who served as president of the university from 1858 to 1861. *Catalog.*
3. Anna Scovel.
4. Julia Tilford, sister of Samuel and daughter of J. M. Tilford. *Catalog.*

———

{ M A Y   5 ,   1 8 6 4 }

E. ANNE BUTLER TO SON SCOT BUTLER

Forest Home
May 5th/64

My Dear Son Scot

We have had rather a lonely time since your Pa and Romy & Chauncey left   Especially of evenings did the house seem deserted, and when Willie Todd proposed boarding out here we were real glad to have him come   He came to the city to seek employment about the time the boys left and succeeded in getting a situation in Fletchers "Trade Palace"[1]

Commencement draws nigh but brings little of interest or excitement with it, so many of the students have gone with the City Reg. that the Anniversaries usually so interesting will have but few attractions. The Mathesians had their spring exhibition last wednesday night but as your Aunt Martha[2] was married that evening neither Demia or Nettie could attend   Your

Aunt Martha's husband has four children one of them however was at its mothers death committed to the care of a sister of Doct Todd's with the wish of the mother that she would have it always as her own. Aunt Mattie has undertaken something of a task in the way of family but I suppose she thinks the merits of the Doct compensate for all that. The relatives are well pleased with the connection as he is a man that stands well every way. He removed from Southport about a year ago. He was Mr Edgar's physician in his last sickness on the farm near Southport

Uncle Robert and "Jimmy" Wallace rode out to see us, being out exercising their brag horse—"Dixy"—Jimmy had a very severe spell of lung fever a few months ago but has quite recovered and at work again. Bob Catterson was married last week to a Miss Norwood[3] They have gone on a bridal trip. Your Uncles have at last thrown the two store rooms into one which makes their place of business quite a big concern. Your Uncle Obe goes to morrow week to Sioux City and Yancton to see after his interest there Your Aunt Mary[4] has about concluded to accompany him. Her health is feeble she is looking very thin & badly and we all wish her to take the trip hoping it will do her good—Your Grandma is rather more feeble than usual, but I am astonished to see her bear the death of Jennie with the degree of resignation that she does. Ma always felt that your Aunt Jennie from feeble health and a delicate constitution was unfitted for the cares and labors of life and I think she draws comfort from the thought that to her can no hardship, no care ever come— "That she is safe"

Capt. Anderson is still at last accounts at Chattanooga. His folks will send him in a few days a box of provisions Nettie intends to add something towards filling it up. She gets letters about twice a week from him

There will be to morrow night at Christian Chapel a strawberry and ice cream supper Those getting it up have not undertaken it for the recreation of the thing for to them it brings a great deal of labor and fatigue but the object is to raise a [subscription] for funds to get a new instrument, an organ if practicable for the Chapel

I have two letters from Chauncey the last written the 27th May. He still writes in good spirits apparently and is perfectly charmed with the appearance of the country south Your Pa writes that he will be home this coming week. He has enjoyed his visit there very much. Uncle Chauncey & Aunt Jennette[5] will return in time for the family meeting

I have been all the while reading every thing that I can find in the papers about Shermans advance, and Know full well Scot that you must have gone through with much that tries mens souls—that you have witnessed human suffering in many trying forms. Scenes of suffering that will long haunt your memory That you will be Kept and preserved from all evil is my constant prayer. That a Kind heavenly father will bless my dear boy and bring him safely through is my daily aspiration to Kind Heaven

Your affectionate Mother
E A Butler

1. On land adjacent to Ovid Butler's first "town" property in Indianapolis, Calvin Fletcher (Ovid's law partner) sold a partial lot to an Ohio business company whose primary incorporator was Fletcher's son, Stoughton. Stoughton developed a subdivision known as Fletcher Place. The first homes in the division were workers' cottages for Irish and German immigrants. A second section was sectioned off into large, comfortable homes for prominent Indianapolis residents, such as Andrew Wallace. The last section was developed into apartments, commercial concerns, local businesses, and retail shops such as Fletcher's Trade Place, where goods could be exchanged or bartered. David J. Bodenhamer and Robert G. Barrows, eds., *The Encyclopedia of Indianapolis* (Bloomington and Indianapolis: Indiana University Press, 1994), 580–81.

2. Martha/Mattie Jeanette McOuat, Scot's aunt, married first Samuel Edgar and after Edgar's death Dr. Robert Nathaniel Todd.

3. Robert F. and Sarah E. (Norwood) Catterson, whose son, George, married Scot's cousin Jean Maitland McOuat.

4. Obed Foote, Sr., married Mary/Mattie Gray McOuat, Scot's aunt and sister of Elizabeth Anne (McOuat) Butler.

5. (Lorinda) Janette Cole, Scot's aunt and sister of Ovid Butler's first wife, Cordelia Dyer Cole. Janette married Ovid's brother Chauncey.

———

{ M A Y   1 6 ,   1 8 6 4 }

E. ANNE BUTLER TO SON SCOT BUTLER

Forest Home
May 16th 1864

My Dear Son Scot

Yours of May 3d was received to day a week ago. I was glad to learn that your pen, postage stamps & photographs had been received, it seems they just made *connection* with your movements, a week or two later and it would have been likely a long while before they would have reached you. From your letter and later newspaper accounts we learn that your wishes in regard to *moving* has been gratified, to me this advance of course encreases my anxieties on your account, but I will be hopeful, and trustful that the kind providence, that has all a long been over you protecting you from dangers seen and unseen, will still preserve you in life and health making you strong to meet whatever of hardship lies before you.

We all feel that the campaign of this year will be the most severe of the war. The determination of the north is only equaled so far in these late battles by the desperation of the south. We are kept in a great state of excitement all the while, the word to day is that Lee had again made a stand for another battle on yesterday morning so we will be all anxiety 'till we hear the result. At the Journal office there is all the while nearly a crowd round the bullitin board eager to read the latest news

The city regiment is about full   they expect to be mustered in this afternoon   They expect to leave this week. About twenty of the college boys have gone in, I saw Sam Tilford[1] at church last night with his new uniform on, with the braid chevrons on his coat sleeve   To day your Pa and I went over to Camp Carrington to see Chauncey as—your Pa was about starting to Illinois. He went into Camp a few days ago and is very full of Military ardor I think that the hundred days experience will content him with being a soldier but nothing but trying it would suffice. Mr Wallace promises to see after him and there are so many that we know that I do not feel so badly about his going as I would other wise

We have letters from Capt. Anderson within a day or so ago, he was well but feeling rather lonely   Col. S[t]reight is still here having orders to remain here to organize three hundred days troops. Capt A. thought that the regiment would be kept doing garrison duty at Chattanooga unless the Col. should come on—

There is a new movement among the ladies, originating at Washington City and called the "Ladies National Covenant," it is for the promotion of economy and the prevention of importations, the pledge runs in this wise

"We pledge ourselves not to purchase any imported article from this time until the close of the war, and we resovele in order to carry out this, pledge that we will not after June 1st 1864 appear on the street at any public or private assembly except in clothes of American manufacture"

There is to be a meeting to night at Masonic Hall to discuss the merits of the movement and Mr Porton and several other gentlemen will address the meeting

Your sister C___ is quite committed to the move   Maria has been making a thorough examination of the matter before going into it   And finds the statements of the merchants so conflicting that but little dependance can be placed on what they say. Some say that nearly all ladies wear is imported, others say that much of goods bearing foreign marks are of american manufacture and have been so marked to meet the demand for foreign goods above that of home manufacture. We cannot but think that as the marks have been heretofore fixed up to suit the whim for foreign goods they will be quite as ready to arrange to meet the present demand for home manufacture—Your Pa left home to day at noon for Ill—

Your Mother in much love
E Anne Butler

1. Samuel E. Tilford, Scot's classmate and an enlistee in Company F, 107th Regiment, Indiana Volunteer Infantry.

———❊———

{ MAY 22, 1864 }

E. ANNE BUTLER TO SON SCOT BUTLER

Forest Home
May 22d 1864

My Dear Son Scot

I am endeavoring to be very patient in my waiting to heer from you and very hopeful too that all is well with you. The word we have of the movements of the army would preclude all hope of hearing either very often or very regularly from you. Nor can there be much hope of a change soon in this particular, for *onward* is the word now with Sherman & will be until Atlanta is reached no doubt—

Yesterday was a day of great stir & excitement in our city, owing to the city regiment leaving—in no regiment has the city been so fully represented as in this   The Col. Major and quite a number of the other officers are natives of this place and the rank and file is largely made up of those to the "manor born"—Scores of persons never hertofore seen on such occasions were on hand yesterday to witness the departure of some dear relative or friend with the regiment—Upon the arrival of the regiment at the depot at five oclock yesterday evening to take the cars for Jeffersonville a long train of freight cars were found by the Governor waiting for the transportation of the regiment. He at once demanded passenger cars, saying that no passenger train should leave on time until such cars were furnished the troops, this caused some delay but at last brought some dozen cars down the track that were soon filled up, when for further cars an order was sent for a Cincinnati train just ready to back in for its regular passengers to come forward and pick up the remaining boys and amid loud cheers for the Gov. they all moved out of sight—

It is thought that these raw troops will be put on garrison duty relieving the veterans who will be sent to the front. This however is not done in every case for we have heard through private sources that some of the new levies of Ohio troops were in the army of the Potomac put in the front & very badly cut up. I expect you will feel badly that Chauncey went but nothing would do but go he must. I have every assurance that as far as possible he will be well cared for Mr Wallace, Romy, Ingram Fletcher and any number of others have given me every assurance that they would look to him. John Duncan & George Gist are in the company made up mostly of the "City Greys " How the privates uniform brings all on a level in appearance these two boys so *exquisite* in their dress toilets, looked with their closely shaven heads as unpretending as to style as the veriest country boy—

I need not tell you the deep anxiety that is felt by every loyal heart for the success of our arms at this great crisis nor yet with what tearful sadness are read the accounts of the terrible sacrifices of life and limb that it costs our noble braves to up hold the right. The work before General Grant is not one of a single day and the thought of the thousand borne dead and dying from the field may be but a small portion of the needed sacrifice before the work is accomplished is heart sickening—But I will not pursue this train of thought further but turn to some home matters that may interest you.

Your Pa I wrote you had gone to Ill. I have not yet heard from him. The family meeting will come off at Aunt Mabel's[1] on the 16th of June   her health is quite poor and on that account some of us thought it best to omit the meeting this year but she was unwilling to have it so saying that although many of the nephews were absent and her own health poor she would rather have the meeting for she thought that by another year some that could meet this year would not be here no doubt meaning herself

Your affec. Mother
E A Butler

1. Mabel (Butler) Pabody, Scot's aunt and Ovid Butler's older sister.

{ MAY 29, 1864 }

E. ANNE BUTLER TO SON SCOT BUTLER

Forest Home
May 29/64

My Dear Son Scot

Yours of 20 inst was truly welcome we had felt so anxious to hear from you. I was sorry to hear that Lieutenant Flooke was wounded. His being wounded indicates I regret to learn that you too in your line of duty are exposed to the shells of the enemy. We will be anxious to hear from you very often for we can expect nothing but a very rough hard campaign for you until Atlanta is reached and will be satisfied with the simple word that all is well with you   But if time and inclination favor [I] would like you to so far throw aside your fear of appearing egotistic as to write more particulary concerning yourself—

I have no letter yet from Chauncey but through George Gists letters to Demia have heard from him several times   The city regiment will it is thought be put to guarding some point on the railroad   To be placed to guard some bridge or out of the way place will not be very agreeable to our city *bucks* but I believe it would be better for the morals of the boys than to be stationed in Nashville or any other town. Gist says Chauncey is well and in good spirits and thinks hardtack "aint so bad"—

The 8th Ind Reg. had a dinner and reception yesterday. They arrived from the front about a month ago but owing to the impatience of the men to get home it was deferred until they passed through on thier return to the field, yesterday was a delightful day, clear & cool after a week of showery weather. This winds up the dinne[r]s and receptions of the Veterans until the war is over the Eight being the last of the reenlisted regiments.

There are now at the Soldiers Home quite a number of refugees ("Poor white Trash") from Tennesse. After the soldiers were through eating the table at one end was arranged for them   In they came a motley crowd made up of women and children of all ages and sizes. I talked a little while with one of the women, who said her husband was conscriped by the rebels and is now a pris-oner in Camp Morton had written about a month ago that he was going to take the oath and as they were about starved out in Tennesse she had begged her way up here bringing her ten children along. I don't know about letting the rebels send thier poor do-less ones here for us to feed while they hold the husbands and fathers as soldiers fighting against us—Nettie wrote you the day we received your last under the spur of your request that all your correspondants would write you without waiting for you to write   I have given *circulation* to this request of yours and—will leave it to time and the good nature of your several correspondants to determine with what effect—

I might write Scot a great deal about our hopes and anxieties in regard to military opperations. How saddened we feel at the terrible sacrifices our soldiers are now making of life and limb—but why should I bring up this topic the realities of which are ever continually pressing themselves upon your hourly experiences. Let me rather by the seemingly idle chat about home and home matters lead your thoughts away for the time being from these sombre scenes. Having no fear that you will construe this to indifferance to the sacrifices made by our boys on the tented field or in the deadly conflict—

Hoping to hear from you very often I will conclude by naming that I received a letter from your Pa a day or two ago that he was enjoying his visit on the "Farm" very much and to name also that your Aunt Mattie is to be married to Doctor Todd next wednesday—

Aff Your Mother
E. A. Butler.

{ J U N E   1 2 ,   1 8 6 4 }

E. ANNE BUTLER TO SON SCOT BUTLER

Forest Home
June 12/64

My Dear Son Scot

It seems a long while since yours of the 20th ult was received and I thought I was prepared to wait very patiently for quite a long while before hearing from you again, but for some days back I have found my self expecting every letter handed me to be one from you and very anxious that it should be so—

Knowing from the reports that have reached us from Shermans Army that you have had a terribly hard severe campaighn our fears and anxieties have been great for your health and safty, but how impotent we feel to help you in any way we can but hope and—pray for your welfare—trusting in the goodness and mercy of God to restore you unscathed to your home when this terrible conflict is over—

We have word that there is much or at least some sickness in the City Reg. at Stevenson.[1] Mr Moores of Merrill's Bookstore died a few days since at Stevenson and I learned this afternoon that Gen. Morris[2] goes tomorrow morning to the Reg. having received a telegram that his son Tom was very sick. Several of the boy[s] have written home very jocosely of having the Tennessee "*quick step*" as they term camp diarrhea, but I fear many a poor fellow will be brought to his grave by this prevelant camp disease

We had our sunday school picnic in the woods northeast of the house yesterday   It was hardly so well attended as usual but the lack of citizens was made up in numbers by the soldiers of the Invalid Corps from Camp Burnside The woods were fairly *blue* with them. They behaved very well and were invited to participate in the games of sport engaged in and seemed to enjoy themselves very much

I wrote you we were going to have a festival at the Chapel on last Monday   It came off according to appointment and was pronounced a perfect success. The walls were prettily decorated with wreathes of flowers & evergreens which were thrown over the clusters of gas burners   The tables also were ornamented with flowers and any quantity of beautiful boquets in handsome vases filled the tables and the piano. The company was select and almost every church was represented by their best members. The proceeds [large ink spot] amounted to $281 out [of] which the expenses deducted left a clear profit of $230   Is not that great splotch of ink too bad—my ink is not good and having taken a pen full and not shaking the pen a g[r]eat drop fell and in trying to wipe it up I have made bad worse—

Demia is now talking of going with Miss Scovel to Nashvill a week or so after commencement. She will likely remain several weeks but does not know certainly how long. Nettie has gone to Kokomo to spend a week or two. Capt's folks were making up a box to send him and she took up some things to add to its contents

I hope it will not be many days before we will hear from you and that the word will be that all is well with you—To morrow Mrs Coburn yours sisters Cordelia Maria & Demia and myself—entend to visit the City Hospital to find out the number of wounded and sick soldiers from Shermans Army after which we will gather up means to furnish them a *treat* of strawberries and some suitable kind of cake. There are there several of the boys of the 33d.   I would like when we go wednesday to Vernon to the family meeting to stop at Franklin to see Lieut. Flook and think I will perhaps

make it out on our way home   It is now late bed time so I will bid you good
for the present

Affectionately Your Mother
E Anne Butler

1. Stevenson, Alabama.
2. Thomas Armstrong Morris, quartermaster general for the state of Indiana.

{ J U N E   1 9 ,   1 8 6 4 }

DEMIA BUTLER TO BROTHER SCOT BUTLER

Forest Home
June 19.1864

Dear Brother Scot:

Once upon a time I wrote you but I am sorry to say I cannot add that
once upon a time I received a reply to said letter. However this does not make a
bit of difference for of course I do not intend to count letters with you.

Where in the world are you and what are you doing! If you had not told
us you could not possibly write soon we would all long ago been very much
frightened about your long silence. Trusting that if all was not right we would
certainly hear from you we hope that you are well &c   Still we are anxious to
hear from you. Chauncy writes us once in a while and seems in high spirits
enjoying a soldiers life finely. I am afraid the ladies of Indpls are going to make
that City Regiment a perfect laughing Stock. They have had a festival and
Concert for the purpose of raising good things to send to the boys. Before the
time arrives however there are so many in the Hospital that they have concluded
to spend the proceeds of the entertainments in procuring Hospital stores. This
is wise enough but I could but laugh at the original plan   Think of boys out

only four weeks and having dainties sent to them. I wrote to Chauncey today and told him if I was a member of that body I would resent being the pet and pride of the Ladies. The Veterans [love ?] them none to much now and what an object of scorn they will be if they do not at least try to brave through three months that which the Vs have endured for three long years

Tom Morris has been very sick at Stevenson. We heard yesterday that he was dead but we have every hope that this is a false report. His father went a week ago to see him. You remember Scot that Thursday was the occasion of our grand family meeting. Between thirty & forty of us went to Vernon Wednesday. There were a hundred present at Aunt Mabels and we had a very very pleasant time. Next year it will be at Hanover. We will then have a basket dinner in the woods. You can then be with us and I know you will enjoy it. There were you & Chauncey Ovid Irby & Rommie all missed from the number. Next year how I hope you may all be with us.

Irby is now very sick down there some where. He was thrown from a horse about a month ago and has been insensible ever since. Willie Todd is now staying with us. He is clerking in Fletchers. This next week is our Commencement week. I do not think it will be specially gay. The Graduates do not amount to much you know. Hillis thinks he is a genius but [. . .] that need not convince you or I of the fact. I am thinking some of going home with Mary Scoval to spend a few weeks. Her home is Nashville you know. The weather here is intensely warm   I don't know what I shall do down there. However I want to go South and this is a good opportunity. Pa wants me to go to Minnesota but having been there I don't feel like going over the same ground again. Pa I suppose will go to Keithsburg after Commencement.

I suppose Ma has told you about our nice Strawberry supper   Davy Beaty says please don't write such things to us. We did not make the supper for fun but for money. I am happy we realized both. Capt Anderson writes all the time like he expected the war to be over this summer   I don't know what makes him think so   I am not so sanguine. Scot do you think there is any way we could get a box to you—If so I am for sending one but perhaps you have plenty good fruits &c there   I hope that country of whose flowers you all boast so much yields also something more substantial. Write soon.

Affectionately Your Sister
Demia

{ J U N E 1 9 , 1 8 6 4 }

E. ANNE BUTLER TO SON SCOT BUTLER

Forest Home
June 19th/64

My Dear Son Scot

Did you think of its being the day of the family meeting last thursday the 16th inst or did you know that that was the appointed day? I had been so taken up with the other matters I very much doubt having told you on what day of the month it was to come off   We had felt here at home very much like postponing it to another year when we hoped to have you and many others now absent present—but your Aunt Mabel was unwilling to give it up so on last wednesday afternoon some thirty of us took the afternoon train for Vernon. Thursday was a delightful day as regards the weather   In numbers the meeting exceeded that of last year by five making the even hundred. Everything passed off pleasantly and would have been we think perfectly delightful if our absent sons had been there and the health of your Aunt Mabel had seemed less precarious   Except your Pa & I the most of the Indianapolis friends remained until Saturday

A week or two ago a project was started to raise funds to send supplies to our city regiment—so according to proagramme [program] a concert was given last friday night and a supper and floral festival the friday previous   Both turned out a pretty fair sum.

Some having friends in the regiment were not at all in favor of the movement thinking that any thing showing favoritism or making it appear a pet regiment would be prejudicial in increasing the feeling of three years men against them and also in with holding from our city boys the oppertunity of showing thier patriotism in taking rough fare in common with their older comrades in arms. Col. Vance[1] in a letter in yesterday's Journal takes the "Thing" by the horns and makes the matter come out in right shape. He acklowledges the kind effort of the ladies in behalf of the 132d Reg & undertakes to designate the articles most needed, which is a long list of hospital supplies, such as bed ticks sheets pillow slips towels comforts window-blinds &c   Together with some light articles of diet fit for the sick only, leaving I should think little or nothing to buy nick-nacks for those in health—

From a letter I got from Chancey I infer that the boys have played "possum" somewhat to get rid of what they thought over much duty. The Col. has commenced a plan as unique as could have been resorted to to lesson the sick list if indeed they are making believe they are sick 'tis to send to the Journal weekly a list of the sick, on saturday the first list of this kind appeared, as a sample I will give one: "Ingram Fletcher Dysentery, not much sick." How would you like to made appear in the papers so. I think the boys are not consulted—

The other day Mrs Col. Coburn, Mrs Bense[2] your sisters Cordelia & Maria and Myself visited our city hospital to learn the number of wounded & sick soldiers there from Shermans Army intending to get up a little treat in the way of strawberries and some kind of delicate cake, we found quite a number from that army wounded at Kingston Resaca &c but after talking with the surgeon concluded it would be better to make no distinction but to raise enough means to give to all alike   So the next day they were all furnished a nice large saucer of berries and full supply of light nice cake at supper.

Through Mr Vawter I learn Lieut. Flook is going round on crutches at Franklin   I think after commencment which comes off this week I will go to Franklin and will try to see him   I have been promising Cousin Eliza Vawter to visit her for a long while and will thus fulfil a promise and be able to hear something about you at the same time.

Your Pa and I are both anxious to hear from you and regret much that so long a time elapses between the reception of letters from you   Hoping this will find all well with you I remain My Dear Son

Your Aff. Mother
E Anne Butler

1. Col. Samuel C. Vance of the Indiana 132nd, in which Chauncey was an enlistee.
2. Mrs. Bence, mother of Anna A. (Mrs. Walter C. Hobbs) and Mary E. (Mrs. Allen Fletcher). *Catalog.*

{ J U N E   2 5 ,   1 8 6 4 }

OVID BUTLER TO SON SCOT BUTLER

Forest Home near Indianapolis
June 25 1864

My Son Scot

The last we have heard from you is by your letter to your Ma of the 8 inst. By it I learn that your paper and postage stamps are exhausted. I wish by all means that you should be able to write home often and I send you enclosed 25 postage stamps. I will also procure and send you by mail a package of note paper which I hope you will receive

You must be aware that we face some anxiety on your account   We do not get very full particulars of the operations of Shermans Army but we get enough to know that it was very actively engaged and has reported fierce conflicts with the rebels and that Hookers Corps has been in the hottest of the fights. We wish therefore to be often apprised of your continued safety. We also ask for more information if possible. We desire to know something of your personal experience in these deadly conflicts. You have not written home latterly At least I have received no recent letter from you. In you letters to your Ma you give us little information concerning yourself beyond the fact that when you wrote you were well and enhanced and even this we have to infer from the fact that you say nothing to the contrary. For this much we are thankful but would prefer that you would be more definite and specific. It would gratify us all and the time will probably come if you survive this war that you would like to refer to a record of these facts and of your inspirations, emotions and feelings while they were transpiring. Then Scot unless it might be an impossibility I hope you will write them out for our present gratification and for your future use

I spent about two weeks pleasantly on the farm in Illinois. I would like to write you somewhat in detail about the farming operation but omit it now. I returned about the 7th inst and my time since has been much occupied in getting my hay here and in the business of the Univeristy. This was Commencement week at the University & yesterday was commencement day. The Graduats were WH Wiley, AC Eaton, WA Cotton & David Hillis all of whom acquitted themselves most creditably. All together I think it the best

Commencement we have had. Of course it will not surprise you to be told that we often thought of you and Chancy in connection with competition exercises of the same character and if God spares our lives I hope most ardently that we shall witness a like creditable graduation for each of you

The family meeting took place at Vernon on Thursday the 16th inst. It was well attended and was a pleasant reunion. We thought that so many of the connection were absent in the Army was perhaps both a joy and a sorrow. While we could but regret their absences we were perhaps a little proud of their patriotism and devotion to their Countrys service in this the hour of her need. The next Meeting is to be on the Third Thursday in June 1865 at your Uncle Chaunceys in Hanover. We hope that before that time the rebellion will be crushed out and that our Countrys service will not require the absence of any of the connection

Capt Anderson is in Chattanooga on Duty there guarding the post. Chancy is at Stevenson, Al. You should open a communication with them if you have not already done so. I suppose you know their address but it will do no harm for me to give them. Capt MT Anderson, Co D, 51 Regt Ind Vol., Chatanooga, Tn. Also Chancy Butler Care of Capt Farlington, Co A, 132 Regt Ind Vol (Nashville, Tn). Our letters to Chancy are sent to Nashville but you can probably reach him better by sending direct to Stevenson or to Chattanooga.

I expect to go again to Illinois sometime in July but do not know how long I shall remain there.

Your cousins Ovid Todd and Irby Todd are in the service. They were attached to Gen H ___[1] staff in some capacity. When near Hampton Irby was severely injured by the fall of his horse. It is said that he is on a severely critical condition by reason of his heart. His Father is anxious to go to him but learns that he cannot get through. Perhaps you may know or can learn something of him. If so let us know as soon as possible.

I would like myself to go to the Front this season if there was an opportunity to do so but I suppose it would not be permitted.

My prayer is that God may protect and preserve you. Remember that we are all anxious to hear from you often & no one is more so than

Your affectionate Father
Ovid Butler

1. Gen. Alvin P. Hovey, commander of the District of Indiana.

{ J U N E   2 6 ,   1 8 6 4 }

E. ANNE BUTLER TO SON SCOT BUTLER

Forest Home
June 26th/64

My Dear Son Scot

The past week has been mostly taken up with University matters it being Commencement week. I attended several evenings the different exercises The boys did well   especially on commencement day did the graduates acquit themselves well—I expect I will have to take back a saying of mine repeated time and again that if my boys are only good I will be content, for as often as I see a college boy display a fair degree of talent—I find myself anticipating a like career for mine

We got a letter from Chauncey a day or two ago   I judge from his and the letters of other boys that they are having a pretty hard time. The Col is over taxing the strenght of his men and the result is much sickness. Gen. Morris returned from Stevenson last monday bringing with him Tom and also Ingram Fletcher. Tom Morris was convalesing when he returned, but Ingram Fletcher is still very sick with camp fever   Chauncey's Capt is on a court ma[rs]hal at Bridgeport and William Wallace is there with him in the capacity of clerk. On last wednesday several tons of sanitary supplies were forwarded to the city regiment besides some seventy boxes sent by the boys friends. We have often of late wished it were practible to send you a box of supplies for we know you must need some things of this kind, but it cannot be done very soon I fear—

In the Journal of saturday is the list of wounded of the 70th & 33d Ind Reg's in which appear the names of Sam Loing [Loring?] wounded in the side and A P May in the Arm. They were brought to Nashville I believe. During commencement week a Mr Reeves and daughter were here from near Fairview Rush Co. who named to us that a young man who makes his home when here with them was home a few weeks ago on veteren furlough—and spoke of you and of being in the same Corps with you, his name is Culver—

Everything seems very quiet in this neighborhood now college is closed and the professors and families will likely soon be off to take a visit off to the country some where. The Hoss family have already gone, The Professor to visit a sick brother, and Mrs H. Julia and Nellie to Greencastle. John Dunn has been mustered out and returned here just a few hours before they left, he has had a very hard time since he returned to his company and his foot troubles him a good deal yet.

Your Pa sent you yesterday a package of writing paper and also a letter. I hope they will reach you safely. I believe I wrote that Demia was thinking of going home with Miss Scovel to Nashville, they think of starting one week from to morrow

Your Cousin Willie Todd has felt very anxious about his brother Irby who was a month or two ago severely injured by his horse stumbling throwing him headlong from the animals back. A few days since Willie received a letter from him stating he was improving but still very weak

I owe you an apology Scot for sending you so miserable an apology of a letter but I have written under difficulties. Such as excessive heat and by *lamp-light* which has attracted all kinds of flying insects moths, millers bugs &c—

Yours of 8 June was truly welcome   We had grown quite anxious to hear from you   If possible write oftener and longer letters

> *Good Night My Dear Son*
> *Your Affectionate Mother*
> *E Anne Butler*

{ J U L Y   3 ,   1 8 6 4 }

E. ANNE BUTLER TO SON SCOT BUTLER

> *Forest Home*
> *July 3d/64*

My Dear Son Scot

I expect we will have a very quiet if not a very dull house for some weeks to come at present our young lady borders having left, Nettie [has] gone for a few weeks to visit in Noblesville, [and] Chauncey away leaves us much reduced in numbers & then to morrow Demia goes home with Mary Scovel to Nashville and your Pa too talks of going again to Illinois—this would seem to leave me and the little ones quite alone but I guess they will come and go by turns before your Pa leaves   Nettie will have returned bringing Miss Anderson a sister of Capt A.s and Viola Cole[1] home with her—and likely by the time these have made out their visit here Demia will be coming back   Your Pa and I have many talks about living more retired and not entertaining so many about us but find it easier to plan than to carry out the same.

Mackie has Obe Foote with him now his father & Mother having gone on a visit to Decotah   A letter was received from them a day or two ago written at Council Bluffs   They had had a pleasant trip so far—Obie & Mack have taken a contract to gather my currants at ten cents a gallon—They "put in" the entire day yesterday from early breakfast until late tea time but as to morrow is the "4th" they feel quite undecided whether to take the whole day for holiday or to make a "divide" between work and play

Demia received a letter from Romy Todd to day   He did not name Chauncey but of course if he had not been well he would have told us. The boys of the City regiment thought they had a pretty hard time before a visit from Forest was expected but now they have the hard work of building stockades added   This with the intense heat—makes it very severe on the boys. I wrote that Tom Morris & Ingram Fletcher were home sick, they are both able to be about now and will soon be returning to thier regiment. The word is that the health is better in 132d but the feeling among the boys towards the higher officers of the regiment is still very bitter   I suppose the trouble is caused by the wish to put the boys through so as to make them a "crack regiment" and in [these?] officers putting on a great amount of style too

Commencement came off a week sooner this year than hertofore this being the new order of things, this will make the week of the fourth seem much quieter than usual especially as we are to have no fourth of July demonstrations in the city this year   Some are going off to Vine Springs to pass the day and others on railroad excursions. Our city will I dare say look much like it was sunday with the stores all closed and no parade of any kind going on

Professor Hosses folks are still absent. Mr Goodwin[2] has lately married a lady of Cincinnatti who like himself edites a paper   Dr Brown & family are sadly afflicted in the death of Tom   He died in hospital at Mephis. His remains were brought here and interred in "Crown Hill Cemetery." He was taken with tiphoid fever—pretty soon after his return with the Red River Expedition and after lingering many weeks death closed his sufferings—

Jim Morrison is in the city Reg as private   Lizzie who was married last Feb is still at home the younger boys too Charley and Sam are at home. Alec is still in the paymaster department but just where I do not know. Bob Duncan told me the other evening that he had bidden farewell to college walls   The graduation speech had frightened him from ever trying to go through

This I hope will find all well with you. Write soon and often

Affectionately your Mother
E. A. Butler

NB If at all practicable I would love to hear from you a good deal oftener Your Pa sent you a package of writing paper Did you get it

1. Scot's cousin and a member of the Cole family of Shelby County, Indiana.
2. Elijah Goodwin, Butler University benefactor, served as a member of the Butler University Board of Trustees. "Trustees."

———————

{ J U L Y   8 ,   1 8 6 4 }

DEMIA BUTLER TO BROTHER SCOT BUTLER

Nashville
July 8th 64

Dear Brother Scot:

I presume Ma has written you of my contemplated visit to this city   So you will not be surprised to see that I am now at what was for a long time your home. I wish you would tell me in what part of the city you were encamped   I would like to visit the place. Mrs Scovel and I have taken several rides out in different directions and I am delighted with the beautiful and wildly romantic scenery. What a city of Soldiers this is. You know Mr Scovel lives opposite the Capitol on Summer Street. All around us soldiers are encamped. They seem very quiet and peaceable.

Mary[1] & I left home on the night of the fourth of July and arrived here the next evening. All were well at home when we left. Janett was in Noblesville Pa was making preparations to go to Keithsburg and ma was laughingly complaining that we were leaving her alone in her glory. Not quite alone for she has about a half dozen contrabands about her. The number of darkies here present to me quite a novel and amusing sight. I went with Mrs Scovel last evening to take some medicine to some sick refugees   I never dreamed of such miserable wretched poverty. They were living in a cellar almost buried in filth and dirt. They are a very low species. Mrs Scovel does much for them but she says they seem to have no gratitude and never receives a "thank you" from any of them.

Scot are you having very hard times. I have felt so anxious about you since Sherman has been so busily engaging the rebels for I feel that you must be in much danger. We hardly know yet whether Maretta[2] is in our possession Hearing so many false reports we are becoming a very incredulous people. It will soon be only six months til your time is out. Wont that be glorious. Do take ever so much care of yourself so that you may pass safely through this comparatively short time.

John Dunn had got home for good a few days before I left. Julia had gone to Greencastle to spend a few weeks. She applied at the Board for a room in the University Building to teach a small school. Mary–Phil Browns Sister also wanted it and when I left the matter was not decided   I do hope Julia will get it for I want Mack[3] & Annie to go to her. I suppose Ma told you Bob Catterson was married. They say his wife is quite pretty. Chauncey still writes home in very good spirits. Tom Browns death was quite sad. Poor boy he died far away from home in the hospital at Memphis.

Scot I wish you would write to me soon. I know you must have much to do so I shall never expect a letter until I receive it. I hope you may have some erand to this place but of course this is almost impossible. Capt wrote that he would be here the Saturday before I came. I would like to have seen him. Janett talks of coming to met him but had no company.

Your Sister
Demia

1. Mary Scovel.
2. Marietta is fifteen miles northwest of Atlanta, Georgia.
3. Thomas McOuat Butler, Scot's youngest brother, called "Mack" or "Mackie."

{ J U L Y   1 7 ,   1 8 6 4 }

E. ANNE BUTLER TO SON SCOT BUTLER

Forest Home
July 17/64

My Dear Son Scot

Since I wrote you a week ago your Pa has left home again for Illinois. Nettie has returned bringing Viola Cole (a sister of Scot Cole's) with her, a sister of Bart. Cole's,[1] Maria Wainwright[2] is also here spending a week or two, Obe. Foote[3] is still here his father and Mother having not yet returned from Dekota— but for these visitors our family circle would be very small indeed.

Day before yesterday I got letters from Demia & Chauncey. Demia is perfectly captivated with the scenery about Nashville and enjoying her visit there very much. Chauncey writes that they are much more pleasantly situated in camp now than at first having got things better fitted up and although they have quite as much duty to perform get along much more comfortably   The regiment however has been relieved and are doubtless by this time at Villa Nova Your Pa had written something to Chauncey in referance to the City Reg. getting spoiled by having too many nick-nacks sent them   (The ladies you remember having got up a festival and concert to raise funds to furnish supplies for this pet regiment)   He writes we need have no fear of injury from that source that the portion that fell to Co. A. was 6 lb butter 10 lb Cheese and four [. . .] of lemons the latter given their lieutenant upon solicitation for the sick—

Chauncey writes that he is *strapped* having lost his pocket book, while in swimming, with all his money and postage stamps—some cavalry man that passed along has the blame of taking it from his pocket. He named in one of his recent letters that Col Vance was endeavoring to induce the boys to reenlist for a year, but the prospect was dull none like him well enough to wish to prolong their connection with him. There will be an oppetunity to send some eatables to him by A L Hunt who goes to the regiment on monday night   I will get up a little box of what ever I can which however must be limited there being so few things that can carry well [over] that distance.

I wish you were where I could do the same for you. You do not say how you fare. Why do you remain so taciturn in regard to every [thing] that concerns yourself? While I do not specially admire egotistical people, I must frankly say that my son Scot tacks too far entirely in the other direction but its useless to expostulate, must draw consolation from the fact that it is not your way to talk much about yourself—

You recollect that your Uncles bought Mr Stringfellow's[4] horse that was sent him in a present from Kentucky in return for the kindness he showed the rebel prisoners here. They have kept him stabled up and been very proud of his gaily ways. Your Uncle Bob got himself a very nice new buggy one of those with no back just a rim of a few inches round the seat. He has taken Demia and Nettie and others out riding several times this summer—last Monday he added a "fly net" to Dixies trappings— this was not agreeable to dixie's notions and after being driven round a few squares he started on the run. Uncle perceiving that he was about to run into some waggons ahead attempted to turn a corner of the street—the turn was too suddenly made—he lost his balance and fell with great force on the left side of his forehead, bruising it severely the reins got entangled round his head and he was thus dragged about a half square bruising his hip and leg very much   Some men came to his assistance—took off the net [and helped] him in. He rode to the doctor and thence home but the word is that Dixie must be sold—the folks at Grandma's are not willing to run such narrow escapes as this   Uncl B. is about the house but does not to go to the shop

Your Grandma's health is much better than a while ago. She wished me when I wrote to remember her in love to you. She always asks about you and is much interested in your welfare. Your Uncle Robt makes frequent inquiries about you too   A brother in law of your Uncle Robt's William Wallace has written home from the City Reg. a letter attacking certain officers of Co. I. of that regiment   This letter brought out a response containing very severe strictures upon *our William Wallace's military career*—mistaking him to be the writer of said letter. William belongs to Co. A. knew and cared nothing about Co. I. or its affairs. Sister Cordelia felt real badly about it, but finally concluded it was well that this occurred as giving William's friends here an oppertunity to explain all about his connection with the 70th regiment and the reasons of his remaining so short a time with it. William has always felt very sensitive about the whole matter for much was said by his enemies in politics in dirision of the shortness of his stay with the 70th   It is folly for him to engage in anything of the kind, his tastes do not lie in that direction & going in as he does without an enlistment he has nothing to hold him to the service but his own will. The Journal came out a day or two ago in rather a warm defence of him and his patriotic efforts to sustain by tongue pen & purse the government. This may paliate the matter but I think William will feel that the Journal used him ill in allowing the attack upon him to appear on its pages at all

Ovid[5] has a heavy weight of responsibility on him in the care of the Clerks Office   He looks worn   Ovid [. . .] wrong end for most any how. He when a youth would never be content unless under engagement bonds to many and the result was that he found himself in honor bound to undertake the care of a wife and the support of a household before he had even accomplished the feat of supporting himself—so he commenced life without profession or trade or any practical way of getting on in the world. He started off wondrous brave and independant on a salary of four hundred a year, would take no help from his father in the way of getting a home, was going to work for a home. Two years found the home farther off than at first—consented to take the same that your Pa had given the rest and was even willing to borrow a few hundred in advance of that sum. He has his lot and house but is unable to save anything from his salary to make the necessary improvements and is not willing I suppose to ask your Pa to advance more. Is dissatisfied   Has not found his right place in the world   And all this comes I think or at least comes in part from too early heart entanglements. So Scot take warning all this is writ for your benefit.

Berry Sulgrove[6] started off full *tilt* to the Baltimore convention promising to forward full reports from that body   The convention met, deliberated, passed resolution and adjourned and still never a line from Berry—poor fellow he was off on a spree, about a week ago a letter came from him saying he would be home in a week or two. His connection with the Journal is said to be closed They will bear with him no longer   Mr Newcomb[7] is now conducting the editorial department. His wife and family have gone to Minnisota to spend the summer

Well Scot I have exhausted all available topics and no doubt your patience also and will bring this to a close. Hoping to get a good long letter from you soon *all about yourself*

I remain affectionately
Your Mother
E A Butler

1. The Cole family of Shelby County.

2. Maria Wainwright, daughter of Samuel Wainwright, a tinner, under whom Scot's uncle Robert Lockerbie McOuat apprenticed.

3. Obed Butler Foote, Scot's cousin.

4. Horace Stringfellow, Jr., first rector of St. Paul Episcopal Church in Indianapolis.

5. Ovid Dyer Butler.

6. Berry R. Sulgrove, publisher of the *Indianapolis Journal* after Ovid Butler. Sulgrove attended the Republican National Convention of 1864, but his known habit of drinking and his unreliable, controversial nature caused much consternation among his followers. He was fired from the *Journal* and resorted to writing laudatory biographies of prominent figures of Indianapolis. In a letter to Demia after the war, Ovid wrote that he refused Sulgrove the opportunity to write about him, as such nonsense was for those who desired to be known as great men who did great things, while he preferred to be known as a Christian man who did what was expected of him.

7. Horatio C. Newcomb, husband of Eliza Pabody, Ovid's cousin, and fellow Butler University benefactor.

E. ANNE BUTLER TO SON SCOT BUTLER

Forest Home
July 24/64

My Dear Scot

Yours of July 14th to me & the one written a day or two previous to Demia came to hand night before last   I was glad to get word from you and very thankful that you are still preserved unharmed and in health through this long and severe campaign   Yours to Demia I will send her to Nashville for I know she would like to get it.

I received a letter from her yesterday. The City Reg. is there. She had seen Chauncey   She writes that he is looking very harty & as brown as he can well be. She still has nothing to say as to the time of her return   Cordelia goes to Nashville to morrow night   William[1] has the blues dreadfully and she fears that he will feel so desperate as to execute some of his threats, such as throwing up the Clerks office and *enlisting* for the war. I do not know whether I wrote you about a newspaper attack that was made on him, supposing him to be the Wm Wallace writing from the Regiment criticizing some of its members rather severely. The writer however was a brother of Jimmy Wallace. Lew.[2] being reported as superseded too has its effect on his spirits, though that I believe is not as bad as the telegram would indicate. He still it is supposed holds the command of Baltimore but his troops were placed under some general that went in pursuit of the rebel raiders   William has I guess some in the regiment that are not very good friends to him   His correspondence is tampered with, letters from him come to hand here opened & those reaching him are long delayed on the way. All things considered Cordelia has concluded to go and spend a week or two with him.

Your uncle Todd[3] found Irby in hospital at Knoxville   They arrived in Vernon about 12 days ago. He has improved very rapidly and is looking quite well again. He is with us now staying a few days. His father was much worsted by his trip south coming back quite sick and is now just beginning to sit up.

I have one letter from your Pa since he left written the day after he left home he had got to "Butlers Grove."   Had had a very unpleasant ride to Chicago the day he left home with the heat dust & cinders besides being quite out of health—but from there he took a sleeping car and got a good nights rest and at the time of writing was feeling very much better. I have no idea when he will be ready to come home   I have promised to join him two weeks before he shall leave there and will take Mackie and Annie with me that they may have a little jaunt—

I have seen nothing of Mate Brown since the day of Tom's funeral   This spring there was considerable improvement in her general health. She could see much better too but it was only in one eye the other is quite blind. She seemed so cheerful and happy when she was going round this spring after her long confinement to the house   So glad that she could see once more. I felt so much for her when poor Tom died. She always had some thing to tell about him and what he had written home about. Now the grave has closed over all that is earthly of Tom. That source of joy and interest is gone from poor Mate

We went to church to day to hear Mr Brewer[4] preach   He is here on his yearly visit   He called out last night to see us. He talks some of giving up preaching for a while and devoting his time during the coming campaign to making Union Speeches but I guess he will hardly make it out, he leaves for other parts of the State in a day or two but will be back in the course of three weeks when he will deliver a Union Speech in this city.

Scot I had no idea until your recent letters informed me that you had drawn no pay. Why have you not written that you needed money   I will enclose in this ten dollars. Do not think it best to risk at this time sending a larger sum

Affectionately Your Mother
E Anne Butler

1. William Wallace.

2. Lew Wallace, son of former governor David Wallace and brother of Scot's brother-in-law William Wallace.

3. Levi W. Todd, Scot's uncle by his marriage to Demia Butler. Their children were Irby, William, and Romy Todd, all Scot's cousins.

4. U. C. Brewer of Danville, a circuit minister and graduate of Butler University.

{ J U L Y   3 1 ,   1 8 6 4 }

E. ANNE BUTLER TO SON SCOT BUTLER

Forest Home
July 31st/64

My Dear Son Scot

Yours of 25 inst. written at Cartersville G.A. was received last night   I had learned through letters from Capt A. of your visit to Chattanooga. On last sunday I wrote you enclosing ten dollars, it would have been better if I had sent you some money sooner, sending at the time I did will be of little use to you now that you have drawn your pay. I hope you have received it however and that it has not been lost on the way—

I had a letter from your Pa night before last written the 25 inst. He was in good health though he had been fearful that he had been rather risking his health by over exertion since he had been at the farm   They have a new reaping machine in operation, which they consider something extra but from some cause has required a great deal of repairing   Your Pa having gone every week day since he has been there with some part of it to Keithesburg to be mended. The distance from the farm to Keithesburg is six miles and he has found it through the heat and dust at times rather severe   The care of so heavy an amount of harvesting without your Uncle Chauncey's help he has found rather onerous but your uncle is there by this time and will in a great measure relieve him—I can not see how farming at that distance from their places of residence can be made profitable in dollars and cents, though to your Pa it seems requisite as amusement and also an acquisition to health—traveling seems indispensable and unless business calls him away from home it is almost impossible for him to get away. As yet he says nothing as to the time of his return home. I had thought of taking Mackie and Annie with me there a few weeks before his return and after spending a week or so there have returned with him—the prospect for that as yet does not appear very promising. Demia says nothing yet about coming home and I could not leave Nettie alone with none about the house but colored servants—

Irby Todd left here friday afternoon for Vernon. He is discharged from the service. His discharge papers were made out at Knoxville but owing to some error had to be corrected here. His father is still very poorly has been quite sick ever since their return from the South with camp diarreahea. Your Grandma has been sick was taken with a congestive chill is now comfortable and will get along now we all think. Her attack was very sudden and unexpected, the first symptom of her indisposition was flightiness of mind after which was crampings and coldness of feet & hands was entirely unconscious for twelve or fourteen hours, but by close attention a return of the chill was kept off and the danger past—

I do not know what the prospects of the university are likely to be this fall at the opening There is a new professor elected for the preparatory school— it was thought for a while that one would have to be hunted up to fill professor Hoss' place but I believe he is disposed to retain it until certain of his election as State Superintendent of Public Instruction They have offered their home for sale [and] will go into the city to live. When over there the other day I went round looking at Mrs Hoss flowers   But found them not looking as of old They showed neglect. Julia is expecting to teach this fall a school of little folks in the University   She has her scholars and room engaged. So I guess they will hardly move to town very soon especially as professor [Hoss] holds his property at six thousand dollars more I think than he can find a purchaser willing to give.

Ovid[1] has a fresh attack of going to town to live   His "Help["] a contraband that just suited him [in] every way left them the other day and he thinks if in town he would have less trouble in keeping help

Hoping to hear from you very soon again and not willing to wait upon the uncertainty of your getting *into Atlanta* will expect you to not defer writing upon any such uncertainties

Affectionately your Mother
E Anne Butler

1. Ovid Dyer Butler, Scot's half brother.

OVID BUTLER TO SON SCOT BUTLER

Butlers Grove Henderson Co Illinois
Sunday July 31 1864

My Son Scot

I have been here something over two weeks superintending the harvesting of the farm. Before I left home I had received your letter to me dated some time the first of this month and was well pleased not only that you had remembered to write me but that your letter evidenced some intelegent appreciation of the Military situation at the time it was written   I was also gratified that you returned the letter I heretofore wrote you from here to have it copied on the letter book[1]

Since I came here your Ma has sent you your two recent letters to her one dated the 14 inst   I was glad to learn that you had received the paper and Stamps I sent you   I was fearful that the Mail would be an uncertain way of sending those things especially the paper but concluded to try it as you could not well do without them. I learn from your letters that you have received no pay for more than a year. You must need some funds before this time   Your Ma writes me that she has sent you $10 and proposed sending another $10 before long

I wrote to her approving her doing so   If you need more I rely upon your letting me know   You have not been troublesome or exacting in these matters and I am disposed to supply what you need   I have confidence in you to believe that you would not spend it in acquiring bad habits

Some severe battles have taken place in Georgia as appears from the papers since the date of your last letter   I suppose that you were at least a witness of the battle of the 20th (Wednesday) as it seems Hookers Corps was hotly engaged and lost heavily   I hope however that no accident has happened to you I do not get the news here very promptly or very fully and am still uncertain whether the Union Army now holds Atlanta. If with the possession of that place the rebel Army of Johnson or rather Hood could be annihilated the rebellion might be terminated speedily   But I have full faith that its end is sure and I hope not distant[2]

Chancy is now at Nashville   The 132 Regt to which he belongs is stationed there. He is I believe still satisfied with soldier life but he has not yet seen any of its real hardships

Your Uncle Chauncys business detained him at home and I therefore came here sooner than I expected to look after the harvesting   I have been expecting him here for the last week but he has not yet come   Under the circumstances I have too much to do in attending to the business and feel that it is wearing on me. We have a large harvest—over 200 acres of small grain   We are about through with cutting but the grain is yet to gather & thrash   I do not know how long I shall be detained here but probably some time. I shall however probably be at home before any letter of yours after you get this can reach me and I want you to write giving me particulars of the Battles and Marches you have been engaged in

I have made considerable investments here in farming lands in connection with your Uncle Chancy in the expectation that he would attend to the farming operations   His protracted sickness last winter and the situation of his family and affairs at home this summer have left him too much away from here and the farming has not been well managed. For this reason my attention is required   Notwithstanding the Mismanagement the prospect now is that the crop will be a profitable one.

I apprehend that no member of my family appreciates the objects and purposes of my investments and efforts here or sympathise with me in them. I am not certain that they are not regarded by some perhaps the most of them as the folly and weakness of my age. I have I suppose enough without engaging in this enterprise to do me the balance of my life   At least I have had no apprehensions of coming to want. But you are I presume aware that my property at Indianapolis was and is wholly unproductive—that the cost of living and the claims upon me every way amounted to a considerable sum yearly which was so much abstracted from the Capital. I desire to put some at least of my property in a shape to make it productive and that would benefit rather than injure my children and the community. I have therefore invested in cheap farming lands here which I feel sure when rightly fixed up will yield a handsome profit. You are old enough and I presume will take interest enough in this matter to be entitled to this much explanation of my motives and purposes for these investments. Therefore I give it here   I am anxious that my children especialy my boys should appreciate them. I feel too that in these times while so much of the labor of this country is necessarily withdrawn to fill the Armies—he who makes earnest efforts to increase those productions of the earth which are essential to feed and clothe these Armies and the population is a public benefactor. It is no time now for any one to be idle who is capable of making any successful efforts and if a man is physically or otherwise disqualified for service in the Army—he may perhaps do something for his country on the farm

But this letter is already too long. I have kept no copy of this and would be pleased if you would return it as you did the other   I conclude by hoping and desiring to hear soon from you and to learn that you are yet well and unharmed

Your Affectionate Father
Ovid Butler

1. Ovid Butler kept handwritten copies of his letters in letterbooks, similar to a carbon copy today. Some of Ovid's Civil War correspondence appearing here is duplicated in Letterbook No. 4, Butler University Archives.

2. Ovid's reference here is to the battle of Peachtree Creek, Georgia, where losses in the siege of Atlanta were great on both sides. Although Gen. Joseph Hooker's corps was relatively ineffective, Union troops were victorious against Confederates Joseph E. Johnston and John Bell Hood. Nearly 20,000 troops were engaged on each side. The Union lost 1,779 troops, while the South lost 4,796. The battle proved that there would be no quick end to the Atlanta campaign and that the only hope for the Confederate army would be a continued effort to attack the North with fewer troops and more effective results. Hood's policy of hard fighting, regardless of the cost, was a disaster, and his late arrival at both Peachtree Creek and Atlanta two days later proved him an incapable field general. Patricia L. Faust, ed., *Historical Times Illustrated Encyclopedia of the Civil War* (New York: Harper and Row, 1986), 565–66; Philip Katcher, *The Civil War Source Book* (New York: Facts on File, 1995), 34–35; E. B. Long, with Barbara Long, *Civil War Day by Day: An Almanac, 1861–1865* (Garden City, N.Y.: Doubleday Co., 1971), 540–43.

{ AUGUST 7, 1864 }

E. ANNE BUTLER TO SON SCOT BUTLER

Forest Home
August 7th 1864

My Dear Son Scot

Since writing you a week ago Demia has returned and last night found the small family of four *Whites* encreased to thirteen. Julia Dunn had come to spend a few days with Nettie in the absence of Proff Hoss and family at Richmond[1] on a visit   Cousin Anne Mathus (Uncle Chauncey's Anne) & husband Cousin Demia Thayer[2] and her husband Will Thrasher and child and your Uncle Chauncey also arrived last night and Obe Foote[3] was out making Mackie a visit. We have had a great many visitors this summer, in this we have never had much lack however.

Demia has had a very pleasant visit in Nashville. She left Cordelia there and it is doubtful whether she comes home until the return of the regiment. The regiments term of service will expire on the 27th of this month but Demia learned from some of the officers that they were expecting to be sent home this week in order to give the boys an oppertunity to reenlist, but I hardly think this will be done. I shall of course be very happy to have it so for although Chauncey has had good health since going out still I feel all the while fearful that he will get sick. Demia learned through Wm. Wallace that Chauncey has acquited himself well and is highly commended by his officers for his faithful & cheerful obedience to orders and that altogether he has done himself much credit in his good conduct since in the service   The word is that the boys of the 132d are not much inclined to reenlist thier experience under Col. Vance has not had the effect of captivating them with the service—

Aug. 8th Monday Morning Your Uncle Chauncey goes on this morning to Keithesburg. I had rather expected to go there myself with the children but as yet get no word when your Pa will be ready to return from there   He has had rather a hard time carrying on the farming operations there this summer and I think he will try to get an efficient farmer on the place after this year There is about half of it rented out it numbers altogether nine hundred acres   I will not this morning attempt to write out this sheet as I want to send it down by the folks as they go to town early this morning. I have no letter from you the past week but hope soon to hear from you. We are having very warm weather and have had a long dry spell   We have had no rains of consequence for months once or twice just enough to lay the dust it is a marvel almost that vegetation looks as well as it does.

Hoping this will find you my dear son safe & in good health is the prayer of

Your affectionate Mother
E. A. Butler

1. Richmond, Indiana, the seat of Wayne County in eastern Indiana.

2. Demia (Thayer) Thrasher, Scot's cousin. Demia's husband, William M. Thrasher, served in the Twelfth Regiment, Indiana Volunteer Infantry.

3. Obed Butler Foote, Scot's cousin.

E. ANNE BUTLER TO SON SCOT BUTLER

Forest Home
August 14 1864

My Dear Son Scot

Yours of August 7th came to hand last night. Your letters have been recd regularly and I wonder that you are not in receipt of those I have sent you from home as I have invariably written you once a week all the while

Demia wrote you since her return from Nashville and your Pa writes me that he has written you from Keithsburg. I have a letter from him just handed me by Ovid written on the tenth. He is still much engaged in farming operations there and is expecting soon to remove a house from one of the places to add to the house that they now occupy as it is much too small to accommodate the number there is of them. Your Pa is not satisfied to trust the heavy interests they have there to Albert & Josephine and until the crops are secured and disposed of he felt it to be necessary for your Uncle Chauncey or himself to be there.

I wrote you last week that your uncle was here on his way there   I had thought that perhaps your Pa would now come home but such is not his expectation. Yet there is as much as both can attend too and when the business is in shape that he can leave   He still proposes that I shall make the visit there with Mackie & Ann. I think your Pa has some thought that you and Chauncey may some day fancy farming and is getting things fixed up there to make it a very inviting place   When you return you will have to visit it before you set in to school. I have written you all along the current news and will not now recapitulate believing that by this time all the delayed letters have reached you   Mate Brown was here not too long ago   She wished to be [remembered] to you with Kind regards   She is in improved health   I saw her at church to day. She has lost the sight of one eye altogether but seems very thankful that she can yet see at all

You say you would like to get the Journal sometimes   I supposed they sent it to you regularly. Your Pa has ordered it several times to be sent to your address. I will try to have it sent to you all the while now there is but little of interest to be found in it. Political speeches is now to occupy its pages mostly. Gov. Morton and the democratic candidate for Governor have commenced the campaign and are *stumping* the state in company. One speaks an hour the other responds in a speech of an hour and a half, the first speaker making the closing speech of half an hour. I will send you some papers with the speeches. Every wednesday & saturday night there is speaking and music at "Circle Park" (Governor's Circle) Gen. Dumont spoke last night—large crowds of gentlemen & ladies attend and the union feeling is on the increase. I got a letter from Chauncey on yesterday   He had been to Chattanooga during the last week. Soldiers from the hospitals who have sufficiently recovered are being sent to the front and Chauncey was one among the squad that was sent as guards with them—one guard to each car. He said that the car to which he was attached held some veterans that were inclined to bear down pretty heavy on the hundred day men to the no small chagrin of Chauncey who could not even take the satisfaction of talking back to them

Cordelia returned from Nashville on friday. I hear no further word of the city regiment getting back before the expiration of their term of service. I will see to morrow about the photographs you name. I am truly thankful Scot that you are still blest with good health, sometimes when I think of the mercy and goodness of our heavenly Father that has thus preserved you through these long years of exposure and hardship my heart is so filled with gratitude and thankfulness that words utterly fail to give expression to my feelings, but the *tears* come unbidden.

Affectionately your Mother
E Anne Butler

{ AUGUST 21, 1864 }

E. ANNE BUTLER TO SON SCOT BUTLER

Forest Home
August 21st 1864

My Dear Son Scot

Yours of August 7th came to hand last tuesday 16th inst   I was rather surprized to learn that you were in receipt of none of my late letters—I have never failed to write you every week and hope notwithstanding their detention my letters will have before this reached you. In the letter sent about the 24th of July I enclosed you ten dollars   I would have sent double the sum but thought it best to wait and learn of the safe transmission of half the amount and at another time send you the additional sum. Your next letter received brought word that you had been to Chattanooga to draw your pay, and I will therefore wait until you are in more need before sending you more—

William Wallace returned home saturday morning bringing a younger sister of Mary Scovels whom Cordelia had invited here to spend the winter & to attend school. The regiment is expected tuesday   their term of service is out on Thursday—we have had any number of times set for their return by Madam Rumor but hope this time that it will not prove all rumor but that by thursday at least I shall have the satisfaction of having Chauncey safe at home.

Thursday I received a letter from your Pa naming the middle of this coming week as the time he wished Mackie & Anne and I to go out to Illinois I will leave home therefore next thursday morning for "Butlers Grove," should Chauncey have returned by that time but if he has not and I can see him by waiting I will of course do so   There has been something said about the city regiment being detained beyond their term of enlistment and it may yet be some time before their return.

Your Pa has had a very busy summer on his farm and is still much engaged   He is now very unwilling to leave things solely in Alberts[1] hands and I fear he will not be able to find anyone suitable to trust with the care of interests now pretty heavy there.

So soon as the photographs you named are done we will forward them to you. We are now fearful that the University will be forced to suspend for a year at least. Not for want of students however but of funds to keep it going. Tuition fees are not depended on to pay the salaries of the professors but a fund made of interest money on stock is the reliance for this   This fund is now used up pretty much to the amount now due, but by suspending a year more funds will have accumulated and it is proposed that the professors act as agents in soliciting more stock for the coming year.[2]

We are beginning to feel somewhat the excitement that might be expected in our political campaign but to this ordinary excitement are being added developments that show we are surrounded by banded traitors that are ready and willing at any moment to precipitate into all the horrors of civil war right here in Indiana. There is much excitement here today sunday as it is on account of some developments made by detectives from New York who traced a large amount of fire arms & ammunition to this city and to day found the same secreted in the Sentinel Building[3]   Several of Sentinel clique have skedadled but as I have not seen any one from town well posted in regard to the affair can give you no particulars. I suppose the copperheads will make the old plea that the[y] want their rights and a free election and took this way to ensure it   I think this move though will surely bring some of these desperadoes to get their des[s]erts. We have strong hopes that the soldiers will get to vote this fall and save us from the calamity of having the copperheads getting things into their traitorous hands   I will send you some papers with some of the developments made by Gen. Carrington of the plots of the "Sons of Liberty" and also the account of Edmund Kirke[4] & Col Jacques visit to Richmond and interview with Jeff Davis.

I hope to hear from you soon   I will not be in Ill. more than ten days or two weeks

Affectionately your Mother
E Anne Butler

We have the report that Col. S[t]reight was killed on the 14th inst a few miles from Chattanooga where his regiment had gone to drive some raiders   Nettie has a letter from Capt. of the fourteenth who had orders then to move. We are anxious to hear farther from Capt A as he doubtless was in the fight. The Cin. Gazette's Cor. does not credit the report of Col S. death

1. Albert Cole, Scot's uncle and brother of Cordelia (Cole) Butler, Ovid's first wife. Albert and his wife, Josephine/Joe/Josie, managed the Butler farm holdings in Keithsburg, Illinois.

2. There is no record of classes being suspended. From time to time Ovid made advances to cover expenses of the university, amounting to thousands of dollars. This may be one of those times. See, for example, the biography of Ovid Butler in M. C. Tiers, ed., *The Christian Portrait Gallery: Consisting of Historical and Biographical Sketches and Photographic Portraits of Christian Preachers and Others* (Cincinnati: The Franklin Type Foundry, 1864). See also Ovid to Scot, November 27, 1863.

3. Offices of the *Indianapolis Sentinel* newspaper.

4. James Roberts Gilmore, who wrote under the pen name of Edmund Kirke and helped establish the *Continental Monthly* in 1862. Gilmore visited Jefferson Davis at Richmond, Virginia, in 1864, having been given a pass by Lincoln to go beyond the federal lines in hopes he could reach a compromise between the warring factions. The visit was unsuccessful. After the war Gilmore entered into business, retiring in 1883 to write biographies, including *Personal Recollections of Abraham Lincoln.*

{ AUGUST 29, 1864 }

E. ANNE BUTLER TO SON SCOT BUTLER

Butler's Grove Henderson Co. Ill.
August 29 1864

My Dear Son Scot

The children & I accompanied by William Wallace arrived here last friday about noon. We are having a very pleasant time and I am feeling very much at home indeed. Your Pa and Uncle[1] have as you may remember, Albert and Josephine to keep house for them though bearing none of the expenses incurred. Your Uncle & Pa furnish every thing and hire all the helps so you see we may well feel at home   Joe is a good cook and like her brother "Lon" great on a "forage" and with all loves good living herself. They have a good vegitable garden plenty of different kinds of apples finest of water melons for the gathering and last though not least these prairie winds gives one the keenest of appitites to enjoy every thing in the eating line.

William proceded the city regiment some ten or twelve [days] before the term of enlistment had expired and not feeling just ready to settled down [to] business proposed to take this trip with me. He and your Uncle Chauency will return to Indiana starting from Keithesburg this evening on a packet for Rock Island. William now thinks he will stop a day in Chacago to look in on the Copperhead convention which is to convene there to day the object of which meeting is to nominate the opposing candidate to Lincoln. It has been thought that there would likely be a division of the party for one part is in favor of coming out for peace on any terms which of course means a recognition of the Southern confederacy, while it is thought the larger part are unwilling to being committed to that platform some from principal and others from policy doubting the success of their party if they should come out squarely on a peace platform. There have been developments lately showing that we have traitors banded together all over the country to resist the draft but the strenght of the government it is thought is sufficient to take care of this fire in the rear of our braves—

We were expecting that Chauncey would get home perhaps last saturday and some time this week any how. I disliked to leave home so near the time of his return very much but feared if I did not go when I was ready otherwise that I would failed to make this trip which I much desired to make and would very much disappoint Mackie and Anne. Your Pa too began to write somewhat impatiently thinking I did not care to come. How long I will stay I have not yet decided   I will stay certainly until thursday and then may leave at the close of the week or the first of next week with the children here if everything were going on well at home I could be contented to stay until your Pa was ready to return but I want to see Chauncey and it is not best I expect for us both to be away long at a time.

Yours to your Pa dated but we judge misdated the 1st August post-marked Nashville 22d inst I brought here to him   Your Pa will write soon or so soon as he can get time   They are very busy   I found them thrashing the wheat when I came this they have finished and are now thrashing the balance of the oats   They have large crops of every kind and are feeling very comfortable over it. The following is their crops this year—

The wheat 2000 bushels

over 3000— bushels of oats

some 4 or 500 bushels of rye

The corn crop will be as much as ten thousand bushels. One cornfield has about one hundred and thirty five acre enclosed of the finest kind of corn I am now expecting a letter from the girls with one from you enclosed   I hope I will not be disappointed

Affectionately Your Mother
E Anne Butler

1. Chauncey Butler.

———◦◦◦———

{ SEPTEMBER 4, 1864 }

E. ANNE BUTLER TO SON SCOT BUTLER

Butlers Grove
September 4th 1864

My Dear Son Scot

By this you perceive I am still in Ill. On next wednesday evening how-ever I will take the boat, with the children, for Rock Island en route for home.

We have had a very pleasant visit, unusually so for me for I have felt at home.

A day or two ago I had a letter from Demia written last monday. Chauncey had arrived at home on the saturday morning before looking rather under the weather. He had been affected with chills but she had got him medicine from the Doctor and that with clean clothes had helped him and his appearance very much. I feel anxious to see him and know just how he is Demia writes that he does not wish to go to school but wants to get to doing some kind of business but he must not leave school with as imperfect an education as his now is–and I hope to encourage him to go into school this fall determined to make some headway with his studies—

Your Pa will not be ready to leave for a few weeks yet. He is having a house moved as an addition to this one at the Grove and a good deal of repairing is to be done to the one we are now occupying. Uncle Chauncey will return in a few weeks to oversee gathering in the corn crop which is very heavy—

To morrow the draft is to take place. Some no doubt feel much uneasiness fearing they will have to go. I suppose we will see too how far the copperheads will dare to go in carrying out their threats in resisting the draft. You have doubtless through the papers learned all about the exposure of thier conspiracy in the northwest. The expose has one good effect in causing the loyal democrats to repudiate and denounce the whole move. At your Grandma's they were very decided in their denunciations. But I must say that nothing short of obedience to the exhortation of "come out of her," as applied to the democatic party can convince me of the sincerity of any heretofore acting with that party in their claims of loving the Union

I will not this evening try to write you at any length   I hope to find a letter from you awaiting—me at home bringing me the ever grateful word that all is well with my dear Son Scot.

Affectionately Your Mother,
E Anne Butler

{ S E P T E M B E R 4 , 1 8 6 4 }

OVID BUTLER TO SON SCOT BUTLER
[A continuation of E. Anne Butler's letter of the same date]

Butlers Grove, Henderson Co Ill
Sunday Sept 4 1864

My Son Scot

As your Ma has left some blank space in this letter I propose filling it by writing you a brief note. Your letter dated the 1st Augt (by mistake I pronounce) but written undoubtedly some time later was recd by me here and afforded me much pleasure   I was glad to hear that you were still safe and well. Otherwise your letter was highly satisfactory giving as you did a more specific statement of your condition and of your service

In a former letter written from this place I advised you that I had come here to attend to the farming operations and have found so much to do that I still remain here   We have raised a heavy crop of small grain   Wheat is harvested & thrashed and much of it sold   Our sales of this years crop of small grain amount to about $2000. Our Crop of Corn will be large and promises well now

Your Mas visit here with Mack & Anna has given me much pleasure and I think she will return home better pleased with the Country and better satisfied with My investment here than she has heretofore been   I shall be detained here after she leaves but how long I do not now know   It is important that some improvements be made on the farm and if I can get them done I wish to attend to them now.

Your Uncle Chauncy and I have made an arrangement by which he takes 100 acres for Albert who will go to farming on his own account in the Spring & leave the house he now lives in   We will then have to get another Manager and another family here   We do not yet know who that will be

As I have little room on this sheet I will not attempt to write more now only to say that if you knew how much pleasure it gives me to receive a letter from you you would I think write me oftener

Your Affectionate Father
Ovid Butler

E. ANNE BUTLER TO SON SCOT BUTLER

Forest Home
near Indianapolis Ind Sep 11th/64

My Dear Son Scot

The children and I arrived safely at home from Illinois last friday evening We had a very pleasant little visit take it all together. I would have been better satisfied if I could have had your Pa return with me but that seemed impossible as the work then in progress required him there to push it forward.

You can scarcely imagine Scot a greater contrast than the life your Pa leads there as compared with that at home. At home no bed but a spring mattress can give repose a quiet room to which to retire is one of the very indispensables of comfort and the morning paper if an hour behind time will discompose [him] for the day. There you find him sleeping "without rocking" on a hastily filled straw bed, eating at table with a dozen or fifteen rough dusty fellows, and getting a paper once a week and then too busy to take time to read it—and you could hardly believe that he enjoys this kind of life, but he really seems to. I think he has undergone a great amount of fatigue and when the weather is inclement there is little in the surroundings within doors to make him comfortable After this year this will be remedied for in fitting up the house this fall two rooms will be set apart for your Pa and uncle's[1] exclusive use to be closed when they are not there to occupy them—

When I arrived at home I found your uncle Chauncey & his wife here, they were returning from Noblesville where they had been to visit Uncle Albert Cole who had been and is still very ill of billious fever. Their expectation is to go to Illinois about the middle of this week They expect Cousin Anne and her husband Mr Mathers to accompany them. I think your uncle would like to have them go there if they should be pleased with the country. He has given Albert a very pretty farm and has another picked out for Anne if they are disposed to go there. I had thought that in case of your Uncle's children going he would think of going there altogether himself, but from what I learned he is talking of buying Ovids house and thinks of spending his winters here and the summers there. Ovid is bound to go to town. He has been a good deal excicised [exercised] about the draft I would judge from a letter he lately wrote your Pa.

I Shall expect your Pa home in about a week after your uncle gets there and then we will all be here at home but you but I hope when another four months has passed you too will be with us

There is but little of news stirring   The Union meetings are still kept up two nights in the week in the open air on saturdays at the Circle Park and on wednesdays in the court house square where they have a large wig wam lighted with gas. The Democrats have not yet commenced their campaign but now that they have held thier conventions and made their nominations will doubtless commence soon. We have strong hopes that our soldiers will be permitted to come home to vote   If not I fear the result, the crisis in national affairs is near at hand and the next few months is looked forward to with intense anxiety by every loyal person   All danger now lies in, it is thought the efforts of home traitors to work to the hand of the rebels in arms if we are able as a government to ride this storm all will be well. To have to pass through a presidential election at this period will try to the utmost the strenghts of our government   We can but hope and trust—

Mary Beaty is to be married on the 25 Oct and it is reported that Sam Tilford & Ollie Grooms, Nan Sister & Pickerell are going to do likewise on the same day of the month

My Sheet is filled up so good bye for the persent

Affectionately your Mother
E Anne Butler

1. Chauncey Butler, Scot's uncle.

{ SEPTEMBER 13, 1864 }

E. ANNE BUTLER TO SON SCOT BUTLER

Forest Home
near Indianapolis Ind. Sep 13th/64

My Dear Son Scot

Enclosed I send you the photographs you wished   I hope the long delay in getting them sent you will cause you no inconvenience   My absence from home prevented me getting it attended to sooner   I had spoken for them before I left home though but not in time to get them from the artists

I wrote you day before yesterday and do not propose to more than write you a note to day. When writing sunday I forgot to name that Orlando Bannaels met his death by an accident very similar to that of his father, that is by the cars. Orlando was an engineer on the train that was thrown from the track by a wind storm and was killed instantly

Affectionately your mother
E A Butler

———◦◦◦———

{ SEPTEMBER 18, 1864 }

E. ANNE BUTLER TO SON SCOT BUTLER

Forest Home
Sep. 18, 1864

My Dear Son Scot

Yours of 28 August is received the contents read with much interest and the assurances it brought of your continued good health and general welfare was truly welcome to my anxious heart.

To day my feelings are too much disturb to write you in my usual gossipping way   Demia is sick and as is usual with me in like cases I am anxious. She has an attack of typhiod fever and this class of fever is very protracted   It has to run its course [and] like measles can not be arrested as many other diseases   So I see much of suffering for her in the weeks to come and for me anxious *anxious* watchings.

I shall expect your Pa home this week   On last wednesday your Uncle Chaunceys folks passed through stopping over night on their way to Keithsburg—they expected to stop at Chicago and also at Davenport[1] and will not likly reach the Grove before saturday. I think when your Uncle gets there your Pa will start home especially when he learns that Demia is sick for now at the opening of college there is much that is necessary to be done in the secretarys office which your Pa will feel that he must do in Demia's place now she is unable to attend to the duties of the office[2]

You have spoken several times of my having misdirected my letters to you. I but followed your directions when I directed them to the 20th Army Corps as I thought and left off "Head Quarters Signal Corps,["] but I now follow the last you gave me and write to Signal Department Army of the Cumberland. I sent you last week the half dozen photograps you sent for. I will write you again some time during the week   For the present good bye

Affectionately Your Mother
E Anne Butler

1. Davenport, Illinois.
2. During the Civil War, Demia served as secretary of Butler University, then located adjacent to Forest Home.

{ SEPTEMBER 21, 1864 }

E. ANNE BUTLER TO SON SCOT BUTLER

Forest Home
Sep 21st/64

My Dear Son Scot

When I wrote you on last sunday I promised to let you know some time through the week how your sister Demia was getting   Within the last two days the violence of the attack is much modified and she does not suffer nearly so much. I think her condition much better than at my last writing and although I can not hope that her attack will be short, I have hopes from what the Doct says that she is not likely to suffer as she did at the first. I wrote you sunday more disponding than I am wont to do but I was quite unnerved and entertained very great anxieties in regard to Demia's sickness   Now that the disease seems to be yielding to treatment & she is so much relieved I am not feeling so fearful of results—but am in hopes she will now get along—slow though it may be—

Nettie got a letter from Capt last night. He writes that all the voters of Ind reg's are expected to come home to vote   Col. Coburn is being expected home   his time was out on the fourteenth. To night the Unionist dedicate a large Wig wam that has been erected in the Court House yard and several celebrated speakers will entertain the crowd—it is capable of holding four thousand persons. There is also to be a grand display of fire works in celibration of Sheridans victory in Shenadoah valley on the 19th and altogether a grand time is expected

Chauncey has gone into College and seems inclined to take hold in earnest   Macky & Anne have commenced going to Julia Dunn[1] and seem much pleased. Your Pa has not yet come but I am in daily expectation of his arrival   I will not now write more   Chauncey is going in to town and is in something of a hurry and I will therefore not detain him

Affectionately your Mother
E A. Butler

1. Julia ran a "small school" within the university. This preparatory school held sessions periodically as the university could afford. See reference to her application for such a position in Demia to Scot, July 8, 1864.

{ S E P T E M B E R   2 5 ,   1 8 6 4 }

E. ANNE BUTLER TO SON SCOT BUTLER

Forest Home
Sep. 25/64

My Dear Son Scot

Owing to Demia's continued sickness and great unwillingness to spare me from her bedside I will not have the time to write you at any lenght. She is still quite sick & suffers a great deal though the Doct. says she is getting along full better than he expected when she was first taken   This morning is the first time she has said that she felt better   Doct says the fever will run one week longer before she will be materially better—

Your Pa got home yesterday morning   He is quite out of health with a bad cold but I hope that with a little nursing up in a warm room he will be over it in a few days   Nettie has been rather expecting that Capt would be home to vote this fall and is feeling some disappointment now as the impression now is that few if any but convalescent soldiers will be furloughed for that purpose.

The draft in centre township came off last friday and substitutes are in great demand. Doct Jameson, Prof Hoss, Parish Webb Grubbs are among those who *drew prizes*   The draft so far has progressed very peaceably notwithstanding the great amount of threatening that the opposition has made that it would bring on a conflict. There is great rejoicing over the Union victories just now and strong hopes that a few months more will finish up the rebellion

Doct Wells was married last wednesday to a Miss Smith of Cincinnati They have not arrived in the city yet as they are making a bridal trip off some where. Daught Beaty is to [be] married a month from to day (25th Oct) if Demia is not well enough by that time to officiate as brides maid & to accompany her on her bridal tour there will be great disappointment to all parties

Excuse farther writing at this time.

Affectionately Your Mother
E A Butler

Yours under date Atlanta Sep came safely today.

{ O C T O B E R   2 ,   1 8 6 4 }

E. ANNE BUTLER TO SON SCOT BUTLER

Forest Home,
October 2d/64

My Dear Son Scot

Since I wrote you last Demia has been improving slowly, so slowly however as to not be yet what can be called convalescent. She has yet some fever about her but it is gradually leaving her, in a few days I hope she will be clear of it and begin to gather some strength

Col. Coburn has arrived here. I have not seen him yet but I learn from those of the family that have that he had been with you a few weeks since. Col. Streight is also here and his wife and child have come to the city to meet him. He has the offer of a brigade and will I suppose accept and go in again this time "for the war"

The draft caught Bob Catterson   Your Uncle Bob says that Bob is going himself and will not try to get a substitute   There has been considerable effort made to raise sufficient funds to get volunteer substitutes to relieve the city from the draft, but with what success is not yet known. Ovid[1] was very much exercised about the draft but as he did not draw a prize he seems much relieved in mind.

I cannot hope Scot to write you an entertaining letter now if indeed I am able at any time to accomplish such a feat. I have sat at Demia's bedside and been confined to her sick room day and night so constantly that I have scarcely a thought beyond its limits unless it is wondering why I do not hear from you oftener and what you are about.

The great topic of interest here now is the State & Sanitary Fair which is to come off this week   If you are in receipt of The "Journal" you will know though quite as much as I do about it. I hope for the honor of the State it will not be a failure.

Hoping to hear from you real soon I will now close

Affectionately Your Mother
E Anne Butler

1. Ovid Dyer Butler, Scot's half brother.

{ O C T O B E R   2 3 ,   1 8 6 4 }

E. ANNE BUTLER TO SON SCOT BUTLER

Forest Home
Oct 23 1864

My Dear Son Scot

We have had but three letters from you since you reached Atlanta   Your communications are rather few and far between, but I will not lecture you on writing often at this time. Yours of Oct 2d came to hand a few days ago. In this you say that you had received no letters from home since the one dated Sep. 18th This is altogether, owing to the stoppage of mails while the rebels were so plenty on the rail road lines. It was stated yesterday in the papers that mail communication was again resumed and we would be again in receipt of the letters of correspondants.

You will find the news in regard to the elections and Sheridans success much better than you had hoped for I know. The friends of the Government are very jubilant & hope ful and the copperheads are just the other way very quiet and subdued—

In regard to the letters sent you from home, I have written you every week once and just after getting home from Illinois I wrote you twice a week   In one I sent you a half dozen photograps   As you have not acknowledged the receipt of them I fear that they have been lost on the way

Demia about two weeks ago got so as to sit up but after trying it two or three days had to go back to bed and be blistered and doctored a while longer. She got out to the table to day for the first time since her sickness. She is very anxious to go to Mary Beatys wedding which comes off next tuesday evening. The invitations are for five oclock (as they leave on the eight oclock train, eastward bound on their bridal trip[)]. I wrote you I believe that Demia was to have gone the trip with them   And a young gentleman friend of the groom was also to have been of the party. Her sickness however broke in upon that arrangement and the bride and groom will take the trip alone.

John Beaty is now home on furlough having received a flesh wound in one of the recent fights in Grants army. I saw at church to day your friend Sam Tilford with his little wife Ollie. Sam to improve his appearance, I suppose had had the barber apply the paint brush to the little tuft of hair pendant from his chin turning it to jetty black while the contrast made his looks look almost red—T. Boaz[1] was drafted and had to pay a thousand dollars for a substitute—from this cause or some other he voted the butternut ticket out and out I learn. Your old shop mate Sam Laing is home. He came with others from hospital to vote, so your Uncle Robt. told me the other day   Your Uncle's have gone to the Kankakee on their annual fishing and hunting excursion—they left last monday and will be gone two weeks.

Hoping to hear from you often and real soon again I remain

Your affectionate Mother
E A Butler

1.William T. Boaz, Butler University class of 1859, was an oil dealer and a resident of Indianapolis. Here Elizabeth Anne refers to the fact that many young men who were drafted bought their way out of service by "buying" a substitute to take their place. "Substitutes" were often young men who made money by selling themselves into service and then not reporting for muster. They might sell themselves again and again under assumed names in different counties. *Catalog.*

DEMIA BUTLER TO BROTHER SCOT BUTLER

Forest Home
Oct 30./64

My Dear Brother:

You will know by this that I have survived that cruel typhoid fever. After struggling with it for seven long weeks I have at last conquered and am now able to go about the house and am rapidly being restored to full and perfect health. I was a very impatient victim for I was so very anxious to get well that I might not have to endure a disappointment which I have since had to submit to. You know I was to be Mary Beaty's bridesmaid and go with them on the bridal tour but I was barely able to be at the wedding and be a silent spectator of the scenes and gaieties in which I so fully expected to participate. The wedding party was very pleasant though small. Ma & Pa were there. Mary looked beautiful in her elegant white satin. Her bridesmaids were dressed in rose color and blue. She had some very handsome silver presents. Berg[1] looked [pale?] for once in his life and really quite handsome. They left for the East that night.

Johnny Beaty arrived at home a few days before the wedding being furloughed on account of a wound in his wrist received in one of the late eastern battles. Ned has grown so tall and they say he has sobered down wonderfully. Although he is very quiet and reserved I doubt very much whether his youthful *folly* and recklessness are entirely subdued. At least I heard the other day that he was a brave lad and a brilliant gambler. Chauncey says he told him that he was going to join the church.

I hope John will reform and be a good boy   His parents are too kind and devoted to him for him to cruelly break their hearts. Oh! you boys little know how anxiously and earnestly you are watched and prayed for in your far distant homes while you brave the stern and fierce ordeal of a thousand temptations. If you knew it and could think of it when the trying hour came your moral courage would never fail nor good resolutions be ever unbroken. But in you Scot I have perfect confidence for I know you will not stoop to any of those bad habits which ruin young men. Come back to us as *good* as when you left a young untried boy.

I was very sorry to hear of Harisons illness. I could sympathise with him fully and only wished that I could send him some of the nice dishes Ma prepared for me. Chicken quails oysters jellies &c I could hardly enjoy think[ing] of him and the many other poor soldiers who longed in vain for such delicacies. I hope however Harison has recovered and is blessed with an appetite as *voracious* as mine for I do think I could gnaw "hard tack" I get so hungry. I look wistfully forward to Thanksgiving and the days of "buckwheat cakes & molasses"   You will be at home then I hope to enjoy them with me if indeed you shall then be long enough from camp fare to enjoy home cooking.

Demia

1. Berg Applegate, enlistee in the Indiana 107th, an Indianapolis resident, and a Butler University student. *Catalog.*

———

{ O C T O B E R   3 0 ,   1 8 6 4 }

E. ANNE BUTLER TO SON SCOT BUTLER

Forest Home
Oct 30th/64

My Dear Son Scot

Yours written from Chattanooga bearing date 22d inst came to hand last night. So you have been on the march again. I had thought when you reached Atlanta that the Army would take a long rest as was the custom in the earlier stages of the war, but this does not seem to be Shermans tactics and it may be that you will not spend much of this winter in the winter quarters

You write that you have had no word from home since mine of the 18 Sep. I am sorry that I wrote you in the discouraging way I did about Demia's sickness as it has happened that you have got no others since. In order to counteract the effect of my "discouraging" letter   I wrote several extra letters, which however has it seems failed to reach you.

I am sorry you did not find Capt. Anderson at Chattanooga, he left with his regiment for Bridgeport a few days before you time of getting there. They will remain there some time likely as they are doing garrison duty. If you had met him there he could have given you all the news from home as Nettie writes him several times a week.

In writing you to day I will not recapitulate the contents of the letters sent you but not perhaps yet received, except in the case of Mary Beaty's marriage and some half dozen others that you know. The first to lead off was your friend Sam. Tilford with Miss Ollie Grooms. Then comes "Pet" Barbour and young Jackson (graduated with Demia). The same week Demia received "cards" to Harry Griffin & Lottie Hillis'[1] wedding at Greensburg and on the following day came Mary Beaty's wedding. She married Berg. Applegate of the firm of Schnull & Co. Whole sale Grocers. This wedding of Mary's has been among her relatives and circle "The Event" of the season—first in the way of wedding outfit   Her wardrobe was elegant and when the present prices in dry goods are considered this means in dollars and cents much more than it once did. The wedding party was "brilliant" and the wedding presents capped the climax. The first grooms man presented a silver water Pitcher & two Goblets lined with gold. The second grooms man gave a *magnificent* castor & stand—others added cake Baskets Pickle castors cake Knives, forks &c all in *silver*—

I saw Kise Fletcher yesterday on the street   He enquired very kindly after you. He is looking quite thin and very rough   he has been out on one of his father's farms at work ever since his return from the six months service and seems to have given up for the present at least all regard for dress or personal appearance—This no doubt pleases some of his family, his father perhaps—but it would not be pleasant to me if he were a son of mine. A man in being a farmer does not need to give up all care how he looks among folks. Why Kise looks like his siege on the farm the past season had been more wearing by far than his six months campaign hard as that was

Chauncy since starting to college this fall has felt very much discouraged, he does not like the study of the languages does not indeed feel the need of education or appreciate its advantages. I wish you were here to engage in study with him now. This time is drawing nigh, November December January and then we will be expecting your return—these are three long dreary months and will bring with them I fear much hard service to you, but I hope you will be kept in health— and that you will be returned to your home in safety is the prayer constantly of

Your Affectionate Mother
E. A. Butler

P.S. In the right place I failed to say that Demia had now recovered from her long sickness but as yet has not gone out except to Mary

1. Lottie Hillis, intermittent student at the university, 1863–65. *Catalog.*

E. ANNE BUTLER TO SON SCOT BUTLER

Forest Home
Nov. 6th/64

My Dear Son Scot

Your welcome letter of the 28th ult. to your Pa came to hand last Monday, we are glad to get letters so regularly from you now and cannot but regret that you are being so long deprived of all news from home, by this time I hope however you have been able to have your mail retained for you at Chattanooga—

I wish you were in receipt of newspapers from home now that you could see the report of the trial of our Indiana conspirators—"Sons of Liberty" that is now going on in the city   They all seem inclined to turn states evidence making a clean breast of it in order to save themselves from severe punishment, that is those that have been already apprehended. Bingham the Sentinel[1] man tells on as few as he can, but enough is already developed to show that we were about the middle of last August in the greatest danger. These conspirators were just ready for the outbreak that would have brought the war to our very doors and but for the efforts of our officials here in ferreting the matter out and making preparations for defense it would have been upon us with all its horrors—and to think these black hearted villains passed along our streets daily looking like innocence itself with this horrid secret and bloody purpose locked in their wicked breasts

Since all these things have come out against the party I have some interest in knowing how your uncles feel about their idol party, but there is a dead silence there.[2] I was at your Grandma's monday but there was never a word spoken in reference to this or to the great fraud that was attempted on the soldiers vote of New York State—

I will be glad when the presidential election is over & yet we may have trouble even after that no doubt is entertained but that Lincoln will be elected but these dissatisfied butternuts may conclude to carry out their plans here yet—But I guess I will for the present dismiss the subject and gather up whatever interest there may be of other matters.

This however is but little   every thing seems on the dull order. Demia is able to go out some but always feels the worse of a trip to town it will take some time yet to bring intire restoration of health to her   Nettie gets word from Capt Anderson every few days   he writes that on Col. Streights return to the regiment he will ask for a furlough. Col. S. left for the front a few days ago with a lot of bounty jumpers

& their agents who were sent from here to be consigned by Col. S. to the underlying *care* of Gen. Sherman. Your old school mate Thurstan Challer is dead—he had been in the service but whether he was at the time of his death I do not know

Demia wrote you this day week ago and helped Annie out in getting up hers, both have I hope come to hand. I sent you a week or so after my return from Illinois a half dozen photographs. I fear you will not get them   if you should not—I can get you more   I suppose your letters and papers will be kept over for you at Atlanta by some one   If not you have lost a pretty good amount of gossip for no doubt each one I wrote had its share. I hope to hear from you in a day or two again. Dont fail to write often

Affectionately Your Mother,
E. Anne Butler

1. Reporter for the *Indianapolis Sentinel*, Democratic competitor of the *Indianapolis Journal*.
2. Refers to the Southern sympathies of the McOuat family.

———⟨∞⟩———

{ N O V E M B E R   6 ,   1 8 6 4 }

OVID BUTLER TO SON SCOT BUTLER

Forest Home near Indianapolis
Nov 6th 1864

My Son Scot

I have your letter dated Chattanooga Oct 28/64 and am much gratified by its receipt and much interested in its contents   The Newspaper accounts of the movements & operations of Shermans Army have been so confused & contradictory that I was unable to gather the facts from them   Your letter gives me a better and clearer idea of what they have been & has quieted some of the apprehensions that I began to entertain for the safety of that Army   The rebel papers however seem very sanguine of Hoods ability to bag Sherman and I apprehend that the rebel forces are still striving to reach Shermans rear and cut off his communications. I hope & believe that he will be able not only to defend himself & maintain his advanced positions, but also to annihilate Hoods Army

But I need not speculate upon the situation for it is undoubtedly continually changing   A little time will probably develop important results

The State election is past and resulted as you of course know in a triumph of the Union Ticket by a large majority. The Presidential Election will be on Tuesday next—the 8th inst. The success of the Lincoln Ticket is regarded as certain in this and in nearly every loyal State   The recent exposure of the so called Order of the Sons of Liberty and the pending Trials of some of the Members of the Order for Treason before a Military Commission here will I think contribute to swell the majority for Lincoln. Harrison, Bingham & Hoffman[1]—prominent Democrats and Members of the Order holding high positions in it have turned States evidence and have made most startling disclosures of its terrible & treasonable purposes. I have not space in a letter for any thing of the particulars but suppose you have seen something of them in the papers which have reached you

By the by Scot I saw in one of your recent letters to your Ma a remark that might indicate that you regarded my voting for Lincoln as hypothetical or doubtful. What could have induced such a doubt   You know something of my past life. You also know something of the convictions which induced me to consent to your entering the service and something of the feelings and opinions I have expressed during the war. To decline now to vote for Lincoln would be to [. . .] myself and to prove false to all my former professions

Lincoln progressed slowly—I have often thought too slowly towards the true and safe political positions upon which alone the war could be successfully prosecuted   But he now stands upon them squarely & firmly and is well entitled to the vote of one who has long been regarded as a radical in advance of the Age I have heretofore cast several votes which were at the time regarded as ultra radical but their highest radicalism was a claim for Freedom in the National [. . .] My vote at the pending election may be, and by reason of my age it is not improbable that it will be my last vote at a National Election. I thank God that I am at last permitted to cast a vote of higher significance & deeper import—a vote claiming National Universal Freedom and that in doing so I have full confidence of the success of the Ticket   Nor is this all that is involved in the present election. Lincolns election secures not only this, but also the Integrity of the Union—for such election will be a national pledge that the rebellion shall be put down and crushed out. I dare not indulge the hope now entertained by many that the result will immediately follow the election. There is yet I fear too much of the Serpents vitality in the rebellion to warrant the conclusion that the Ballot box will at once extinguish it   How long it may live and what terrible things it may yet inflict I do not know—but if the Nation wills that it shall perish—it must die sooner or later   The election of Lincoln will be the expression of such a National will

The fact that the rebels are about to arm their slaves to fight for them raises in my mind an apprehension of a more protracted struggle than for sometime past I had anticipated but that fact will not—cannot change the final result—A Free Nation—one and indivisible, is as I read the signs of the times Gods purpose as the result of the present conflict

But enough of this and I have room for little more on this sheet. I suppose you must be needing some things which you cannot well get there and which we might send you if we knew what they were and could feel assured that they would reach you. Write what you need and whether the transportation would be regarded as safe   Our letters have it seems failed to reach you latterly and we fear there would be no certainty in the transportation   May God bless preserve and protect you

Your Affectionate Father
Ovid Butler

1. John T. Hoffman (1828–1888), New York judge closely aligned with William "Boss" Tweed and the Tammany Society who earned recognition for his handling of the 1863 New York riot draft cases. He was elected mayor of New York City (1866–68) and twice governor of New York (1869–72). Following the Tammany Hall scandal and Tweed's conviction, Hoffman escaped to Germany and died there. He is buried in New York.

{ N O V E M B E R   2 6 ,   1 8 6 4 }

E. ANNE BUTLER TO SON SCOT BUTLER

Forest Home
Nov. 26th/64

My Dear Son Scot

It is now nearly two weeks since I last wrote you. Yours of the 17th written at Nashville was duly received, you had then a long hard trip ahead but I hope when this reaches Chattanooga you will have arrived safe and sound there.

Last monday night week Capt. Anderson arrived on sick leave furloughed for twenty days and on thursday 17 inst Nettie presented him with a son—Mother and child doing well. Thanksgiving we had a family gathering, which by including some visitors that Cordelia had and brought with her made the round number of (30) thirty

Our Democratic folks in the city are having a gay time since the election they have been having one dance after another for the last week or two and some times two in one evening   It looks real droll after the grand Expose of the "Sons" and the defeat of little "Mac" Old Capt Cain and lady are going the rounds to all of the parties and Mrs Cain though about 50 still "Trips the light fantastic toe"

Mrs Duncan gave Mary Beaty Applegate a reception on her return from her bridal trip   Demia was there   John Beaty has returned to his regiment to serve out the remainder of his term of service   Ester Wallace is now home from boarding school to spend thanksgiving week   She had a party last night which Chancy attended   It was made up of the half grown girls and lads of her acquaintance. Col. Coburns card offering his services in the law appeared in to days Journal. He has been since his return up to the election engaged making political speeches to help the Union cause

We were all very much surprized at Charley Davage connecting himself with our church a few weeks ago. He goes into business in the grocery line in one of the rooms of the new building opposite the post Office put up this summer by Ketchem Major and Doct. Jamison

This is rather a poor excuse for a letter but it is the best I have been able to do writing in Nettie's room and constantly almost, interrupted by calls to wait on her—

Hoping to hear from you soon I remain

Your Affectionate Mother
E Anne Butler

{ D E C E M B E R   5 ,   1 8 6 4 }

E. ANNE BUTLER TO SON SCOT BUTLER

Forest Home
December 5th 1864

My Dear Son Scot

I have not much expectation that this will likely reach you in a very rea-sonable lenght of time owing to the military situation about Nashville, but will never-the less send it on its way hoping that *some* time it may *come* to hand.

Capt Anderson left to join his regiment last thursday morning—will likely arrive in time to engage in the battle that in the last accounts seemed pending near Nashville—this thought brings many anxieties for his welfare and we will await in anxious suspense the news from there. Your own safety has I fear been any thing but secure in this trip you under took from Nashville. Among all the ills imaginable to which you might be exposed that of being taken pris-oner to me now seems the most terrible. After reading the horrors of the Andersonville prison pens one would think death in any form would be prefer-able to being committed to the mercy of such a foe.

Your trip, though, (as I hope safely made by this time), has no doubt been a very hard and toilsome one and I draw hope from the advance of the sea-son & also the near expiration of your term of service that it is about the last time that you will have hardships of this kind to undergo—Some eight or ten weeks and you will be home "God willing" after three long years of travel toil and pri-vation. Well, can *home* "make you happy?"   I hope that *civilization* has not lost its charm for you—that home and home folks will not seem too tame for enjoy-ment to our soldier boy altogether. We have great plans laid off for the coming year. Demia expects your companionship during a sojourn of a few months at "Butlers Grove" the coming summer and she will no doubt try to "*impress*" you as her escort to Minneapolis, as she thinks of making a short visit there   Doct. Butler still resides there and is urgent in invitations to us to visit them—

We have not much local news now of interest. At church to day I saw Joe Pope & his wife, she informs me they are home now for a while. He, you remember was rather compelled to resign his position as brigade quartermaster owing to neglect of duty, since he has been on Gen Hovey's[1] staff, but from some cause he is now out of the service. Your Uncle Chauncey & Aunt[2] are not yet returned from Illinois but we will be expecting them along about the last of the week. My time has been very little at my own disposal the greater part of the time since my return from Illinois, first with Demia's long sickness and latterly with Nettie and her baby and I feel that my letters to you need to be apologized for in lacking in interest as they have been and hurriedly written as they have necessarily been. Nettie and babe are getting along finely and the little one is a great "mug." He is named Thomas Butler but called Tommy for short.

Demia is wearing her hair short. She was compelled, to her great regret to have it cut off, after her sickness it combed out by great hands full and to prevent baldness she had to be shorn—

I fear I will not get any word from you for some time as the enemy is between Chattanooga and Nashville, but I hope that this state of things will not last long   We are all waiting with much impatience for news from Sherman and must learn before many days his where a bouts. The rebel papers ignore his presence in Georgia so we get no information thence   in this they follow the plan made up on Shermans first advance, to give us no information as to his movements knowing only through that source we could learn any thing in regard to him until he reached the coast.

Your Affectionate Mother
E Anne Butler

1. Joe Pope was dismissed because Gen. Alvin P. Hovey, as commander of the District of Indiana, recruited only single men. His recruits became known as "Hovey's Babies."
2. Lorinda Janette (Cole) Butler.

———

{ D E C E M B E R   1 8 ,   1 8 6 4 }

OVID BUTLER TO SON SCOT BUTLER

Forest Home near Indianapolis
Sunday Evening Dec. 18th 1864

My Son Scot

The last letter we have from you was yours to your Ma dated Nashville Nov 17th—more than a month ago   You were then about starting back to

Chattanooga   We have no word from you since and are as you must be aware quite anxious to know how you have fared & how you now are   The advance of Hood has cut the communication between Nashville & Chattanooga and this we suppose accounts for our hearing nothing from you   We hope & believe however that Chattanooga is safe & well supplied & that no personal injury has happened to you   I think that the recent battles & Union victories near Nashville have opened or will soon open the communication & expect to hear from you soon   I pray God that the information may be such as we desire.

We rejoice at the recent triumphs of the Union Arms at all points according to our latest information but we rejoice with fear & trembling knowing that the safety of those near and dear to us is involved in the conflicts resulting in these victories. Capt Anderson was of course in the battles near Nashville. His Regt belongs to the 3d Division of the 4th Corps   That Corps it seems was in the hardest of the fight   We have not since heard from him & are waiting with some anxiety some word from him. Owing to the absence in the rebel prisons of many of the Officers of his regiment he was serving as Lieut. Colonel. The Capts health is not good   He was at home on sick leave the latter part of Nov. While here Nettie presented him with a Son—born the 17th November. He left for the front the first of this month and was in the trenches before Nashville until the advance of Thomas' Army[1] on the 15th inst   We hope to hear favorably both from him & from you soon

Well Scot your term of service is drawing to a close   I need not tell you how anxious we all are for that close   I believe that thus far you have come up well and bravely under the hardships and privations of a soldier life and that you have promptly & faithfully discharged your duty in the humble place you have filled   I trust you will continue to do so to the end. Then both yourself & your friends will have the satisfaction of knowing that for three long years of your youth you have served your country faithfully neither for the honors of the Office or for any pecuniary consideration but simply & purely from motives of patriotism   This service is I think sacrifice enough for you to make unless the necessity for further sacrifice shall be greater & Sterner than I now apprehend that it will be   Of that necessity you can judge best after your discharge & after you return home   In any event I desire you to return wholly uncommitted as to continuing in or reentering the service after your present term expires   If the question of reenlistment is to be considered at all, it can best be considered then and here

I write this under an apprehension that it may not reach you not only for the reasons that the communication has been cut by the rebels & may not yet be opened but also for the reason that I do not know how or where to address you. Your former instructions to direct to "Headquarters Signal Corps Army of Georgia" are I presume inappropriate to the present circumstances

Shermans Army now at or near Savanah is I suppose the Army of Georgia. You are now under Thomas but his army is with him South of Nashville—pressing Hood. From all the information I have I suppose you are at Chattanooga but with what Corps or what portion or division of the Army I do not know   I shall direct this simply to "Signal Corps Chattanooga Ten."   If you get it write promptly and let us know how & where to address you that we may feel some assurance that you will get our letters

While Capt Anderson was here he and Nettie named their boy Thomas Butler Anderson. Nettie & the boy are doing very well. I wrote you on the 6th Nov which letter I hope you received. Your Ma has written you occasionally but the knowledge that the communication was closed has prevented her writing regularly

We had a pleasant Thanksgiving Dinner at which the family including Delia, Maria & Ovid & their families were all present. You were remembered and much missed. Had you been here the family circle would have been complete.

Remember Scot that we are anxious to hear from you soon. We too are anxious to see you safe at home but for this we will wait for patience and hope till the expiration of your term of service praying too and trusting in God that we may not there be disappointed

Your Affectionate Father
Ovid Butler

1. Here Ovid refers to Gen. Henry Thomas's attempt to break through the Confederate lines at Missionary Ridge in order to control the Mississippi River.

{ J A N U A R Y 4 , 1 8 6 5 }

E. ANNE BUTLER TO SON SCOT BUTLER

H. G. Scovel's Summer Street
Nashville Ten January 4th/65

My Dear Son Scot

My being in this city will be a matter of surprize no doubt to you, but when I tell you that Capt. Anderson was severely wounded in the battle of the

16th before this place it will be explained—When through a letter from Mrs Scovel we learned the condition of Capt. it was thought best that I should come to him as Nettie was too feeble either to take the trip or to render him any service in the way of nursing   His wound is doing remarkably well and we expect to leave for home to morrow or next day—we will go on the hospital train as he is not able to go through in a sitting posture.

I will give you now the particulars of Captain's getting wounded—if you have read an account of fridays fight you will remember that a certain hill which the rebels still held was assaulted by Col Streights brigade and a brigade commanded by Col. Post or at least these two brigades led the assault—that in the first attempt to take the hill our forces were repulsed but afterwards rallied and carried the hill driving the rebels pell mell. Capt. was wounded in the first attack just in front of the rebels works a few moments before our forces were driven back—he was in command of one wing of the 51st Reg. and was struck by a rifle ball as he was turning to give some command to his men the ball entered a few inches to the left of his spine coming out above the point of the hip on the right side. I said coming out, I should rather say was put out for it was lodged near the surface and was taken out by the surgeon on the field—and a terrible jagged looking thing it is, about an ounce and a half in weight an english bullet. Well when he was struck his horse gave a plunge or two and as Capt fell—after lying there a while he found his position very perilous   Our forces had all fallen back and were shelling the hill and when ever the shells fell short of the rebel works they fell plunging in every direction within a few feet of him. Finding he could move himself he commenced rolling himself down the hill, when he reached the foot of the hill he crawled on his hands and feet to the skirmish lines of our forces—where in the course of time his wound was dressed and he was taken to a farm house. The agents of the Christian commission were on the field looking after the wounded and Capt. hearing one called "Scovel" enquired if he knew H. G. Scovel. This gentlemen was a nephew of H. G. Scovel, and brought word to the family that Capt wished to be taken to their house, he was brought saturday the day after the battle which is now about three weeks [ago]. Since being brought here he has received every kindness & attention imaginable by one and all of the family—

On last friday night I left home for this place accompanied as far as Louisville by William Wallace he seeing me safely aboard the Nashville train. In returning home we expect as I named to take the hospital tran which leaves at 7 oclock in the morning and if we can make connection with the Indianapolis night train will take a sleeping car at Jeffersonville. The trip will be attended no doubt with some perpexities for Captain is very helpless, but I do not fear but that we will get along very well. The surgeon says he will not be able to walk for three or four months even with crutches, but Capt. and all of us do not feel disposed to murmer at this and are but too thankful that it is as well with him as it is—

I have not my Dear son written to you with any regularity for some time now—there seemed so little probability of my letters reaching you in any sort of time if at all that I had not heart in writing. It seemed so long a while since we had heard from you when yours of Nov. 29 came to hand just a week ago, that I had grown very anxious about you and although that letter had been a month on the way and gave no satisfaction as to your present condition, still as it brought word that you had made the trip safely through from this place to Chattanooga it relieved very many anxieties in regard to you. When I contemplate all that you have undergone in the three years now nearly expired I hardly can find words to give expressions to the emotions of gratitude that fill my heart. While the spirit has been riven of so many thousand's of mothers, Our Heeavenly Father in his great Mercy has spared me my boy—"Give thanks and rejoice Oh my soul for *His* goodness endureth forever"—

Of the home folks all were in usual health. Your Pas health is perhaps as good as usual but as each winter passes by he grows less and less inclined to go abroad and is disposed more and more to find comfort at his own fireside alone going very seldom abroad. I find too Scot that upon you & Chauncey will depend the happiness of your father's declining years. I fondly hope for the sake not only of him but your own that his hopes in regard to you boys will be fully realized   I believe in former letters I have given you all the local and family news and will not now repeat that already written. On the night I left home I called to see your Grandma who had had a severe attack of Nueralgia   She was then able to sit up but felt very much prostrated—Doct Wells had been very sick too but was recovering

Well Scot a few more weeks, if all goes well and you will be "Home again." Will you be like a fish out of water? it will not surprize me if you are— and will you be able to take to books? Hoping to hear from you very soon and to see you face to face before many weeks I am as ever

Your Affectionate Mother
E A Butler

{ J A N U A R Y   1 6 ,   1 8 6 5 }

E. ANNE BUTLER TO SON SCOT BUTLER

Forest Home
Jan 16th 1865

My Dear Son Scot

We arrived safely at home on last wednesday morning—our trip from Nashville was rather tedious as we came by water to Louisville. We were kept waiting from thursday evening until saturday afternoon for the boat to leave N. After we got aboard thursday the "Robert Moore" it and all the other boats lying there were seized by the government to transport troops up the Tennessee   We left this boat at Paducah, having gone on to that point thinking that if we had to lie over long waiting for a boat to Louisville the accommodations would be better than at Smithland. We had just time to dine and rest a while when the "Darling" one of the four regular packets running between Memphis and Cincinnati came along, we got to the Galt House in town to take supper and get aboard the "Bus" for the night train, and also in thus making this connection escaped the dangers and horrors of the fire at the Galt House, for in a few hours after our leaving it a fire broke out and before morning it was a mass of ruins. The night before the boat left Nashville Captains father joined us. His brother in law Doct. Martin Surgeon of the 52d Ind Reg finding himself unable to join his regiment came along and Miss Mary Scovel at my invitation accompanied me home to attend school, so we made quite a formidable party and except some apprehensions in regard to the Guerrillas who might take a fancy to our boat we had a very pleasant trip and in getting Capt through comfortably and safely was intirely successful—he is getting along now very well   Occasionally he suffers considerable pain but most of the time he is comfortable.

Yours to your Pa of the 8th & tenth inst came to hand saturday night & found your Pa much out of health on my return and although not confined to his room is still any thing but well. We are all rather on the complaining order owing to very bad colds

Your return is getting narrowed down to weeks now   Tell me when your *papers* say your time is out and if there is likely to be any delay in your being mustered out and in short the prospect generally of your time of return

The folks are about to start to town and I will now close this to send by them   Write soon and tell me all I have asked about your getting home

Affectionately Your Mother
E A Butler

{ JANUARY 22, 1865 }

OVID BUTLER TO SON SCOT BUTLER

Forest Home near Indianapolis
Sunday Jany 22d 1865

My Son Scot

Your letter of the 4th to the 10th inst came promptly to hand   It is a gratification to us to have so full an account of your route from Nashville to Chattenooga—and of the hardships endured and dangers encountered upon that route. We had previously by your letters to your Ma of the 29 Nov and 1st Jany been advised of your having got through safely about which we had felt much apprehension   But your last letter enables us to go over the route with you and in some degree to sympathise with you in the difficulties and dangers of the March. But there is in the future an abundant compensation for all the trials and hardships we may manfully endure and all the dangers through which we may safely pass. The remembrance of them will be vivid and pleasurable when the impressions made by the monotonous incidents of ordinary life shall have wholly faded from the Memory. The mind and heart grows very rapidly under circumstances of difficulty and danger and I have often thought that one hour "under fire" was more effectual for the development and maturity of the Mental and Moral nature than years of ordinary life. Evidently we should not wantonly seek dangers. It would be criminal foolhardiness to do so. But if it comes to us in the discharge of duty it should be welcome and we should be thankful for the lessons it teaches us

I might pursue these reflections much farther but I have other matters to write about   Your Ma has written you since she returned from Nashville and if you got that letter you already know that she brought Capt Anderson home with her   The Capt was badly wounded but his wound is doing well and he begins to hobble about his room on Crutches   It will probably be some time before he can walk without them   He and Nettie talk of going to Kokomo to his Fathers this week

Your Ma has been in poor health since her return from Nashville and is now sick in bed   We feared she was having an attack of fever but she seems better now and the Doct thinks she will be well in a day or two. I have been having poor health for a week or two but it is nothing I think more than is usual for me at this season of the year

So much has been heretofore said about the prospect of the speedy winding up of the rebellion that I almost fear to say what I think now upon that subject   But the recent brilliant successes of the Union Arms and the manifest weakness of the rebel forces at the points at which if they would be successful they should be strongest would seem to justify the hope—even the apearance that the days of the rebellion are numbered and that its time is short   But there is a Power higher and more potential than the power of the Social Good or of the President or of both combined   Who holds in His own Hand the issues of this conflict and He will dispose of them for the accomplishment of His own purpose. The whole history of the war so far shows that God is in it—controlling its events and that His purpose is not or at least has not hitherto been the purpose of *either* the North or of the South. But it is written in letters of blood upon the unrolling canvas of the conflict and whenever the Nation shall be willing to accept peace upon His terms—it will come and will be abiding   As I read His purpose those terms are the utter abolition of Slavery—the putting away that sin—the blotting out that stain   Then—in the language of inspiration shall "our peace be as a river" and a future will open before us—more briliant and more glorious than any Nation has yet enjoyed.

We are all waiting for the expiration of your term of service, hoping to see you return in health and safety but we would not shorten the period by a day or an hour which may be necessary to gain you a full and honorable discharge from the three years service. That term of service will in the future be regarded as more creditable—more honorable than any less period—You probably know something of the operation of "red tape" and can guess at what time you will probably get your discharge   Write and let us know about what time to expect you.

Your Affectionate Father
Ovid Butler

{ J A N U A R Y   2 6 ,   1 8 6 5 }

E. ANNE BUTLER TO SON SCOT BUTLER

Forest Home
Jan 26th/65

My Dear Son Scot

Yours of 21st inst. came to hand last night. Was very glad to learn that we might begin to look for you home at least a week sooner than we had hoped for   I had rather been under the impression that your mustering out would be about the 7th of February. With good luck you will a week from to night be on your way home. This the *last week* will seem almost interminable to us all at home and until you have got started for home to you none of the shortest—

Nettie and Capt. with their *Knap sack* "The general"[1] left home for Kokomo to visit his fathers at noon to day. Nettie went regretting that she would not be here on your arrival—but as Capt. could now get round pretty well on his crutches it was time for him to visit his mother who is no doubt very anxious to see him after all the perils he has been through—

I was not at all well when your Pa wrote you last sunday and am not feeling quite my self yet but expect to be fully recovered in a day or two   We are having a long continuation of severely cold weather which completely penns me up indoors and no one feels just right if they do not take a run out in the weather once in a while   Demia has been keeping me company in this respect having a very severe cold in her head—she has not sat up more than a third of her time for quite a number of days   On my return from Nashville I found your Pa quite poorly too but I am happy to inform you we are all decidedly on the "*mend*" and expect to be in full health and spirits to welcome you home on your arrival

This will wind up this long years "talk" we have been holding on paper. To me it has been a great comfort—without it how could this long separation from my boy been at all bearable. In a few days more you will be "home again" and then farewell to the thousand and one anxieties that ever follow those in the tented field but not farewell to a mothers anxieties for her son these only end with life—

I believe there is nothing of local interest worth mentioning. The Journal keeps you I suppose pretty well posted in every thing of a public nature and in the private social circle there is literally nothing astir

Fondly hoping that you will have a pleasant and safe trip home I remain

Your Affectionate Mother
E Anne Butler

N.B. If you have possibly the time call at Mr H. G. Scovel's on Summer Street. Entrance to his office is on Park Street opposite the Capital. He has two daughters here you know one at your sister Cordelia's and one with us and would no doubt be glad to send some word to them and be glad to have you call any how—

1. Thomas B. Anderson, Scot's nephew and the oldest son of Marion Thomas and Janett (Butler) Anderson.

Postscript

In the postwar decade Ovid Butler continued to expand and beautify his beloved Forest Home. He served as an elder to the Christian Church (Disciples of Christ) and as an incorporator of Crown Hill Cemetery in Indianapolis. He also retained his position as chairman, board of trustees for the university and served as the university's chancellor until his death in 1881 at the age of eighty.

Ovid's lifelong commitment to education and his visions for the future of the nation continued to overshadow all his other postwar interests. He lived long enough to see his soldier son Scot return from the war, complete his education, and become a member of the university teaching staff. Scot twice served as Butler University president and became a member of the board of trustees.

Elizabeth Anne outlived her husband by less than a year. In 1882 she was buried beside her husband in Crown Hill Cemetery, Indianapolis. Her death certificate reads that she died of old age. She was sixty-three.[1] Demia (1867) and Janett (1868) died within a year of each other, both from the postwar diseases that plagued the nation. Demia was twenty-five years old and Janett, twenty-two. Chauncey married Anna Scovel and lived with his wife and six children, dying at the age of eighty-nine in 1937.

Scot was discharged from the army on February 1, 1865. He spent the next six months regaining his health and working with his uncle Chauncey on Ovid's farm near Keithsburg, Illinois. That fall he returned home to the gothic towers of the university building located on twenty-five acres of his father's Forest Home property. Here he began his lifelong career in academia. Scot completed his undergraduate work at Butler University, receiving his bachelor's degree in 1868, his master's in 1870, and his LLD in 1896. From 1869 to 1872 he was an instructor, a tutor, and director of the primary department at Indiana University in Bloomington, Indiana, homestead of his wife Julia Wesley Dunn whom he had married in 1868.[2]

In 1873 Ovid sent Scot, Julia, and their young family to Europe, where Scot continued his education at the University of Heidelberg, Germany, and visited other schools of advanced education throughout Europe. On his return in 1875 Scot became a professor of Latin and classical literature at Butler, a post he retained until his retirement in 1907. For two separate terms he was president of the university, one from 1891 to 1904 and another from 1906 to 1907. Scot served as professor emeritus from 1907 to 1931 and was a member of the board of trustees from 1905 until his death on January 14, 1931.[3]

Meanwhile, Butler University continued to grow and expand its program, drawing students from all over the country. Enrollments doubled to more than two hundred by the 1870s. The city of Indianapolis had grown up to surround the initial campus, and there was little benefit to expanding the then current building.[4]

In 1877, over Ovid's great protest, the school's name was changed from North Western Christian University to Butler College in honor of its founder and major benefactor. The year before it had relocated to the community of Irvington, where the new campus could once more become a "University City." Here students could focus on their academic pursuits and were removed from the "delights" of Indianapolis.[5]

On the young Butlers' return from Europe they, too, moved to the new campus and settled into "The Big House," a large Victorian home located at 124 South Downey Avenue.[6] When Scot was once asked, "What will you ever do with such an enormous house?" he replied, "We'll fill it with children!"[7] He and Julia raised six children in their Irvington home: Georgia Elgin, Evelyn Mitchell, John Scot, Elizabeth Anne, Ovid, and Cordelia. An infant daughter, Janet, had died and was buried in Germany; but daughter Georgia and her husband, Perry Hall Clifford, lived on with Scot and Julia, raising grandson Scot Butler Clifford there. According to the Butler children, life at "The Big House" was ideal.

Irvington was country farmland at the time the university relocated there. Butler students carried lanterns as they tracked through the mud to and from evening classes. The "Big House" itself, located on three acres of farmland, had a small creek running through it with a large barn facing Julian Avenue. Horses, cows, and dogs roamed freely through the property. Scot and Julia's grand home provided a fascinating playground for the six young Butlers, who were apparently not distracted by "Papa's" lofty position.[8]

The young Butlers were cultural icons of the Irvington community. Julia was very active in literary clubs such as the Demia Butler Society, where scholarly papers, poetry, and literature were read and discussed by neighborhood women. Scot brought men and women of letters to "foster literary and social culture" in the community.[9] Among them was Henry Van Dyke, who came to open the Athenaeum which Scot had organized in 1910. Other speakers included Charles W. Elliott, Henry James, Woodrow Wilson, and William Butler Yeats.[10] Scot, too, gave lectures and sermons for the community usually held in the university's chapel.

Strongly influenced by his European experience, Scot Butler expanded the university's curriculum in advanced studies in the vein of his father's broad, progressive educational policy. Under Scot's direction, the university made available courses "in every branch of liberal and professional education," as Ovid had sought to do in the original charter.[11] While the College of Liberal Arts and Studies has always been the mainstay of the university, a College of Religion grew from the old department of Bible, and the College of Education developed from a merger with Teachers' College of Indianapolis in 1930.[12]

Since the beginning of the university, courses in law and business had been available only on an adjunct basis. These courses now became an integral part of the college curriculum, available under the newly instigated concept of electives. Scot continued to introduce new subjects to the school's curriculum, including sociology, public speaking, home economics, journalism, and physical education. Typically art and music were offered, as Irvington, through its identification with the university, became known as a community of arts. The university also offered extension classes to the city schools of Indianapolis. Summer sessions became available, particularly in the field of teacher training. Ministers on the faculty began preaching at nearby churches on Sundays.[13]

Scot reversed the school's financial debt, incurred during the postwar depression, while drawing a staff of renowned professors to it. Under his tenure on the board of trustees, the university associated itself with the University of Chicago participating in an "umbrella policy" that protected smaller schools from being absorbed by larger state-funded universities. Butler University benefited from this joint venture in several ways. First, the agreement brought it a greater exposure to the University of Chicago's faculty and staff. Second, the University of Chicago advised Butler University in developing its choice of course offerings. And finally, a student could receive an additional degree from the University of Chicago by attending that school for one-quarter of his undergraduate work.[14]

Scot modernized the university's concept as a liberal arts school for advanced studies, reversed its financial difficulties, and attracted well-known professors and lecturers. The university was the first to endow a chair always to be held by a female professor and the second to have a woman employed as a professor in an American university. It was among the earliest to have women serve on the board of trustees and to serve as chairman of that board.[15]

Scot rarely wrote or spoke publicly about himself; but when he did it was often about his Civil War experience and how it had influenced him. In one posthumously published article from his "Recollections" he wrote:

> What did I derive, what quality of mind, what purpose of soul, what fear of the Eternal God did I derive from my service in the army? . . . There is this thing about it all: I believe that in war a man's faith in the Power not ourselves is developed, is strengthened to meet whatever fate life brings. . . . That was many years ago. The past dies? Ah, but its spirit lives and bears one silent company evermore.[16]

Ovid's last wartime letter to Scot, dated three months after Scot's discharge from the army, is filled with Ovid's characteristic love for the betterment of mankind, his university, and his home. It reads, in part:

> In attending to these matters, you must not neglect your studies. Your education is your present first concern & to it all else must be subordinate. Push that to the utmost time which will leave your health unimpaired. Education is a power which I am anxious you should possess, if you will use it for the benefit of Man. If employed in works of crime and mischief, it were better it were not possessed.

> *Your Affect Father*
> *Ovid Butler*[17]

Under Scot's influence the school that bears his father's name continued to reflect Ovid's vision of a growing, progressive, liberal university on the edge of the new western frontier. Scot rigorously upheld his father's ideals and brought Butler University into a new age of education as a major influence among private colleges and universities throughout the state of Indiana.

Scot is buried with the rest of his family in Crown Hill Cemetery, Indianapolis.

1. Elizabeth Anne outlived five of her eight children: Georgia Anna, Demia, Janett, Thomas Lockerbie, and Thomas McOuat.

2. Scot Butler, "Recollections," holograph manuscript held by the editor. Also see Catharine Merrill Graydon, "Scot Butler," *The Butler Alumnal Quarterly* 20 (Apr. 1931): 7–12.

3. Ibid.

4. George M. Waller, "Butler University Historical Sketch," unpublished manuscript, June 1990, Butler University Archives, Indianapolis, Ind.

5. Lola Blount Conner, "The Scot Butler Homestead," unpublished manuscript held by the editor. A copy of the manuscript is in the Butler University Archives.

6. The home was demolished in 1958 to make way for the administration building of the Disciples of Christ Extension. There is a stone marker at that location to designate the site of the university's Irvington location, however.

7. Conner, "Scot Butler Homestead."

8. Ibid.

9. Ibid.

10. Ibid.

11. Waller, "Historical Sketch of Butler University."

12. Ibid.

13. Ibid.

14. Ibid.

15. Ibid.

16. Butler, "Recollections."
17. Ovid Butler to Scot Butler, May 1, 1865, Irvington Historical Society, Indianapolis.

Appendix

The oxen stood quietly, ready to remove this extended family of twenty westward from their upstate New York home to the nation's new northwest. As with many pioneer families, this was not the Butlers' first move in search of new opportunities to improve their lot. Visions of increasingly available land and the Butlers' own determination to take part in shaping the new territory took this family from Massachusetts to Vermont to New York and, finally, to Indiana.

Among this large family was a boy of sixteen whose future accomplishments would affect many walks of life in the city of Indianapolis. Ovid Butler became the founder of a major university, a prominent lawyer, a newspaper publisher and editor, an outspoken foe of slavery, and a pillar of the Christian Church (Disciples of Christ). Under his father's influence Ovid dedicated himself to the vision that God had chosen him to work for the good of humanity. But the history of his family in America began in 1659 New England.[1]

Ovid's particular line of descent is from James Butler I (died 1681) to James Butler II (ca. 1674–1735) to Amos (called Asaph) Butler (1729–1806) to Joel Butler (1752–1822) to Chauncey (variant spellings Chancey, Chancy, 1775–1840), Ovid's father.

The exact date of James I's arrival in this country is not known, but it is likely that he made the voyage here in the first half of the seventeenth century, perhaps under the auspices of the Massachusetts Bay Company.

Little more is known of James except that his name appears in the Lancaster, Massachusetts, land records of 1659 and the tax lists of Woburn, Massachusetts, for 1676 and 1678. At some point James Butler married a certain Mary. Following the Indian raid and massacre of Lancaster, James removed his family to Billerica, Massachusetts, where he died and was buried. The notice of his death reads: "James Butler Sen., Irishman, dyed 20,01,80."

James II was born in Lancaster, Massachusetts, about 1674 and died there in 1735, having served in the courts and holding local political offices. James II was married twice. His first wife, a certain Lydia, bore him ten children before dying about 1723. His second wife, Hannah Wilson, was twenty-five years James's junior. They married the same year that Lydia died. Hannah bore James four more children, the youngest of whom was Asaph (variant Aseph, also called Amos).

Asaph was also born in Lancaster in 1729, spending most of his life in Massachusetts. He first married Jane McAllister about 1750/1751 in Lancaster. She bore him eight children, including four sons: Joel, Amos, Ezra, and James, all probably born in Massachusetts. The Butler family then moved to Vermont, where Asaph settled in Windsor in 1771. On Jane's death Asaph married Lydia Allen, who gave him two more daughters.[2] His headstone is located in Waterbury, Vermont, and is dated 1806.

The Rev. Joel Butler, first child of Asaph and Jane, was born in Bolton, Massachusetts, in March 1752. He died September 13, 1822, in Geneva, Indiana, and was buried in the Old Geneva Cemetery. In 1771 Joel married his only wife, Mabel Thompson. In their forty-nine years of marriage Mabel bore her husband just three children: Ora (also called Asa, b. 1772), Eunice (b. 1773), and Chauncey (b. 1775). Joel preached the Baptist word throughout New England and New York, before traveling westward with his son, Chauncey, and family in 1817.

Joel was an active patriot in the American Revolution, holding first a private's rank in the Vermont militia and later a colonel's commission in the colonial army. While serving in the regular army, smallpox began to decimate his ranks, and he ordered that the men under his command be inoculated against the disease. Although his action saved many lives, the inoculations were against the law, and Joel's commission was revoked. He retired to private life at his home on Grand Island on Lake Champlain, New York, before his westward travels.[3]

Joel and Mabel's youngest child, Chauncey, married for the first time Deodemia (Demia) Bullen in 1798. This marriage brought forth eleven children. Chauncey and Demia lived for a time in Augusta, Oneida County, New York. After the birth of their third child and first son, Ovid, they moved to Smith's Mill on Sandy Creek in Jefferson County, New York.

"While I was quite young my father removed to a village at Smith's Mill on Sandy Creek near Adams, Jefferson County," Ovid wrote in his autobiographical notes.[4] Here the family engaged in making potash for fertilizer. The potash was made by running wood ash through running water before being further refined. According to Ovid, the task was hard and dirty with little reward.

Within three years the Butlers moved to Smithfield, Madison County, New York, near the falls of Canasaraga Creek, where Ovid and his Baptist father labored in sawmills, on farms, and in the making of fertilizer. Ovid remembered this, too, as unpleasant work.

In 1807 or 1808 the Butlers settled in the village of Canasaraga, near Sullivan, where Ovid spent his youth helping Chauncey operate the family's gristmill and prepare gypsum, also used in the making of fertilizer. "Work in the gypsum quarries constituted a material part and, as I recollect, the most disagreeable part of the manual labor of my youth," Ovid continued.[5]

Pioneers were families on the move, constantly seeking out new and better ways of life. From Canasaraga, Chauncey moved his family just one and a half miles onto Chittenango Creek, purchasing a farm and building a sawmill. Ovid became a "pretty good ox driver" as he hauled logs to his father's mill during New York's logging season. He spent his youth in New York farming, sawing, and attending to the lumberyard.

Ovid gives little insight into his early education, but he did leave behind a record of his early interest in law and politics. His father was appointed postmaster and justice of the peace in Canasaraga, the thoroughfare between Albany and Buffalo. The mails and newspapers of the day passed through Canasaraga, carrying with them the political and social excitement growing out of the War of 1812. Ovid wrote:

> The eagerness with which information was sought and the rapidity with which it was diffused by the circulation of newspapers fostered . . . in me a taste for desultory reading and, indeed, there can be little doubt that in witnessing the petty trials, the legal conflicts before my father, as justice of the peace, a direction was given to my own thoughts, feelings and purposes which afterwards controlled me in the choice of a profession.[6]

In 1812, when Ovid was eleven, his mother died and was buried in Canasaraga. A year later Chauncey married Polly Norcross, the widow of his brother, Ora. The two families' Bible records now became that of a single family. The Bible shows how the union of these two families, plus children of their own, amounted to a family with twenty-two children. Ovid inherited eleven half brothers and sisters. Some of these were also his cousins! The last entry in the old Bible was made in 1819 with the death of Polly's last child, Ira.[7]

Indiana's 1816 statehood brought about an unforeseeable change in the Butler family's future. The opening of the Indiana Territory meant land, and land meant upward mobility. The twenty-plus members of the pioneering Butler families—the Reverend Joel Butler, his wife Mabel and family, and the Reverend Chauncey Butler, his wife Polly and extended family, left "York State" in 1817 for

Pittsburgh, Pennsylvania. Not content with what Pennsylvania had to offer, the families continued to search for a homestead by oxcart and flatboat, reaching Indiana by way of the Ohio and Allegheny Rivers. After an arduous and danger-ous journey, the Butlers landed at Madison and settled in Jennings County.[8]

It was fall when Joel, Chauncey, and their families arrived in Madison. There the families sold the boat and remained throughout the winter while the men blazed a trail to an Indian trading station named Geneva. The village grew quickly during the years after the Butlers arrived. It soon became a thriving town with two hotels, several businesses, and many homes. Joel and Chauncey built a two-room log house with a passageway in-between. The first wedding of Jennings County took place in this cabin. It is supposed that either Joel or his son Chauncey, both Baptist preachers, officiated. Chauncey, like his father, had been ordained a minister in the nearby Baptist church. In 1820 the state legis-lature proposed the layout for the new state road running from Madison to Indianapolis. When Geneva lost the bid as one of its way stations, the town dwindled and finally died out. Its rivals, Vernon and Scipio, absorbed what was left of a once thriving town. Five years after their arrival in Geneva, Joel died. He, his wife Mabel, and several other family members are buried in the town cemetery, now extinct. In 1825 Ovid moved on.[9]

Ovid turned to teaching as a livelihood; but his self-taught education and lack of training did not serve him well. He tried several positions in the primitive backwoods schools of Jackson County, Indiana, and Shelbyville, Kentucky; but he was removed from his position in Shelbyville when the par-ents complained about his strict discipline and irksome ways. The future founder of a prominent university never entered the classroom again as a teacher. He returned to his father's home in Vernon, where he ran a local store and attended Vernon Seminary for his advanced education.

Ovid developed an interest in the law and studied under Judge Avery Bullock. Although he was a diligent student, Ovid failed in his first attempt at practice in Greensburg, Indiana. In September 1825 Ovid wrote that there was lit-tle likelihood of success in his chosen profession. "I was a stranger without a friend or influence in the county and absolutely without means."[10] His peers considered him to be a great counselor but not a talented or eloquent orator. Even his daugh-ter, Maria, described him as an immensely private man. Butler University gradu-ate W. W. Woollen wrote, "Mr. Butler in stature and build was rather under size; his movements were not hasty; his speech was chaste and well chosen."[11]

From 1825 to 1836, however, Ovid extended his practice on the circuit court and was admitted to the United States Court and the Indiana Supreme Court. He moved his practice to Shelbyville, Indiana, and built a profitable practice, based on "sound judgment, vigorous power of reasoning and careful preparation of cases," and became a leading attorney in the state of Indiana.[12]

By 1836 Ovid's reputation had spread to the capital city of Indianapolis. Calvin Fletcher, the first lawyer to be admitted to the bar in the state, invited Ovid to join him in practice there. In partnership with Fletcher, Ovid developed a very lucrative business administering office affairs and advising associates and clients. In the beginning his cases were restricted to local disputes. With time, however, Ovid's case work expanded as did his bank account. During this era he was twice a candidate for the state legislature but was defeated. After his unimpressive start in politics, Ovid confined himself to holding only local offices.

Even before the Butler family settled in Jennings County, the pioneering family of Judge Abel Cole of Shelby County was rising to prominence. When Ovid turned to the study of law, he also turned to the study of Cordelia Dyer Cole, the judge's daughter. They were married in the spring of 1827 in Jefferson County, Indiana. Before Cordelia's death in 1838, she bore Ovid six children, three of whom died in infancy. The three surviving children were Cordelia (Delia), Maria, and Ovid Dyer.

Two years after Cordelia's death Ovid married a young widow named Elizabeth Anne (McOuat) Elgin, daughter of Thomas and Janette Smith (Lockerbie) McOuat and granddaughter of George Murray and Anne (Blacklock) Lockerbie. The union of these families brought forth a fruitful marriage destined to meld the political and social ideals of three distinct families, two Democrats and a staunch, radical Republican.

THE GEORGE MURRAY LOCKERBIE FAMILY

George Lockerbie (also Lockerby) was born in Annan, Dumfriesshire, Scotland, on April 15, 1771. Nearby is the little town of Lockerbie, today known for the tragic Pan Am 747 crash of 1988. In the eighteenth century, however, the town was named after a certain Lockerbie, famous for his custom of "locking by" his wife and valuables when he went away.[13]

As tradition has it, the people of Annan were known as an "argumentative, clear headed, contentious lot given to intellectual pursuits more than other people."[14] The Lockerbies were known for the courage of their convictions. George became a writer, and some of his articles against conditions in Scotland led to his arrest and imprisonment. He defended himself and was acquitted. Lockerbie, his wife Anne (Blacklock), and three of their eventual thirteen children came to America in search of greater political freedom. In October 1809 the family arrived at Philadelphia on the ship *New York*, settling in Germantown, Pennsylvania, where they lived until 1812. Lockerbie then moved his family to Lexington, Kentucky.[15]

While in Lexington, Lockerbie, an already wealthy Scotsman, set up a cotton gin and bought the required number of slaves to run it.[16] Although Lockerbie was a Democrat by political association, morally he never accepted slavery. By 1831 he had sold his gin and moved to Indianapolis.

Here he lived on his daughter Janette McOuat's farm until his death in 1856. When Janette parceled off the land into city lots and sold them as Lockerbie's Addition, she named Lockerbie Street in honor of her father.[17] Lockerbie was also the street on which well-known author and poet James Whitcomb Riley (1849–1916) and Butler relative Booth Tarkington (1869–1946) lived.

In 1886 Tarkington's sister, Mary Booth (called Haute), married Ovid Butler's grandson, Ovid Butler Jameson. Tarkington's novels *The Magnificent Ambersons* and *Penrod* were based on Indianapolis society. The *Penrod* characters, Penrod and Sam, were modeled after Tarkington's nephews (Ovid Butler's great-grandsons), Booth and Donald Ovid Jameson.[18] The Lockerbie Street neighborhood had such a profound effect on its artistic residents that in his later years Riley wrote:

> Such a dear little street it is, nestled away
> From the noise of the city and the heat of the day,
> Oh, my Lockerbie Street! You are fair to be seen—
> Be it noon of the day, or the rare and serene
> Afternoon or the night—you are one to my heart,
> And I love you above all the phrases of art.[19]

THE THOMAS McOUAT FAMILY

Thomas McOuat, of Stirlingshire, Scotland, immigrated to America sometime between his birth in 1794 and 1809, when he settled in Kentucky. Although the exact date of his arrival is unknown, thorough research indicates that Thomas was the first McOuat to arrive in this country. Here he met and married George Lockerbie's daughter Janette.

Thomas became interested in land speculation in the new state of Indiana. Indianapolis was named the capital in 1820, chosen for its central location and for the fact that it lay on the White River, erroneously believed to be navigable, even though only a handful of pioneer families and some Delaware Indians inhabited the village. On October 10, 1820, McOuat attended the first land auction for the city and purchased several lots. He traveled by the only keelboat to successfully run up the White River.

Ten years later, in the spring of 1830, McOuat bought a stock of goods at Louisville and shipped them to Indianapolis, this time traveling on *The*

General Hanna, a double-decker, lower-cabin steamer. He booked first-class passage for a trip fraught with disease, danger, and loneliness. The White River, even with the spring rise of water, proved to be nonnavigable by the deep-hulled boat, and McOuat did not arrive at his destination until June. His family, whom he had packed on horseback for the trip overland, must surely have worried about his safety, having received no word from him since his departure four weeks earlier. The McOuats settled on a farm on what is now the corner of East and Tenth Streets. Today that property is a mere mile from the heart of the tenth largest city in the country.[20]

Between 1818 and 1838 nine children were born to Thomas and Janette. All but two survived. The McOuats were a tightly knit family, and Elizabeth Anne, the oldest, remained close to her seven siblings, George, William, Robert, Andrew, Mary, Martha, and Jean, during the years covered in this collection.

The oldest son, George (1821–1872), always said he never had time for a wife, and so, never married. Instead, he became a very successful businessman, a deputy U.S. marshal, and a leader of the Democratic party. George's most time-consuming profession, however, was caring for the large, extended McOuat family after his father's death in 1838.

The second and third sons to survive were Robert (1827–1883) and Andrew (1830–1895). In the six years between George and Robert, two sons (Thomas and William) were born. Thomas died at age fifteen, and William died in infancy. Robert and Andrew, however, grew to become leaders of the Indianapolis community. Both were tutored privately and attended the Marion County Seminary ("The Old Boys' School)," known for its class and style. At age seventeen, Robert entered an apprenticeship as a tinner and then went into business with Andrew. George funded his brothers' business, which was built on property originally purchased by their father. Together the brothers were quite successful.

In 1850, during the gold rush in California, Robert left the business in Andrew's charge and traveled overland to the gold mines, walking the final distance from Salt Lake City and carrying his provisions and baggage on his back.[21] Like many others, Robert was unsuccessful in the goldfields. He proceeded to San Francisco and took a job as a tinner with a large firm, but he found the climate "uncongenial" and returned to Indianapolis. The 1874 Indianapolis city directory lists McOuat, Foote & Co., dealers in stoves and house furnishing goods, at 61–63 West Washington Street. The company's building still stands today. It is a large, gray granite building with the name "McOuat" engraved along the top.[22]

In 1880 Robert sold his interest in the business to Andrew, who operated it until his retirement in 1887. Andrew married Ellen McCrosson in 1853, and they had a long marriage blessed with ten children. Andrew's last son, Mack Butler McOuat, was born in September 1872. Ellen died at his birth. After his retirement, Andrew left Indianapolis to spend the rest of his years in Wayne Township at "Ellerbie Farm," the 245-acre home he purchased in 1883. He died of heart failure in 1895 at the age of sixty-five.

Meanwhile, Robert became interested in the manufacture of car wheels and formed a partnership with John May under the firm name of McOuat & May. For two years the new firm was quite successful, but in 1882, having sold large contracts to a manufacturing company that reneged on its obligations, McOuat & May was forced into bankruptcy.[23] Following the bankruptcy, Robert returned to his brother's firm. He married Ellen C. Wallace in 1851 and, although childless, Robert and Ellen "adopted" their nieces and nephews, the children of Ovid and Elizabeth Anne. Aunt Ellen and Uncle Robert were obvious favorites of the Butler children, who wrote of their sorrow for their uncle on Ellen's death in 1863.

Elizabeth Anne's sisters were Mary, Martha, and Jean. Mary was born in 1833 and lived to be nearly one hundred years old. She married Obed Foote, Jr., whom she outlived by forty years. Foote's staunchly Southern politics, as well as the McOuats' support of the Democratic party, caused great "offishness" between Elizabeth Anne and her McOuat relatives, including her mother. Martha McOuat, born in 1835, married "the good doctor" Samuel Edgar at Christ Church, Indianapolis, in 1856. Nothing is known about their marriage except that they had three children before Samuel died in 1860, and that Samuel was "a good man." Four years later Martha married Dr. Nathaniel Todd, a widower with four children. Todd's youngest child was raised by his first wife's sister on his wife's request, a common practice of the time. The remaining three children, along with Martha's three, formed a family with six youngsters. Martha and Robert had five additional children, and Martha (McOuat) Todd raised eleven children. Jean, born in 1838, married David Reynolds in 1863. She died in New York the following year giving birth to their only child, Jennie, who married George L. Hilt and moved to Minnesota.

ELIZABETH ANNE McOUAT

Elizabeth Anne, the oldest daughter of Thomas and Janette Smith (Lockerbie) McOuat, was born November 18, 1818, in Lexington, Kentucky. Her marriage certificate to George Elgin shows that Elizabeth Anne was not yet eighteen when they married, and that her Grandfather Lockerbie was present and "gave surety," or oral permission, for his granddaughter's marriage. In September 1836 they were married in the First Presbyterian Church in Indianapolis. The couple settled in Lincoln County, Kentucky, and later moved to Scott County.

From Elizabeth Anne's early correspondence with her father, Thomas, and her Grandfather Lockerbie,[24] it appears that George (only known as Mr. Elgin or "your gudemon") was a horse trader by occupation, buying his herds in Kentucky and driving them to Missouri or Georgia for sale. Elgin's many trips kept him far from home for months at a time. Eighteen-year-old Elizabeth was lonely and disapproved of her husband's long absences, writing,

> This is the first and last time yes, the *very last* that I will ever give my consent to your going to the South Nay more, I will exert all my power of *persuasion, supplication, and entreaty*, to prevail on your remaining with me. For indeed I would rather live upon half allowance, possessing your dear society, than possess all the wealth and riches of the South with out it. . . . Pa wished to know how it would do to buy a drove in Ind. I could write him nothing about it but I am in hopes he will not get horse driving in his head.[25]

Not only was she young and far from home, but she was also thrust into a deeply Southern society of which she had little kin. Elgin bought a small inn to supplement their income, and Elizabeth Anne was its keeper. Her grandfather's letter of manners reveals his expectation of this vulnerable young woman.

GEORGE LOCKERBIE TO ELIZABETH ANNE (McOUAT) ELGIN

Indianapolis, September 20, 1836

My Dear Child,

> . . . I shall not insult your understanding by a long moral series of good advices, but allow me to exercise the privilege of a grandfather to point out some of the duties which belongs to the new station which you have assumed in society and also some remarks on the nature and present moral organization of that society. . . .

> You are no longer to be considered a girl where frivolities may be overlooked as the efforts or sportiness of giddy youth, but you are now commencing to act the part of the head of a family, and it will require all your judgment and all your prudence

to fill that high and honorable station with that matronly dignity which will command the respect of your husband and
friends generally. . . . [I]n your domestic relations try to avoid
every thing like [. . .] and exercise all your philosophy to get
the complete command of your temper. . . . [Your husband]
in his intercourse with the world may oftentimes meet with
rascals who may do him much wrong and in a vast variety of
ways may bring much trouble to the generous and confiding
heart.—But what can produce such constitution as the sincere
and affectionate condolence of a faithful wife.

Your loving grandfather,
George Lockerbie [26]

Thomas McOuat, age forty-three, died of congestive chills on August
24, 1838. He was buried next to his fifteen-year-old son, Thomas Harvey
McOuat, who died five days earlier of the same cause.[27]

On September 6, 1838, the following obituaries appeared in the
Kentucky Gazette, one below the other without a single line to separate them:

On the 25th ult., in Indianapolis, Indiana, MR. THOMAS McOUAT,
formerly of this city.

In Georgetown, Ky., on the 30th ult., MR. GEO. M. ELGIN, of
Congestive fever, aged about 37 years.[28]

Mr. George M. Elgin of Georgetown, Kentucky, was, of course,
Elizabeth Anne's husband. Within ten days she had lost her brother, her father,
and her husband. One year earlier she had delivered a stillborn baby. Six weeks
after her husband's death, on October 16, 1838, Elizabeth Anne gave birth to
George's first and only child, whom she named Georgia Anna Elgin. Georgia
Anna did not live to see her twenty-first birthday, dying of congestive fever on
March 18, 1861.

After the deaths of her father, her brother, and her husband, Elizabeth
Anne and Georgia Anna left Kentucky to be with her McOuat and Lockerbie
families in Indianapolis, where she met and married Ovid Butler. Their marriage
in 1840 satisfied the needs of both Ovid and Elizabeth Anne. The 1838 death
of Cordelia, Ovid's first wife, left Ovid a widower with three children ranging in
age from three to twelve. Ovid was a wealthy man with a statewide reputation
for his commanding knowledge and capable abilities. Elizabeth Anne was the
daughter of a successful tradesman in the stove and tinware industry with an
infant daughter to support. While the marriage benefited both parties practi-
cally, their letters also reveal the deep love and affection they felt for each other.

In four years the "giddy" teenager had become the wife and widow of a horse trader, an innkeeper, the mother of a stillborn baby and an infant daughter, a bereaved daughter and sister, the wife of a prominent lawyer, the mother of four children, and a growing influence on Indianapolis society. Elizabeth Anne died in 1882, outliving Ovid and seven of her nine children. Her letters prove her to be a warm, loving woman who continued to bear illness, death, and disaster with dignity.

Between 1842 and 1857 Elizabeth Anne bore Ovid seven children: Demia (1842–1867), Scot (1844–1931), Janett "Nettie" (1846–1868), Chauncey (1848–1937), Thomas Lockerbie (died in infancy), Thomas "Mack" (1854–1872), and Anne Elizabeth "Annie" (1857–1937).

1. Butler is an Anglo-Irish surname deriving from Middle English *buteler* and, in turn, from Old French *boutellier*. In both cases the word was applied to the position of: 1) a keeper of wines and liquors; 2) a cup or bottle bearer; or 3) a butler in the traditional sense of a household manservant. The first recognized bearer of the surname Butler in English history was Theobald Fitz Walter, the first butler of Ireland. In the twelfth century King John bestowed on Fitz Walter the title of Lord of Ireland and the office of his "butler." In his later years Fitz Walter was sometimes spoken of as *Le Botiller* or *Butler*, which then was adopted as the surname of his descendants. "History of the Butler Family," unpublished manuscript by Scot Butler 2nd of Winchester, Va. (undated).

2. Joel Butler Papers, SC 0161, Indiana Historical Society. There is conflicting information on the early years of the Butler family. Ovid lists Asaph as Amos Butler in his genealogical notes; records from *A History of Bolton, Massachusetts* list him as Asaph as does the genealogy of Sally (Butler) Thayer, Ovid's sister. Another source says Asaph was born in Templeton, Massachusetts, rather than Lancaster.

3. DAR Patriot Index–Centennial Edition (Part 1), p. 456; "Frances E. Emerson, State Historian, Indiana D.A.R.," *Indiana Magazine of History* 10 (Mar. 1914): 114; Lewis Cass Aldrich, ed., *History of Windsor County, Vermont, with Illustrations and Biographical Sketches of Some of Its Prominent Men and Pioneers* (Syracuse, N.Y.: D. Mason & Co., 1891), 293–95. For more information on Joel Butler see Jacob Piatt Dunn, *Greater Indianapolis: The History, the Industries, the Institutions, and the People of a City of Homes*, 2 vols. (Chicago: Lewis Publishing Co.), 2:1165; John Ellsworth Goodrich, comp., *The State of Vermont: Rolls of the Soldiers in the Revolutionary War* (Rutland, Vt.: Tuttle Co., 1904), 28, and DAR Registration No. 142333 for Anne Butler Thomas. Also see Ovid Butler Papers, held by the editor, and Scot Butler 2nd, "Ovid Butler—Hoosier Pioneer," published in part by The Butler Society of North America, *News Bulletin* (November 1990): 15.

4. Ovid Butler holograph autobiography held by the editor.

5. Ibid.

6. Ibid.

7. The Bible no longer exists, but a microfilm copy is available through the LDS Family History Center Library, Salt Lake City, Utah. A copy is held by the editor.

8. Butler autobiography.

9. *This Is Jennings County* (Vernon, Ind.: Jennings County Historical Society, n.d.).

10. Butler autobiography.

11. *Butler Alumnal Quarterly* 6, no. 4 (Jan. 1918): 277.

12. Ibid.

13. *Lockerbie's Assessment List of 1835*, Eliza G. Browning, ed., Indiana Historical Society Publications, vol. 4, no. 7 (Indianapolis: E. J. Hecker, 1909), 399–433.

14. Ibid.

15. John H. B. Nowland, *Early Reminiscences of Indianapolis: With Short Biographical Sketches of Its Early Citizens and a Few Prominent Business Men of the Present Day* (Indianapolis: Sentinel Book and Job Printing House, 1870), 231–33.

16. United States Federal Population Census for the State of Kentucky, Fayette County; George Lockabye, U.S. Archives, Washington, D.C.

17. Many artists and writers currently reside in the Lockerbie Square area. The neighborhood is part of an ongoing renovation and development program that began in the 1970s.

18. Haute Tarkington was named for Terre Haute, Indiana, where she was born and raised. She was known in the family as "Hautie." Haute frequently attended Butler University functions. The editor's father Ovid M. Butler recalls stories of Hautie, known for her flamboyant clothes and her "ebullient manner." She often wore flower and plume-decked hats and yellow or ivory satin gowns and carried enormous fans. For more on Haute (Tarkington) Jameson, see "The Indiana Woman," reprint by the Irvington Historical Society, 1995, originally published as "Irvington Edition of the Indiana Woman," August 7, 1897, vol. 4, no. 12. The original is located in the Indiana State Library.

19. *Pictorial and Biographical Memoirs of Indianapolis and Marion County, Indiana, with Biographies of Many Prominent Men of Other Portions of the State, Both Living and Dead* (Chicago: Goodspeed Brothers, Publishers, 1893), 141.

20. The White River runs from the Wabash River to Indianapolis. See Nowland, *Early Reminiscences of Indianapolis*, 229–30, for a detailed description of this journey, and *Looking at Lockerbie* (Indianapolis: Old Northside Historical District), 41–43.

21. B. R. Sulgrove, *History of Indianapolis and Marion County, Indiana* (Philadelphia: L. H. Everts and Co., 1884).

22. This was the office building of the McOuat Stove and Tinware Manufacturers.

23. Sulgrove, *History of Indianapolis and Marion County,* 160; W. R. Holloway, *Indianapolis: A Historical and Statistical Sketch of the Railroad City* (Indianapolis: Journal Print., 1870), 356.

24. Correspondence between Elizabeth Anne McOuat and George Lockerbie, Lockerbie file, located in the Indiana State Library, Indianapolis.

25. Elizabeth Anne (McOuat) Elgin to George Elgin, October 23, 1837, Thomas McOuat Collection, SC 2241, Indiana Historical Society, Indianapolis.

26. George Lockerbie to Elizabeth Anne (McOuat) Elgin, Lockerbie file, located in the Indiana State Library.

27. In 1869 both Thomas and his son were reburied in Crown Hill Cemetery in the McOuat lot for which Janette McOuat paid $10,000. Coincidentally, the cemetery was incorporated in 1863 by a committee that included McOuat's in-law Ovid Butler. The Butler and McOuat lots face each other at Crown Hill.

28. *Kentucky Gazette*, September 6, 1838.

Name-Place Glossary

Janett/Net/Nettie (Butler) Anderson (1846–1868), Scot Butler's sister. An intermittent student, she was a member of the freshman class of 1863. She married Marion Thomas Anderson, "her captain," at Forest Home on January 14, 1864, while Anderson was home recuperating from battle wounds and illnesses suffered during his escape from Libby Prison. She and her husband had two sons, Thomas Butler and Joseph E., before her death in 1868 from typhoid.

Marion Thomas Anderson (1839–1904), Scot Butler's brother-in-law and husband of Scot's younger sister, Janett Butler. He was born November 13, 1839, in Clarksburg, Indiana. Anderson enlisted as a sergeant, Company C, Fifty-first Regiment, Indiana Volunteer Infantry, in 1861 and resigned as a captain on June 15, 1865. In February 1863 he was captured along with Col. Abel Streight's regiment in Ohio and was held prisoner in Libby Prison, Richmond, Virginia, known second only to Andersonville in its notoriety. He served seven months there in retaliation for the executions of rebel spies made by Gen. Ambrose E. Burnside in Kentucky, an incident connected with the murder of Gen. John Hunt Morgan. Anderson was one of the seventy-five officers who drew lots for those who would be hanged the following morning, and on December 11, 1863, he and 108 other prisoners of war made their successful escape from that prison. He was severely wounded on December 31, 1863, during his escape. Anderson married Janett Butler on January 14, 1864, at Forest Home, Indianapolis, Indiana, while recovering from his wounds there. He returned to his unit and was awarded the Congressional Medal of Honor for heroism on December 16, 1864, at Nashville, Tennessee, where he led his regiment over five lines of the Southern works, fell, and was severely wounded by a bullet penetrating his spine and exiting through his side. He recovered but resigned that summer. After Janett's death in 1868 Marion remarried and moved to Washington, D.C., where he served as a clerk for the War Department. Citation, Medal of Honor, United States Archives, Washington, D.C.; Military Records of Individual Civil War Soldiers, United States

Archives, Washington, D.C.; Marion T. Anderson file, American War Soldiers, United States Archives, Washington, D.C.

Thomas B. Anderson (also known as General, Knapsack, and Tommie) (1864–1885), Scot Butler's nephew and the son of Marion Thomas and Janett (Butler) Anderson.

Berg Applegate, personal friend of the Butler family, who married Mary J. Beaty on October 25, 1864. He served as a private in Company E, 107th Regiment, Indiana Volunteer Infantry in 1863 and was recognized for distinguished service. After the war he returned to school and graduated in the Butler University class of 1879. *Catalog of Students Not Alumni, Butler College, 1855–1900* (Indianapolis, Ind.: Butler University, n.d.) (hereafter cited as *Catalog*); 1870 United States Federal Population Census Index, Indianapolis, Marion County; Military Records of Individual Civil War Soldiers, United States Archives, Washington, D.C.; Berg Applegate file, American Civil War Soldiers, United States Archives, Washington, D.C.

Alonzo/Lon M. Atkinson of Wabash, Indiana, an intermittent student of the university and Scot Butler's classmate. He enlisted from Rush County, Indiana, on August 12, 1862, in Company G, Sixteenth Regiment, Indiana Volunteer Infantry and was wounded on August 30, 1862, at Richmond, Kentucky. He was discharged because of wounds suffered on December 22, 1862. After the war he served as a member of the Butler University Board of Trustees (1870–99) and as board president (1890–95). Alonzo M. Atkinson file, American War Soldiers, United States Archives, Washington, D.C.; Gisela S. Terrell, comp., "Alphabetical Listing of Butler University's Board Members, Board of Directors (July 27, 1852 to February 23, 1961) and Board of Trustees (since March 2, 1961)," Butler University Archives, Indianapolis (hereafter cited as "Trustees").

Mary, Davey, and John Beaty, close personal friends of the Butler family. Daughter Mary was Demia's best friend, while sons Davey and John served in Indiana regiments during the war. Although she never graduated, Mary was a member of the university class of 1860. She married Berg Applegate on October 25, 1864, as detailed in the letter above dated October 30, 1864. Willard Heiss, ed., *Indiana Source Book* 3 (Indianapolis: Indiana Historical Society, 1982), 210.

Mrs. Bence, mother of Anna A. (Mrs. Walter C. Hobbs) and Mary E. (Mrs. Allen Fletcher). *Catalog*.

Allen R. Benton, Butler University president of the faculty and benefactor and president of Fairview Academy in Rush County, Indiana, before his association with Butler University. Henry K. Shaw, "The Founding of Butler University, 1847–1855," *Indiana Magazine of History* 58 (Sept. 1962).

Joseph J. Bingham, editor of the *Indianapolis Sentinel,* the Democratic competitor of the *Indianapolis Journal. Indianapolis City Directory, 1887–1890.*

William T. Boaz, Butler University class of 1859. He was an oil dealer and a resident of Indianapolis. *Catalog.*

Braxton Bragg (Bragg/General Bragg) (1817–1876), commander of the Confederate Army of Tennessee. See entry for Chickamauga, Tennessee.

U. C. Brewer of Danville, a member of the Butler University class of 1851 and a circuit minister. *Catalog.*

Bridgeport, Kentucky, located outside Frankfort, between Lexington and Louisville.

Thomas A. Brown, enlistee with Chauncey Butler, Jr., in May 1864 in the Indiana 132nd Infantry. Brown was a student of the university's English Department from Indianapolis. Members of the Brown family appear frequently in these letters and include Dr. Ryland Thomas Brown (professor of natural sciences, Butler University), his wife, Matti, and children Mary, Tom, Phil, George, and Lidi. Mary and Lidi (Leonidas E. Brown) were intermittent students of Butler University, class of 1878. Carolyn Brown, "Dr. Ryland Thomas Brown," *Indiana Magazine of History* 23 (Mar. 1927): 92–106; *Catalog.*

Nancy Burns, the first woman to graduate from Butler University (1856) and arguably the second woman to graduate with a classical education in the United States. She was also the first woman to serve as a full voting member of a university board of trustees. She married Alonzo Atkinson, who also served as a member of the Butler University Trustees (1870–99) and as board president (1891–95). Shaw, "Founding of Butler University"; "Trustees."

Ambrose Everett Burnside (1824–1881), noted for his lackluster career as commander, Army of the Republic. He was a native of Indiana who, prior to the Civil War, left the army to manufacture a carbine rifle. Federal contracts for the rifle failed to appear, forcing Burnside into bankruptcy. (Eventually the rifle was sold to thousands in the Civil War.) With the onset of the Civil War, he raised a regiment and was assigned to various commands with the Army of the Potomac and the Army of Ohio. Following his successful search for Confederate raider John Hunt Morgan, Burnside advanced to Knoxville. For his actions there he received the thanks of Congress. His performance thereafter, however, showed poor leadership ability and a lack of commitment. Following his disastrous performance at Fredericksburg, Burnside was relieved and replaced by Joseph Hooker on April 15, 1865, the day of Lincoln's death. Under protest, Burnside agreed to remain in the army in subordinate positions. Following the war he served as governor of Rhode Island and as a U.S. senator. He is noteworthy for having invented the Burnside breech-loading rifle in 1856 and for his muttonchop whiskers, still called sideburns today. In his memoirs, Ulysses S. Grant described Burnside as a man "not fitted to command an army. No one knew this better than himself." Mark M. Boatner III, *The Civil War Dictionary* (New York: Vintage Books, 1991), 107; Emma Lou Thornbrough, *Indiana in the Civil War Era, 1850–1880*, The History of Indiana, vol. 3 (Indianapolis: Indiana Historical Bureau and Indiana Historical Society, 1965), 157; Patricia L. Faust, ed., *Historical Times Illustrated Encyclopedia of the Civil War* (New York: Harper & Row, 1986), 96–97.

Annie Butler/Anne Elizabeth Butler (1857–1938), Scot Butler's full sister. Annie was the youngest daughter of Ovid and Elizabeth Anne (McOuat) Butler and later a member of the Butler University class of 1877. She was a favorite of the Butler household on whose *sun shiney* personality the family focused while Scot was away. She married Dr. David Owen Thomas in 1885 at Forest Home, and they made their home in Minneapolis, where both she and her husband dedicated their lives to the Christian Church. In 1925, while Annie was away on a church trip to Asia, David died suddenly. Her passage home to bury him took three months. See the Indiana State Library, Indianapolis, for her diary and a journal she kept during her trip to Asia.

Chauncey Butler (variant spellings Chauncy/Chancy) (1807–1875), Scot Butler's uncle and Ovid Butler's brother. Chauncey married Lorinda Janette Cole, sister of Cordelia Cole (Ovid's first wife), about 1828. Chauncey was a well-respected and beloved member of Indianapolis society. There is some reference in Ovid's biographical notes that Chauncey was an invalid, having been maimed in an accident as a young man. A laudatory account of Chauncey's life reads, "Few people won so much love as he did. Generation after generation has passed, and still the memory of his dear name is cherished and still the stories of his loving kindness are told among us, with words of affection and admiration." Maria Butler Jameson, "A Genealogy of Five Generations of the Butler Family, 1906," original typescript held by the editor.

Chauncey Butler (variant spellings Chauncy/Chancy) (1848–1937), Scot Butler's full brother.

Cordelia Butler. See entry for Cordelia/Delia (Butler) Wallace.

Demia Butler (1842–1867), Scot Butler's full sister. During wartime staff shortages and financial duress, Demia served as secretary of Butler College. She was the first woman to graduate from Butler University with a full four-year degree in the classics. In 1866 she married George Ellis Townley, but Demia died just a year after her marriage and just ten months before her sister, Janett. After Demia's death in 1867 Ovid named a Chair of English at Butler University in her honor, the first in the nation always to be held by a female professor.

E Anne/EA/Elizabeth Anne (McOuat) Butler (1818–1882), Scot Butler's mother. She was the daughter of Thomas McOuat and Janette Smith Lockerbie. Elizabeth Anne married Ovid Butler in 1840. Scot Butler was their second child and first son. See Butler Family History and McOuat Family History in the Appendix.

Janett/Net/Nettie Butler. See entry for Janett/Net/Nettie (Butler) Anderson.

Mabel Butler. See entry for Mabel (Butler) Pabody.

Maria Butler. See entry for Maria (Butler) Jameson.

Maria Butler (1863–1872), Scot Butler's cousin and daughter of Ovid Dyer and Martha (Meeks) Butler.

Martha/Mattie (Meeks) Butler (died 1927), Scot Butler's sister-in-law. Martha married Ovid Dyer Butler, son of Ovid Butler and his first wife Cordelia Cole. For more information on Martha (Meeks) Butler, see *Butler Alumnal Quarterly* 16 (Jan. 1928): 195.

Ovid Butler (1801–1881), Scot Butler's father. He was the son of Chauncey and Demia (Bullen) Butler. See Butler Family History in the Appendix.

Ovid Dyer Butler (1837–1919), Scot Butler's half brother and youngest son of Ovid Butler and his first wife Cordelia Cole. Ovid Dyer married Martha Meeks in 1860. They had one daughter, Maria Butler, born November 22, 1863. Ovid Dyer served as secretary of Butler University from 1858 to 1861, when he retired to join the 107th Regiment, Indiana Volunteer Infantry. He later served as a member of the board of trustees from 1869 to 1882. "Trustees."

Thomas (Mac/Mack/Mackie) McOuat Butler (1854–1872), Scot Butler's full brother and the youngest son of Ovid Butler and Elizabeth Anne McOuat. Mackie died from diphtheria contracted while transporting his mother to and from the homes of her various children, who also suffered from this postwar disease.

William F. Butler, Scot Butler's uncle and Ovid Butler's brother.

Butler's Grove (the Grove). Several letters were written from here, the Butler farm of nine hundred acres in Keithsburg, Mercer County, Illinois, south of Davenport on the Mississippi River.

Bob Catterson/Robert Francis Catterson (1835–1914), whose son, George, married Jean Maitland McOuat, Scot Butler's cousin. The son of an Irish immigrant, Bob was a successful Civil War veteran, rising from private to brigadier general during his service in the Fourteenth and Ninety-seventh Regiments, Indiana Volunteer Infantry. Some of his service included action in the West Virginia campaign, the Shenandoah Campaign, Antietam, Chattanooga, and Atlanta. Following the war he organized a black militia unit to fight the Ku Klux Klan in Arkansas and was elected mayor of Little Rock (1872–74). He was later unsuccessful in farming and selling farm equipment in Minneapolis and died of a stroke in San Antonio, Texas, at the local veterans' hospital in 1914. Robert Francis Catterson genealogy file, privately held by the editor.

Sarah E. (Norwood) Catterson, wife of Robert F. Catterson and mother of George Norwood Catterson. George married Jean Maitland McOuat, Scot Butler's first cousin, in 1887.

Chickamauga, Georgia. The two-day battle of Chickamauga took place in the wooded fields of Georgia, twenty miles south of Chattanooga, Tennessee, on September 19–20, 1863. Scot Butler was actively involved in the action under Capt. Jesse Merrill's detachment of the Signal Corps, U.S.A., Department of the Cumberland. Chickamauga was one of the last important victories of the South, Gen. Braxton Bragg commanding the Confederate Army of Tennessee against Gen. William Starke Rosecrans. Northern casualties numbered 16,200, while Southern casualties numbered 18,500. Bragg, who was seeking to keep his army free for action, evacuated the city and withdrew to Georgia, with Rosecrans recklessly pursuing him. Bragg had received reinforcements by rail from Virginia, and his forces numbered approximately 66,000. He fell on Rosecrans savagely at Chickamauga. Bragg's forces held their line so well that in the end Rosecrans's entire army had to retreat to Chattanooga, where the Southern victory trapped Rosecrans's army. The defeat's importance was that it kept the North from opening its supply lines into Georgia. John Bowers, *Chickamauga and Chattanooga: The Battles That Doomed the Confederacy* (New York: Avon Books, 1994).

John Coburn (1825–1908), colonel of the Thirty-third Regiment, Indiana Volunteer Infantry, was a distant cousin of Scot Butler's through Coburn's wife, Caroline (Test) Coburn. Coburn was born in Indianapolis and was educated in the Seminary on University Square and Wabash College, from which he graduated with honors in 1846. After serving as clerk for his father, an Indiana Supreme Court justice, he studied law and was admitted to the bar. He practiced law with his schoolmate and lifelong friend, William Wallace (brother of Lew Wallace), who married Cordelia Dyer Butler, daughter of Ovid Butler, in 1847 at Forest Home. Coburn was appointed, and later elected, circuit court judge prior to the Civil War. A noted public speaker and writer, he strongly supported the Union and advocated the use of force to sustain it. At the outbreak of the Civil War he was appointed colonel of the Thirty-third, in which Scot Butler also served, and saw immediate action in October 1861 in the battle at Wild Cat, Kentucky, where his regiment engaged Gen. Felix Zollicoffer, who was killed in the battle. Coburn continued to serve in Kentucky and Tennessee with his regiment, which was part of the Army of the Cumberland. In 1863 he was stationed first in Nashville and then Franklin, Tennessee, where during a major action at Thompson's Station, Tennessee, he was captured and sent to Libby Prison in Richmond, Virginia, from which he was later exchanged. He rejoined active service as a brigadier general and served in Gen. William T. Sherman's campaign on Atlanta. He was honored by being designated the officer to accept surrender of the city. He was mustered out of the Union Army in 1864. After the Civil War he was elected to Congress, serving four terms. His service in Congress included the chairmanship of the powerful Committee on Military Affairs. Among his accomplishments in this capacity was the bill to provide military headstones for all Union soldiers. Before returning to Indianapolis to practice law, he was U.S. District Court Judge in the Montana Territory. He died in Indianapolis and was buried in Crown Hill Cemetery.

Cole family of Shelby County, Indiana. In 1827 Ovid Butler married his first wife, Cordelia Cole (1809–1838) of Hanover, Indiana. Cordelia died leaving Ovid to raise three of their surviving six children (Cordelia, Maria, and Ovid Dyer). The extensive Cole family remained an integral part of the Butler family and included Albert, (Lorinda) Janette, Anne, Viola, Bart, and Scot Cole after Ovid married Elizabeth Anne (McOuat) Elgin in 1840.

Albert Cole, Scot Butler's uncle and brother of Ovid's first wife Cordelia Cole. Albert and his wife, Josephine (Joe, Josie), managed the Butler farm holdings in Keithsburg, Illinois.

Anne Cole, Albert and Cordelia Cole's sister, who married a Mr. Mathers, first name unknown.

Barton/Bart W. Cole, an 1871 graduate of Butler University. Barton served as secretary-treasurer of the school from 1869 to 1871 and again from 1915 to 1918. During the war years he was a U.S. Postal Service employee.

(Lorinda) Janette Cole, Scot Butler's aunt and the sister of Ovid Butler's first wife, Cordelia Cole. Janette married Ovid's brother, Chauncey.

Scot Cole, Scot Butler's cousin. Cole served as a private in E Company, 109th Regiment, Indiana Volunteer Infantry.

Connersville, Indiana, twenty-five miles southeast of Richmond, Indiana.

Thomas Leonidas Crittenden (1819–1893), a lawyer and U.S. consul to England. At the outbreak of the war, he was appointed brigadier general of Union volunteers and commanded the Fifth Division, Army of the Ohio at Shiloh. The following July Crittenden was promoted to major general of volunteers. He commanded the Twenty-first Corps at Stone's River, Tullahoma, and Chickamauga, where William Rosecrans criticized him for his poor performance. He resigned from the army in December 1864. Following the war he served as state treasurer of Kentucky. He was the brother of Confederate general G. B. Crittenden.

Charley Davidge, Scot Butler's classmate, who entered Butler University in the fall of 1862. Although he never graduated, Davidge remained in Indianapolis at least through 1900. *Catalog*.

Robert P. Duncan (born Indianapolis, 1847), Scot Butler's distant cousin through Col. John Coburn. Duncan enlisted on July 9, 1863, as a private in Company H, 107th Regiment, Indiana Volunteer Infantry and was recognized for his distinguished service at the end of the war. He entered Butler University in 1863 and was an intermittent student during the war. Butler University Trustees, *Directory of Alumni and Students: Butler University*, Archives, Butler University, Indianapolis (hereafter cited as *Directory*), 203. See also Shaw, "Founding of Butler University."

John E. Dunn, brother of Julia Wesley Dunn.

Julia Wesley Dunn (1845–1937) married Scot Butler on November 3, 1868, in Bloomington, Indiana. Julia's later letters from Europe reveal a bright, well educated, well traveled, if somewhat homesick, young mother. Born in Portland,

Maine, in 1845, Julia moved with her family to Indiana in 1847. Her family was very active in Indiana politics. Julia's father, George G. Dunn, was a congressman from the Sixth Indiana District from 1847 to 1849, and from the Third District from 1855 to 1857. Moses F. Dunn, Julia's uncle, was a representative in the Forty-fifth and Forty-sixth General Assemblies. Julia's grandfather, Samuel Dunn, settled near Bloomington at an early age. The present Indiana University campus is part of the Dunn family farm. The family cemetery still remains in a nook of the campus. In 1871 Julia moved with Scot and their three daughters to Germany, where Scot studied Latin at the University of Heidelberg for two years. While in Germany, one daughter, Nettie, died, and Julia bore one son, John Scot. Julia traveled extensively throughout Europe, developing an interest in economics and literature. On the Butlers' return to Indianapolis, where Scot served as professor of Latin and Butler College president, they moved into 124 Downey Street, Irvington (now Indianapolis). The house was later demolished; but in its place now stands a landmark of the Butler College Irvington campus and the Scot Butler home. A collection of Julia (Dunn) Butler's letters is held by the Irvington Historical Society, Indianapolis, and a second collection is owned by the editor. "Reviews and Notes," *Indiana Magazine of History* 9 (Dec. 1913): 309–10.

Samuel A. Edgar/Sam Edgar (1829–1860), Scot Butler's uncle by marriage and the first husband of Martha/Mattie Jeanette McOuat.

George Manning Elgin (died 1838), first husband of Elizabeth Anne McOuat. The couple settled in Kentucky, where George traded horses and traveled often and for long periods of time to Missouri where he sold his stock. He died following a long illness, just six weeks before his daughter, Georgia Anna, was born. After his death, Elizabeth Anne returned home to Indianapolis, where she married Ovid Butler in 1840.

Margaret/Mollie Elgin, Scot Butler's cousin through his mother's first marriage in 1836 to George Manning Elgin. The McOuats and the Elgins, both from Scott County, Kentucky, had strong Southern political leanings. The McOuat-Butler ties to the Elgin family remained strong throughout the era. See correspondence of Elizabeth Anne (McOuat) Elgin Butler to the Elgin family, Indiana Historical Society, Indianapolis, Indiana.

Ingram and Stephen Keyes Fletcher, sons of Calvin Fletcher, Ovid Butler's former law partner in Indianapolis. Ingram and Stephen Keyes served in Company A, 132nd Regiment, Indiana Volunteer Infantry and were transferred to the Signal Corps with Scot. Ingram Fletcher and Stephen K. Fletcher files, American War Soldiers, United States National Archives, Washington, D.C.

Fletcher's Trade Place. See footnote in above letter dated May 5, 1864.

Lt. Henry R. Flook of Hall, Indiana, served in Company A, Thirty-third Regiment, Indiana Volunteer Infantry and was transferred to the Signal Corps along with Scot Butler. Henry R. Flook pension file, American War Soldiers, United States Archives, Washington, D.C.

Mary Gray (McOuat) Foote (1833–1926), Scot Butler's aunt. She was a daughter of Janette Smith (Lockerbie) and Thomas McOuat and was Elizabeth Anne (McOuat) Butler's sister. Mary married Obed Foote in 1851.

Obe/Obed Foote/Obed Foote, Sr. (ca. 1821–1883), Scot Butler's uncle. He married Mary Gray McOuat (sister of Elizabeth Anne [McOuat] Butler) in 1851. Obed was a Democrat who had strong affiliations with many other Southern sympathizers in Indianapolis. He often vexed Elizabeth Anne with his insulting political comments, alienating her from her McOuat family.

Obie/Obed Foote/Obed B. Foote (b. ca. 1853), Scot Butler's first cousin and son of Mary Gray McOuat and Obed Foote.

Franklin, Indiana, located in southeast Indiana and the site of a Butler family homestead. Each year the Butler family held a "gathering," or family reunion, in either Franklin, Vernon, or Indianapolis. See Indiana State Library clippings file for a description of one such reunion.

George J. Frenyear (Frenyer), hospital stewart, chaplain, and a private in Company A, Fifty-first Regiment, Indiana Volunteer Infantry. He served with Marion T. Anderson, Janett Butler's husband. Frenyear was captured following Abel Streight's Raid on Rome, Georgia, at the battle of Cedar Bluff, May 3, 1863, and died during his imprisonment.

Margaret/Mollie Frybarger of Connersville, Indiana, a student in the university's preparatory school. *Catalog.*

George Washington Gist, born in 1843 in Henry County, Kentucky. In May 1864 he enlisted with Scot Butler's brother, Chauncey, as a private in the 132nd Regiment, Indiana Volunteer Infantry. Gist was an intermittent student at the university. *Catalog.*

Elijah Goodwin of Indianapolis, an original benefactor, the treasurer, and later president of the Butler University Board of Trustees from 1855 to 1868. He married Marcia Melissa Bassett, who also served on the board from 1869 to 1873. "Trustees."

Greencastle, Indiana, the seat of Putnam County in central Indiana. Like Franklin, it was laid out in 1822. Greencastle is the home of De Pauw University, which still includes a school of music referred to in these letters. The First Methodist Church of Indiana, built in Charlestown in 1807, is restored on its campus.

Guys Gap, Tennessee, located on the Mississippi River, twelve miles southwest of Shiloh. It is significantly south of Murfreesboro.

Hanover, Jefferson County (southeast Indiana), the home of Chauncey Butler, Ovid's brother, and Hanover College (founded in 1827).

Benjamin (Ben Harrison/Mr. Harrison) Harrison (1833–1901), United States senator (1881) and president of the United States (1889–93). Originally from Ohio, Harrison moved to Indianapolis in 1854 following his admission to the bar. He ran successfully for city attorney of Indianapolis in 1857. Harrison became secretary of the Republican State Central Committee in 1858 and was elected reporter of the Indiana Supreme Court in 1860. He was twice reelected. Later he was an unsuccessful candidate for governor. Ovid Butler and Harrison were close, personal friends, as Harrison was law partner to Butler's son-in-law, William Wallace, and closely aligned politically. Their relationship to Gov. Oliver P. Morton was beneficial to all three. During the war Harrison's tour of service closely mimicked Scot Butler's, and Ovid could more easily follow Scot's survival through Morton and Harrison. Harrison was appointed commander of the Seventieth Regiment, Indiana Volunteer Infantry in August 1862 but saw little action through the winter of 1862–63 as his regiment performed reconnaissance duty and guarded the railroads in Kentucky and Tennessee. When the Atlanta campaign got under way in May 1864, Harrison saw action at Resaca, Cassville, New Hope Church, Lost Mountain, Kennesaw Mountain, Marietta, Peach Tree Creek, and the siege of Atlanta. His regiment took part in the "March to the Sea" and then transferred to Tennessee, where Harrison commanded a brigade in the battle of Nashville in December 1864. He was brevetted a brigadier general in January 1865. Thornbrough, *Indiana in the Civil War Era,* 129, 164.

Thomas Andrews Hendricks (1819–1885), future governor of Indiana. Hendricks and Ovid Butler were personally acquainted through their practice of the law from 1825 to 1835 in Shelbyville, Indiana. Politically a Democrat,

Hendricks later became a member of the Indiana state legislature and the United States House of Representatives. Thornbrough, *Indiana in the Civil War Era,* 226–27.

Samuel K. Hoshour, Butler University professor. He served as president of the university from 1858 to 1861.

George Washington Hoss, Julia Wesley Dunn's uncle. Hoss was a professor of mathematics and engineering at Butler University. He also taught at Indiana University in Bloomington.

Alvin Peterson Hovey (1821–1891), general, U.S. Army. Orphaned at an early age, he worked as a bricklayer, schoolteacher, and lawyer and served as an officer in the Mexican War. He became a state supreme court judge, served as U.S. District Attorney, and was defeated in the 1858 election for Congress. Hovey was commissioned colonel of the Twenty-fourth Regiment, Indiana Volunteer Infantry and saw action under Lew Wallace's command at Shiloh. He was promoted to brigadier general. Hovey then served as liaison officer between Gen. Ulysses S. Grant and Gov. Oliver P. Morton. He again saw action in Atlanta. Following the war, he was elected to Congress and later became governor of Indiana.

Maria (Butler) Jameson (1831–1911), Scot Butler's half sister. She was the daughter of Ovid Butler and his first wife Cordelia Cole. Maria married Patrick Henry Jameson on June 20, 1850.

Patrick Henry Jameson/P. H. Jameson (1824–1910), Scot Butler's brother-in-law. Jameson was a prominent Indianapolis physician and philanthropist who married Scot's half sister, Maria Butler, in 1850 at Forest Home. During the war Jameson was in charge of state and local troops in hospital camps including Camp Morton in Indianapolis. From 1863 to 1866 he was acting assistant surgeon general in the army and from 1861 to 1869 served as physician to the Indiana Institution for the Deaf and Dumb. He was a member of the Butler University Board of Trustees from 1870 to 1909 and board president in 1873. Jameson served on the Indianapolis committee to prepare a bill for public school reformation in 1899. He was also a member of the executive committee of the Progressive Citizens Education Society.

Jennings County, located in southeast Indiana. The county was organized in February 1817 and named for Jonathan Jennings, the first Indiana governor. Vernon was soon thereafter chosen as the county seat. It was also home to Vernon, the homestead of the Chauncey Butler family.

The *Journal,* an Indianapolis newspaper established in 1853 and considered the mouthpiece of the Whig party. In 1854 the owner sold it to a company of which Ovid Butler was a member and principal financier. In 1858 Ovid Butler sold his interest to Berry Sulgrove.

Keithsburg (Mercer County, Illinois), south of Davenport on the Mississippi River and the sight of Butler's Grove, Ovid's farm of nine hundred acres. Ovid would retreat to Butler's Grove when he needed a "getaway" or when his farms needed tending. In his daughter Maria's account, Ovid slept on a dirt floor and labored in his dress shirt and waistcoat. This is curious in light of his "failing health," which he used as a reason for not writing Scot more frequently.

Knightstown (Indiana), twenty miles east of Indianapolis on U.S. Highway 40.

Libby Prison, a Confederate prison for federal officers just outside Richmond, Virginia. It was second in notoriety only to Andersonville. The 45,000-square-foot structure was originally the Libby & Son Ship Chandlers & Grocers building. The Libby family was evicted so that the building could be used as a Confederate prison on March 26, 1862. By 1863 the prison was full to capacity. Although escape was nearly impossible, 109 Union officers, including Marion Anderson, fled via a tunnel on December 11, 1863. This was the only successful escape known to occur from Libby Prison during the war. Shelby Foote reports that President Abraham Lincoln toured Richmond just after the surrender. "William Crook, White House guard, remembered the crowd passing Libby Prison, empty now, still with its old ship chandler's sign attached. 'We'll pull it down!' someone offered, but Lincoln shook his head. 'No. . . . Leave it as a monument,' he said." Following the war the eccentric Civil War historians Charles Gunther and William H. Gray purchased the prison for $23,300, dismantled it, and had it reassembled in Chicago in 1889. It first became The Libby Prison War Memorial Museum, located on Wabash Avenue between Fourteenth and Sixteenth Streets. The city later built an outside wall around the building, and it became the Chicago Coliseum. It was demolished in the mid-1900s. Chicago Historical Society; Chicago Department of Tourism; Shelby Foote, *The Civil War,* 3 vols. (New York: Random House, 1974): 3:897.

George Murray Lockerbie (1771–1856), Scot Butler's great-grandfather and grandfather to Elizabeth Anne (McOuat) Butler. Lockerbie was born in Scotland and immigrated to the United States in 1806. He and his wife, Anne Blacklock, had thirteen children, seven of whom died before him. One remaining daughter, Janette Smith Lockerbie, married Thomas McOuat in 1818. See Lockerbie Family History in Appendix.

Andrew W. McOuat (1830–1895), Scot Butler's uncle, son of Thomas McOuat and Janette Smith Lockerbie, and brother of Elizabeth Anne McOuat. Andrew married Ellen McCrosson, who bore him ten children during their long marriage.

Elizabeth Anne McOuat. See E Anne/EA/Elizabeth (McOuat) Butler.

Ellen (Wallace) McOuat (1832–1863), Scot Butler's aunt by marriage and wife of Robert L. McOuat. Robert was a son of Janette Smith Lockerbie and Thomas McOuat, a brother of Elizabeth Anne (McOuat) Butler, and Scot's uncle.

Janette Smith (Lockerbie) McOuat (1800–1870), Scot Butler's grandmother. She was born in Dumfries, Scotland, to writer and politician George Murray Lockerbie and Anne (Blacklock) Lockerbie. She immigrated with her parents in 1809 to New York, settling in Philadelphia, where she lived several years until traveling west to Kentucky where she remained with her family until 1830. Janette married Thomas McOuat in 1818 and bore him nine children, including Scot's mother, Elizabeth Anne. During her long lifetime she outlived her seven brothers and sisters by more than twenty years, lived another thirty years after her husband's death in 1840, and saw at least four of her nine children buried. Janette died in Indianapolis and is buried in Crown Hill Cemetery there. Religiously she was an Episcopalian, having signed the first writ of Association for St. Paul Church in Indianapolis. Politically she was a Democrat and a Southern sympathizer.

Martha/Mattie Jeanette McOuat. See Martha/Mattie Jeanette (McOuat) Edgar Todd.

Robert Lockerbie McOuat (1827–1883), Scot Butler's uncle, son of Thomas McOuat and Janette Smith Lockerbie, and brother of Elizabeth Anne McOuat. He married Ellen C. Wallace on April 8, 1851, but their twelve-year marriage was childless, and she died suddenly in 1863. Robert married Eugenia Frances Burford in 1865.

John Hunt Morgan (1825–1864), a well-known Confederate general who was noted for his daring, hair-raising raids. In 1863 Morgan and his Kentucky Raiders invaded Indiana, marauding, pillaging, and burning towns in his path in order to draw Gen. William S. Rosecrans's army from Tennessee. Ovid's interest in Morgan's raid concerns the Butler homesite in Vernon, Jennings County, southern Indiana, where many Butler relatives still lived. During the Indiana raids, 400 men gathered in Vernon to ward off Morgan and his 2,200 cavalrymen. It was the only town in southern Indiana not destroyed by Morgan's Raiders. Morgan escaped but was later surrounded in Greeneville, Tennessee, and shot by Union troops. Faust, ed., *Historical Times Illustrated Encyclopedia of the Civil War,* 510; Robert G. Barrows and David J. Bodenhamer, eds., *The Encyclopedia of Indianapolis* (Bloomington and Indianapolis: Indiana University Press, 1994), 324.

Thomas Armstrong Morris (1811–1904), the first quartermaster general for Indiana and a West Point graduate from Indianapolis who had had a successful career as a civil engineer and railroad magnate before the war. He was also commissioned the first brigadier general from Indiana, but he resigned after a few months in the field because of accusations by Gen. George McClelland that Morris's slowness was a hindrance to McClelland's army. Morris was one of a few officers with prior military training that trained and commanded raw recruits. Under his command, five of the first regiments of the original three-month volunteers were organized into a brigade and sent to western Virginia to drive the South out of what became West Virginia. After the war Morris returned to his railroad interests. From 1866 to 1869 he was president and chief engineer of the Indianapolis and St. Louis line, and in 1870 Morris became receiver for the Indianapolis, Cincinnati and Lafayette Railroads. Morris was largely responsible for the planning and building of the Union Depot in Indianapolis. Thornbrough, *Indiana in the Civil War Era,* 127, 143.

Oliver Perry Morton (1823–1877), Indiana's "War Governor" and a personal, social, and political ally of Ovid Butler. He was elected lieutenant governor in 1860 and became governor in 1861 when Gov. Henry S. Lane was elected to the U.S. Senate. Morton was a strong Unionist and antislavery man in accord with Abraham Lincoln on the issue of secession. Having conferred with Lincoln shortly before Fort Sumter was fired on, Morton telegrammed Lincoln offering him 10,000 men for the Union army, the first offer of troops from any state. Many regard Morton as one of the foremost war governors, evidenced by Indiana's contribution of 200,000 soldiers to the Union army. When the legislature, which included a large number of members with strong peace sentiments, tried to embarrass Morton by limiting his executive war powers, Morton refused to call the legislature into session and financed the government with loans guaranteed personally from individuals and counties throughout the state. Morton was known as the "Soldier's friend," and his frequent trips to camps and hospitals undoubtedly contributed to the level of care received by Indiana troops. James A. Garfield said of Morton, "On a hundred battlefields his name was the battle cry of the noble regiments he had organized and inspired with his own lofty spirit." Morton was elected governor in his own right in 1864 and, despite a stroke in 1865, went on to serve in the United States Senate from 1867 until his death in 1877. Morton's last public appearance was as a speaker at

Crown Hill Cemetery in Indianapolis, where he gave an address honoring the soldiers buried there. A statue of Morton honoring his service stands in statuary hall in the State Capitol building.

Horatio C. Newcomb, husband of Eliza Pabody, Ovid Butler's niece through his sister Mabel Butler. Horatio was an Indianapolis philanthropist and fellow benefactor of Butler University.

North Western Christian University (North Western Christian College), later renamed Butler College and then Butler University. The school was located adjacent to Forest Home until 1875 when it moved to Irvington (later incorporated into Indianapolis) and finally located in Fairview Park in Indianapolis, Indiana, in 1928. Shaw, "Founding of Butler University."

Sarah E. Norwood. See Sarah E. (Norwood) Catterson.

Mable (Butler) Pabody (1799–1877), Scot Butler's aunt and Ovid Butler's older sister. Mabel married Ezra Fitch Pabody in 1820 and lived all her married life in Vernon, Jennings County, Indiana, the Butler homestead.

David Reynolds, husband of Scot Butler's aunt Jean/Jennie McOuat. Reynolds was in charge of organizing, equipping, and commissioning all Indiana volunteers. After the war, he developed an interest in his brother's business of designing mechanical improvements in milling. He went back to his native state of New York and then to England and France to introduce these new appliances to the developing international markets. In 1865 Reynolds moved to Minneapolis and invested in land speculation. Politically, he was a Democrat. He married Jennie McOuat on April 2, 1863. She died a year later in Rochester, New York, leaving a daughter named Jennie. The daughter moved to Minneapolis with her father and married George L. Hilt.

Jean/Jennie Maitland (McOuat) Reynolds (1838–1864), Scot Butler's aunt and Elizabeth Anne (McOuat) Butler's sister. She married David Reynolds of New York in 1863 and died the following year in childbirth. She was buried in Crown Hill Cemetery and later reburied in Minnesota. See Elizabeth Anne's letter above, dated May 5, 1864, for her mother's reaction to Jennie's death.

Richmond (Indiana), the seat of Wayne County. The city was founded in 1806 by soldiers who served under George Rogers Clark. The Quaker community located there founded the Friends' Boarding School, which in 1859 became Earlham College.

Ringgold Gap, Georgia. The battle of Ringgold Gap was fought on November 27, 1863. Ringgold Gap provided an entrance for the Union army through the Smokey Mountains into northern Georgia on the way to Atlanta. The Northern army, commanded by Maj. Gen. Joseph Hooker, attacked the Southern army, commanded by Maj. Gen. Patrick Cleburn, which held the Gap. At the end of the fighting, Northern casualties far exceeded those of the South, thus leading some to declare the battle a Southern victory. However, the Southern army was depleted to the point that it could not risk a repeat of the battle, so it withdrew. The Northern Army occupied Ringgold Gap, and a door to Atlanta was opened.

William Starke Rosecrans (1819–1898), known as "Old Rosy." Rosecrans graduated from West Point in the class of 1842. He was best known for his command of the Army of the Cumberland, when in the Tullahoma Campaign he drove the Confederates from Chattanooga while suffering fewer than five hundred casualties. He was loved by his men but was hard on his senior officers. Known for his micromanagement of troop movements and his hatred for committing his beloved men to battle, his command at the Battle of Chattanooga gave the Confederates under Gen. James Longstreet the opportunity to break the Union lines and ultimately defeat the Union army. As a result, Rosecrans was relieved of his command and for the remainder of the war commanded the Department of Missouri. The following year James Garfield asked Rosecrans to run as Lincoln's vice president, but Rosecrans refused. He served as a member of the House of Representatives from California, died in Redondo, California, and is buried at Arlington National Cemetery.

Anna Scovel (1849–1894), Scot Butler's future sister-in-law and wife of Chauncey Butler, Scot's younger brother. Chauncey and Anna were married in 1870. Her sister, Mary, also attended the university.

The *Sentinel,* the Democratic newspaper of the Civil War period published in Indianapolis.

Sentinel Building, headquarters of the *Indianapolis Sentinel* newspaper.

Mary Ella Sharpe, a close friend to Demia and Janett Butler. Mary Ella was married twice, first to Joe Moore and second to Robert Duncan. She was a member of the Butler University Board of Trustees from 1870 to 1873. "Trustees."

Edward Shaw, Indiana Sanitary Agent. Shaw worked for his father, B. C. Shaw, owner and president of Shaw's Carriage Company at 26 to 34 East Georgia Street, Indianapolis, before entering the sanitary business. His children were students of the university and active members of its board in later years. Cline & McHaffie, *The People's Guide: A Business, Political and Religious Directory of Marion Co., Indiana* (Indianapolis: Indianapolis Printing and Publishing House, 1874), 130.

Shelby County (Indiana). The land was originally part of a large, unsettled territory called the New Purchase, which became a part of the Delaware Indian reservation in 1818. The county was officially established in 1821 and named for Isaac Shelby, twice governor of Kentucky and a resident of Indianapolis.

Sigournean Literary Society. Literary societies were common in nineteenth-century normal schools. Men and women met weekly in their respective club rooms to enjoy sociability and read papers. The societies taught expression through declamation, composition, and debate with faculty members as critics. The Sigournean was unique for its emphasis on the art of conversation. Societies were a required part of campus life, providing a valuable complement to classroom work. Each society presented a yearly exhibition of its work as part of graduation ceremonies. When courses in literature, composition, and public speaking became available at the turn of the century, literary societies withered. Scot Butler regarded societies as the most important extracurricular activity of the university. In fact, he noted, it was such an accepted part of the educational process that it could be considered "co-curricular." Exercises in declamation and composition were required of every student not a member of one of the societies. Other Butler societies included the Mathesian, the Pythonian, and, later, the Demia Butler Society. *Butler Alumnal Quarterly* (Oct. 1914); Butler University biographical file on Lydia Short; Binder, Butler University Archives section OCFS S45. See also Scot Butler, *Butler Alumnal Quarterly* (Jan. 1913).

Sons of Liberty. This secret society, reported to have lodges in forty counties in Indiana, was founded on a "devotion to states'-rights principles as embodied in the Virginia and Kentucky Resolutions." Many Democrats believed that secret organizations were necessary in order to preserve constitutional liberty against the "despotism" of the Lincoln and Morton administrations. They were also reported to be the basis of what might become a Democratic move to establish a Northern confederacy by enticing Peace Democrats to riot against the Northern cause. Other such societies referred to in these letters were the Order for Treason and the Knights of the Golden Circle. For a general discussion of secret societies active in Indiana during the Civil War, see Thornbrough, *Indiana in the Civil War Era,* 213–19, and Frank L. Klement, *The Copperheads in the Middle West* (Chicago: University of Chicago Press, 1960).

Abel D. Streight of New York (ca. 1829–1892), a book and map publisher. He settled in Indianapolis in 1859. He joined the Union army in 1861 and was appointed commanding officer of the Fifty-first Regiment, Indiana Volunteer Infantry, under whom Marion T. Anderson served. Streight was held prisoner of war at Libby Prison in Richmond, Virginia, from late 1863 to early 1864. He is known for his daring escape from that prison when he and 107 other soldiers dug a tunnel from their barracks under the prison grounds. He retired in 1865 as a brigadier general. From 1876 to 1877 and again from 1888 to 1889 he served as an Indiana state senator.

Horace Stringfellow, Jr., the first rector of St. Paul Episcopal Church in Indianapolis, supported the building of the church not only financially but also physically as he worked side by side with the McOuats on the church's construction.

Berry Sulgrove, an experienced newspaperman and biographer. Sulgrove had been associated with the first owner of the *Indiana Journal* and became its editor in 1854. He purchased Ovid Butler's interest in the *Journal* in 1858 and continued as editor until 1863. Sulgrove was closely associated with Oliver P. Morton, and in 1864 the *Journal* was sold to William R. Holloway and Company, the owner having been Morton's private secretary during the war.

Bayard Taylor (1825–1878), American author. Scot Butler became personally interested in Taylor when the author lectured at the Masonic Hall in Indianapolis on February 19, 1859. Taylor was an American traveler and author noted for his books recording his travels in California, Mexico, Egypt, Asia Minor, Syria, India, China, and Japan. He served as a correspondent to the *New York Tribune.* In 1878 Taylor became ambassador to Berlin, where he died. Fellow student Lydia Short wrote of Taylor's lecture:

> Bayard Taylor, Esq., lectures this evening. We are going; everybody is going. . . . There we go, wending our way to Masonic Hall with the bustling current tearing along helter-skelter, all in the same direction. Did you ever! . . . Here he comes. What a stillness reigns as he moves up the aisle and mounts the rostrum. . . . He is a large man, very tall, with a well-built constitution, tho' not disposed to corpulency; a well-developed, tho' receding, forehead; . . . very black hair, with short whiskers and trim mustache of the same hue. . . . Though having undergone many privations in foreign lands, we would judge him not to be wholly insensible to the luxuries of life—good brandy not

excepted. He is no orator, tho' expressing himself in the most glowing and brilliant words, his style is purely graphical, his voice is of the most exquisite clearness, indicating the soundest of lungs. His articulation and intonations were very good, but rather awkward in gesticulation. In some of his quotations from Byron and Tennyson his delivery was masterly. "Pages from a Diary," by Mrs. Lydia (Short) Braden, *Butler Alumnal Quarterly* (Oct. 1917): 145–61.

Thaddeus Test, Scot Butler's cousin through the Wallace family. He was a brother of Caroline (Test) Coburn and in-law of William and Lew Wallace.

Demia Thayer. See Demia (Thayer) Thrasher.

Henry Thomas (1816–1870), Union general. Following a distinguished career in various assignments of the war, Thomas was appointed commanding officer of the Department of the Cumberland in which Scot served. Thomas was particularly known for his military genius at the Battle of Nashville, December 15–16, 1864, where regimental captain of the Indiana Fifty-first, Marion T. Anderson, received his career ending wounds.

Demia (Thayer) Thrasher, Scot Butler's first cousin. She was the daughter of Sally Butler (1805–1870) and Spencer Thayer (1799–1878). Demia married William M. Thrasher, who served in the Twelfth Regiment, Indiana Volunteer Infantry. She died in 1924.

J. M. Tilford, president of the Indianapolis Printing and Publishing House. Son Samuel E. Tilford enlisted in Company F, 107th Regiment, Indiana Volunteer Infantry in July 1863. He attended the university and worked for his father as a bookkeeper in his father's business, located on the Circle at Meridian Street. Following the war Samuel lived in Irvington, where he continued his education at Butler University. Cline & McHaffie, *The People's Guide,* 345; *Catalog.*

Todd/Butler family. Irby, Jerome Jillete (Romy), Ovid, and William (Willie) were Scot Butler's cousins and children of Ovid's youngest sister, Demia, who married Indianapolis physician Levi W. Todd.

Martha/Mattie Jeanette (McOuat) Edgar Todd (born about 1835), Scot Butler's aunt and daughter of Thomas McOuat and Janette Smith Lockerbie and sister of Elizabeth Anne (McOuat) Butler. Martha married first Samuel Edgar and on his death, Dr. Robert Nathaniel Todd, a prominent Indianapolis physician and philanthropist.

Robert Nathaniel Todd (died 1883). He was a physician and Scot Butler's uncle by marriage and husband of Martha/Mattie Jeanette McOuat, Elizabeth Anne's sister.

United States Sanitary Commission. Prior to 1861, there were many relief societies throughout the country, all independent of each other with no system or method of organization. Churches, schools, and parlors were filled with the making and collecting of goods for soldiers at the front, but their work was useless without a means to collect and distribute the contributions. Recognizing this aimlessness, a group of women, with the support of the New York Medical Association, met at the New York Infirmary to draw up a request for organization to Secretary of War Edwin M. Stanton. Grateful for the relief from the demands being made on his department for sanitary care, he immediately approved the organization of a national volunteer group that would include the original Sanitary Commission and would "inquire with scientific thoroughness into the subjects of diet, cooking, cooks, clothing, tents, camping grounds, transports, transitory depots, with their exposures, [and] camp police. . . . Every thing appertaining to outfit, cleanliness, precautions against damp, cold, heat, malaria, infection; crude unvaried, or ill-cooked food, and an irregular or careless regimental commissariat, would fall under this head." Supplies, including food, clothing, bandages, hospital furniture, and cordials and delicacies for the wounded and sick, were collected from homes and local communities. The local branch then opened, sorted, inventoried, repacked, and shipped the goods to one of two national collection points that determined their destination. Supplies were distributed to any and all, regardless of state or color of uniform, "be it Union soldier or Confederate prisoner." "Articles of Organization," Advisory Committee of the Board of Physicians and Surgeons at the Hospitals of New York," n.d., as cited by Jan P. Romanowich, www.netwalk.com/~jpr, "The Beginnings" (accessed Feb. 22, 2004). The original document, "Articles of Organization," is an undated printed pamphlet.

Samuel C. Vance, colonel of the 132nd Regiment, Indiana Volunteer Infantry, in which Chauncey Butler was an enlistee. Vance was a watchmaker who settled in Indianapolis in 1859. Politically he was a Republican. Cline & McHaffie, *The People's Guide,* 351.

Vernon (Jennings County in southeast Indiana) (once Geneva), the Chauncey Butler, Sr., homestead from 1817 to 1838, lies on the Ohio River. Many of the Butler descendants remained there to live out their lives as did the Vawter family, cousins of Scot Butler. The unusual provisions of Vernon's 1815 land grant stipulated that it remain the county seat forever.

Cordelia/Delia (Butler) Wallace (1828–1866), Scot Butler's half sister and daughter of Ovid Butler and Cordelia Cole (Ovid's first wife). Cordelia married William Wallace, son of David Wallace and brother of Lew Wallace, in 1847.

Lew Wallace (1827–1905), born in Brookville, Indiana, the son of West Point graduate and Indiana governor David Wallace. He was also the brother of William Wallace, who married Ovid Butler's daughter Cordelia. Lew was best known as the author of *Ben-Hur: A Tale of the Christ* (written in 1880), one of the best-selling novels of all time, but he would have preferred to have been remembered as a military man. He did not pursue a formal education but was drawn to the military, where he first saw service as an officer in the Mexican War (1846–48). Wallace was a state senator when the Civil War broke out and accepted Gov. Oliver P. Morton's appointment as adjutant general. During the Civil War he attained the rank of major general in the Union army when his troops captured Fort Donelson, Tennessee. In 1864 Wallace was also instrumental in delaying Gen. Jubal Early's invasion of Washington, D.C., so that a successful defense of the city could be mounted. In 1865 he was a member of the court that tried those involved in the assassination of Abraham Lincoln. Among many commands he served as colonel of the Eleventh Regiment, Indiana Volunteer Infantry and brigadier general of volunteers in the Union army. Although a scapegoat for Ulysses S. Grant's surprise at the Battle of Shiloh and relieved of his command, he continued to gain the support of Morton, who appointed Wallace to set up the defense of Cincinnati when the Confederates threatened to invade Indiana. In later life Wallace was a lawyer, a state legislator, governor of the New Mexico Territory, and U.S. minister to Turkey (1881–85). He was a prolific writer who drew on his travels and experiences. He is buried in Crawfordsville, Indiana.

William Wallace (1827–1891), Scot Butler's brother-in-law and husband of Cordelia Butler, Scot's half sister by Ovid and Cordelia Cole (Ovid's first wife). William was an Indianapolis attorney and son of David Wallace, governor of Indiana (1837–40). William and Cordelia were married in 1847 in Indianapolis, presumably at Forest Home. He was the brother of Lew Wallace, Civil War general and author of *Ben-Hur.*

Estis Wallingford, first lieutenant and adjutant to the Thirty-third Regiment, Indiana Volunteer Infantry during the entire length of the war.

Graham A./H. Wells (Doct. Wells), husband of Georgia Anna Elgin (1838–1861), daughter of Elizabeth Anne (McOuat) Butler by her first husband George Manning Elgin.

Chancey Wilkinson, Scot Butler's first cousin and son of Robert Wilkinson and Eunice Butler, Ovid's sister. Chancey served in both the Third and Seventh Regiments, Minnesota Volunteer Infantry. He enlisted as a corporal on September 27, 1861, at the age of twenty-six in Company A, Third Infantry Regiment. He received a disability discharge from that regiment on March 29, 1862.

Yankton (South Dakota), located approximately sixty miles west by northwest of Sioux City, Iowa.

Bibliography

UNPUBLISHED MATERIALS

SCOT BUTLER'S MILITARY SERVICE

Butler, Scot. "Recollections of the Civil War." Unpublished manuscript. Transcribed and edited by Barbara Butler Davis. Irvington Historical Society, Indianapolis, Ind.

_____. "A Soldier's Summer in the Cumberland Gap." Unpublished manuscript. Transcribed and edited by Barbara Butler Davis. Irvington Historical Society, Indianapolis, Ind.

_____. Scot Butler papers and correspondence regarding his Civil War service and pension record. Irvington Historical Society, Indianapolis, Ind.

National Archives, Washington, D.C. Scot Butler Service Records, U.S. Signal Corps.

_____. Scot Butler Service Records, Thirty-third Regiment, Indiana Volunteer Infantry.

_____. Scot Butler Pension Record, File No. X-C-2-637-653.

FAMILY HISTORIES, GENEALOGICAL NOTES, AND BIOGRAPHIES

"Affidavit Concerning Some Descendants of Joel Butler." Source unknown. Original document, 1775, held by the editor.

Butler, Ovid. Handwritten family vital records. Held by the editor.

Butler, Scot. "History of the Butler Family and Genealogy by Scot Butler in Indianapolis," circa 1880. Eighty-three-page handwritten manuscript from autobiographical notes left by Ovid Butler, Letter Book 4, and compiled by his son Scot Butler. Held by the editor.

_____. "Genealogy of the Descendants of Ovid Butler." Handwritten circa 1880. Held by the editor.

_____. Eighteen-page handwritten Butler family genealogical notes circa 1880. Original held by the editor.

_____. "Butler Family Burials at Crown Hill Cemetery in Indianapolis." Handwritten original held by the editor.

Clark, Grace. "Julia (Dunn) Butler, 1845 to 1937: A Speech in Her Memory." Original typescript held by the editor.

Elgin, George, and Elizabeth Anne (McOuat). Elgin Family Bible dated December 8, 1836, Georgetown, Kentucky. Original Bible held by the editor.

Helming, Emily M. "The Butler Family," dated 1953–54. Unpublished typescript contains compiled biographical material. Original typescript held by the editor.

_____. "Ovid Butler and Butler University, Compiled from Records of the University," April 1944. Original typescript. Butler University Archives, Indianapolis, Ind.

_____. "Scot Butler, Ninth and Eleventh President, 1844–1931." Original typescript held by the editor.

Jameson, Maria Butler. "A Partial Record of the Butler Family Made Out from Biographical Sketches and Notes Found among the Papers of Ovid Butler, of Indianapolis, Indiana, and Copied by His Daughter, Maria Butler Jameson in October, 1907." Original typescript held by the editor.

_____. "A Genealogy of Five Generations of the Butler Family, 1906." Original typescript held by the editor.

Larabee, W. H. "History of the Dunn Family from W. H. Larrabee to the Descendants of John Wesley Dunn, August 1909, Contributed at the Request of Julia Dunn Jameson." Original typescript held by the editor.

Recker, Elizabeth Anne (Butler). Spiral notebook of handwritten genealogical information, 1952. Held by the editor.

_____. "Birthday Book."

FAMILY HOMESTEADS

Alig, Leona T. Personal letter, April 30, 1974, regarding the status of Forest Home. Location of the original unknown. Copy held by the editor.

Conner, Lela Blount. "The Butler Homestead." Original typescript held by the editor.

Goodwin, E. M., M. O. Ross, and Fred C. Lockwood. Correspondence dated December 1943, amended by Anne Elizabeth (Butler) Townsend regarding Butler family residences and burials in Old Geneva, Indiana. Original typescript. Indiana State Library, Genealogy Division, Indianapolis, Ind.

PERSONAL LETTERS, 1836–1986
(EXCLUDING SCOT BUTLER LETTERS)

Butler, Ovid. Letter to Levi Butler, July 20, 1858. Indiana Historical Society, Indianapolis, Ind.

_____. Letter to Levi Butler, August 9, 1863. Indiana Historical Society, Indianapolis, Ind.

Butler, Scot 2nd. Letter to Scot Martin, July 21, 1986. Held by the editor.

Fox, John L. Letter to Miss Dunn, November 25, 1966. Indiana State Library, Indianapolis, Ind.

Lockerbie, George. Letter to Janette Smith (Lockerbie) McOuat, September 20, 1836. Indiana Historical Society, Indianapolis, Ind.

_____. Letter to Elizabeth Anne (McOuat) Elgin, March 4, 1838. Indiana Historical Society, Indianapolis, Ind.

_____. Letter to Elizabeth Anne (McOuat) Elgin, March 12, 1838. Indiana Historical Society, Indianapolis, Ind.

Martin, Scot. Letter to Scot Butler 2nd, June 23, 1986. Held by the editor.

Recker, Elizabeth Anne (Butler). Letter to Elizabeth Anne (Butler) Wangelin, April 15, 1964. Location of original unknown. Copy held by the editor.

BUTLER UNIVERSITY

Waller, George M. "Butler University Historical Sketch," June 1990. Unpublished manuscript. Butler University Archives, Indianapolis, Ind.

MISCELLANEOUS

Butler, Ovid. Autobiographical notes found in Letter Book 4. Butler University Archives, Indianapolis, Ind.

_____. "Selected Letter Drafts of Ovid Butler with Introduction." Edited by Steven Jameson Schmidt. Typed transcript.

"Inventory of Holdings on Ovid Butler in the Indiana Historical Society Library." M0036 BV 1011, Ovid Butler Collection. Indiana Historical Society, Indianapolis, Ind.

INDIANA DOCUMENTS

Crown Hill Cemetery, Indianapolis. A selection of original documents.

_____. Rights of burial. A selection of original documents.

_____. Butler family burial lots, 1865–1973.

_____. McOuat family burial lots, section 13, lot 1.

_____. McOuat family interment record, deeded by Crown Hill Cemetery to Janette Smith McOuat, 1869.

Marion County, Indiana, Board of Health (Indianapolis). A selection of original documents.

Marion County, Indiana, Clerk's Office (Indianapolis). A selection of original documents.

CHURCH RECORDS

St. Paul Episcopal Church Parish Registers, 1870–1910. Indiana State Library, Indiana Division.

PUBLISHED MATERIALS

BOOKS

Bodenhamer, David J., and Robert G. Barrows, eds. *The Encyclopedia of Indianapolis.* Bloomington and Indianapolis: Indiana University Press, 1994.

Bowers, John. *Chickamauga and Chattanooga: The Battles That Doomed the Confederacy.* New York: Harper Collins, 1994.

Brown, Hilton U. *A Book of Memories.* Indianapolis: Butler University, 1951.

Brown, J. Willard. *The Signal Corps, U.S.A. in the War of the Rebellion.* New York: Arno Press, 1974.

Burgess, Lauren Cook. *An Uncommon Soldier: The Civil War Letters of Sarah Rosetta Wakeman.* New York: Oxford University Press, 1995.

Cathcart, Charlotte. *Indianapolis from Our Old Corner.* Indianapolis: Indiana Historical Society, 1965.

Cline & McHaffie. *The People's Guide: A Business, Political and Religious Directory of Marion Co., Indiana.* Indianapolis: Indianapolis Printing and Publishing House, 1874.

Cottman, George S. *Centennial History and Handbook of Indiana.* Indianapolis: Max R. Hyman, 1915.

Darlington, Jane E., comp. *Marion County, Indiana, Mortality Records.* 2 vols. Indianapolis: Marion County Printing Office, 1989.

Davis, Kenneth C. *Don't Know Much about the Civil War.* New York: Avon Books, 1996.

Dunn, Jacob Piatt. *Greater Indianapolis: The History, the Industries, the Institutions, and the People of a City of Homes.* 2 vols. Chicago: Lewis Publishing Co., 1910.

Dyer, Frederick Henry. *A Compendium of the War of the Rebellion.* 3 vols. New York: T. Yoseloff, 1959.

Faust, Patricia L., ed. *Historical Times Illustrated Encyclopedia of the Civil War.* New York: Harper & Row, 1986.

Foner, Eric. *Free Soil, Free Labor, Free Men: The Ideology of the Republican Party before the Civil War.* New York: Oxford University Press, 1995.

Funk, Arville L. *Hoosiers in the Civil War.* Greencastle, Ind.: Nugget Publishers, 1993.

Hale, Hester Anne. *Indianapolis: The First Century.* Indianapolis: Indianapolis Historical Society, 1987.

Hays, Samuel P. *American Political History as Social Analysis Essays.* Knoxville: University of Tennessee Press, 1980.

Heiss, Willard, ed. *Indiana Source Book*, vol. 3. Indianapolis: Indiana Historical Society, 1982.

Holliday, John H. *Indianapolis and the Civil War*. Indiana Historical Society Publications, vol. 4, no. 9. Indianapolis: Edward J. Hecker, Printer and Publisher, 1911.

Holloway, W. R. *Indianapolis: A Historical and Statistical Sketch of the Railroad City*. Indianapolis: Indianapolis Journal Print., 1870.

Indiana at Chickamauga, Report of the Indiana Commissioners: Chickamauga National Military Park. Indianapolis: Wm. Buford, 1901.

Jennings County Historical Society. *This Is Jennings County*. Vernon, Ind.: Jennings County Historical Society, n.d.

Katcher, Philip. *The Civil War Source Book*. London: Arms and Armour Press, 1992.

_____. *Lincoln's Unsung Heroes*. London: Arms and Armour Press, 1997.

Keller, Allan. *Morgan's Raid*. Indianapolis: Bobbs-Merrill Co., 1961.

Klement, Frank L. *The Copperheads in the Middle West*. Chicago: University of Chicago Press, 1960.

Kline, Mary-Jo. *A Guide to Documentary Editing*. Baltimore: Johns Hopkins University Press, 1987.

Lockerbie's Assessment List of Indianapolis, 1835. Edited by Eliza G. Browning. Indiana Historical Society Publications, vol. 4, no. 7. Indianapolis: E. J. Hecker, 1909.

Long, E. B., with Barbara Long. *The Civil War Day by Day: An Almanac, 1861–1865*. Garden City, N.Y.: Doubleday and Co., 1971.

McPherson, James, ed. *The American Heritage New History of the Civil War*. New York: Viking Press, 1996.

_____. *For Cause and Comrades: Why Men Fought in the Civil War*. New York: Oxford University Press, 1997.

_____. *What They Fought For, 1861–1865*. New York: Anchor, 1995.

Merrill, Catharine. *The Soldier of Indiana in the War for the Union*. 2 vols. Indianapolis: Merrill and Co., 1866.

Mitchell, Reid. *The Vacant Chair: The Northern Soldier Leaves Home*. New York: Oxford University Press, 1993.

Nowland, John H. B. *Sketches of Prominent Citizens of 1876: With a Few of the Pioneers of the City and County Who Have Passed Away*. Indianapolis: Tilford and Carlon, Printers, 1877.

_____. *Early Reminiscences of Indianapolis: With Short Biographical Sketches of Its Early Citizens, and a Few of the Prominent Business Men of the Present Day*. Indianapolis: Sentinel Book and Job Printing House, 1870.

Pictorial and Biographical Memoirs of Indianapolis and Marion County, Indiana, with Biographies of Many Prominent Men of Other Portions of the State, Both Living and Dead. Chicago: Goodspeed Brothers Publishers, 1893.

Raines, Rebecca Robbins. *Getting the Message Through: A Branch History of the U.S. Army Signal Corps.* Washington, D.C.: Center of Military History, United States Army, 1996.

Seeds, Russel M. *History of the Republican Party of Indiana.* Indianapolis: The Indiana History Co., 1899.

Smith, O. H. *Early Indiana Trials and Sketches.* Cincinnati: Moore, Wilstach, Keys and Co., Printers, 1858.

Stampp, Kenneth M. *Indiana Politics during the Civil War.* Indiana Historical Collections, vol. 31. Indianapolis: Indiana Historical Bureau, 1949.

Sulgrove, B. R. *History of Indianapolis and Marion County, Indiana.* Philadelphia: L. H. Everts and Co., 1884.

Sword, Wiley. *Mountains Touched with Fire: Chattanooga Besieged, 1863.* New York: St. Martin's Press, 1995.

Tafft, Henry Spurr. *Reminiscences of the Signal Service in the Civil War.* Providence: The Society, 1903.

Terrell, W. H. H. *Report of the Adjutant General of the State of Indiana.* 8 vols. Indianapolis: A. H. Conner, State Printer, 1865–69.

Thomas, Edison H. *John Hunt Morgan and His Raiders.* Lexington: University Press of Kentucky, 1975.

Thornbrough, Emma Lou. *Indiana in the Civil War Era, 1850–1880.* The History of Indiana, vol. 3. Indianapolis: Indiana Historical Bureau and Indiana Historical Society, 1965.

Tiers, M. C., ed. *The Christian Portrait Gallery: Consisting of Historical and Biographical Sketches and Photographic Portraits of Christian Preachers and Others.* Cincinnati: The Franklin Type Foundry, 1864.

Trapp, Glenda K. *Index to the Report of the Adjutant General of the State of Indiana.* Evansville, Ind.: Trapp Pub. Service, 1986–1987.

Turner, Ann, ed. *A Chronology of Indiana in the Civil War, 1861–1865.* Indianapolis: Indiana Civil War Centennial Commission, 1965.

United States Veteran Signal Corps Association. *Roster of Signal Corps, U.S.A. 1861–1865, Issued by the U.S. Veteran Signal Corps Association, Civil War Division, November 1910.* [Stoneham, Mass., 1910].

Vinovskis, Maris A. *Toward a Social History of the American Civil War.* New York: Cambridge University Press, 1990.

Welcher, Frank Johnson. *Coburn's Brigade: The Eighty-fifth Indiana, Thirty-third Indiana, Nineteenth Michigan, and Twenty-second Wisconsin in the Western Civil War.* Carmel, Ind.: Guild Press of Indiana, 1999.

Winslow, Hattie Lou, and Joseph R. H. Moore. *Camp Morton 1861–1865: Indianapolis Prison Camp.* 1940. Reprint, Indianapolis: Indiana Historical Society, 1995.

WPA, comp. *Index to Death Records, Marion County, Indiana (1902–1920)*, vol. 1. Indianapolis: Indiana State Printing Office, 1939.

WPA, comp. *Index to Marriage Records, Marion County, Indiana*. Indianapolis: Indiana State Printing Office, 1939.

NEWSPAPERS

"A Family Reunion of the Ovid Butler Family." *Indianapolis Daily Evening Gazette*, June 22, 1863.

"Calvin Fletcher and Ovid Butler." *Union Title News*, March 1947.

"Evelyn Mitchell Butler and the Demia Butler University Chair of English." *Indianapolis News*, date unknown. Clippings file, Indiana State Library.

"Forest Home." Unidentified newspaper clipping, January 26, 1972. Held by the editor.

Guthrie, Wayne. "University Named for Ovid Butler." *Indianapolis News*, October 5, 1971.

Hanna, Agnes M'Culloch. "Forest Home." *Indianapolis Star*, date unknown. Clippings file. Indianapolis Public Library.

Indianapolis Daily Journal. Various issues.

"Ovid Butler's Open Minded Nature and Compromise Position on Secession." *Indianapolis News*, December 14, 1960.

Savin, Harold. "Butler U's 'Friends' 1st Met 120 Years Ago." *Indianapolis Star*, August 13, 1967.

Scherrer, Anton. "Our Town: The Progressiveness of Ovid Butler." 1939. Unidentified article. Clippings file, Indianapolis Public Library.

"Scot Butler." *Indianapolis Star*, January 16, 1931.

"The Scot Butler Homestead." Unidentified and undated article. Clippings file, Indiana State Library.

"Second Female Professor in US appears at Butler." *The Butler Collegian* (September 14, 1995).

"Side Lights on Ovid Butler." *Indianapolis Star*, date unknown. Butler University Archives.

"The Status of Forest Home." *Indianapolis Star*, July 25, 1979.

NEWSLETTERS AND PERIODICALS

"A Biographical Sketch of Ovid Butler." *Christian Standard* (August 6, 1881).

Butler, Evelyn M. "Ovid Butler." *Butler Alumnal Quarterly* (April 1923).

Butler, Scot 2nd et al. "Ovid Butler—Distinguished American." *The Butler Society of North America* (November 1990).

Coburn, John. "Founder's Day Biography on Ovid Butler." *Butler Alumnal Quarterly* (January 1925).

"Dispute within Christian Church." *Christian Standard* (June 19, 1897).

Esarey, Logan. "The Pioneering Aristocracy." *Indiana Magazine of History* 12 (September 1916): 270–87.

Graydon, Catharine Merrill. "Remarks on Ovid Butler's Nature." *Butler Alumnal Quarterly* (September 1881).

Money, Charles H. "The Fugitive Slave Law in Indiana." *Indiana Magazine of History* 17 (September 1921): 257–69.

"Ovid Butler and Indiana Christian Home Missionary Society." *Christian Record* (November 1849).

"Ovid Butler and Northwestern Christian University." *Christian Record* (April 7, 1850).

"Ovid Butler: Founder's Day." *Butler Alumnal Quarterly* (April 1916).

"Ovid Butler's Descendants Attending Butler University." *Butler Alumnal Quarterly* (date unknown).

Rodgers, Thomas E. "Civil War Letters as Historical Sources." *Indiana Magazine of History* 93 (June 1997): 105–10.

"Scot Butler Memorial Issue." *Butler Alumnal Quarterly* (April 1931).

Shaw, Henry K. "The Founding of Butler University, 1847–1855." *Indiana Magazine of History* 58 (September 1962): 233–63.

"South Side Christian Church." *Christian Record* (March 14, 1896).

OBITUARIES

Mrs. E. Anna [*sic*] Butler. *Christian Record* (August 26, 1882).

Chauncy Butler. *Indianapolis News*, October 4, 1937; *Indianapolis Star*, October 4, 1937; *Indianapolis Times*, October 9, 1937.

Chauncy Butler. *Indianapolis Star*, October 3, 1937.

Evelyn Mitchell Butler. *Indianapolis News*, undated. Indianapolis Public Library.

Scot Butler. *Indianapolis News*, January 15, 1931.

Scot Butler. *World Call* (March 1931): 35.

Scot Butler. Unidentified article. Indianapolis Public Library clippings file. Held by the editor.

Mrs. Scot Butler (Julia Wesley Dunn). Dated by hand 1937. Source unknown. Held by the editor.

Thomas McOuat Butler. *Christian Standard* (May 18, 1872).

David Owen Thomas. *Butler Collegian* (February 13 and 17, 1925).

Genealogical Charts

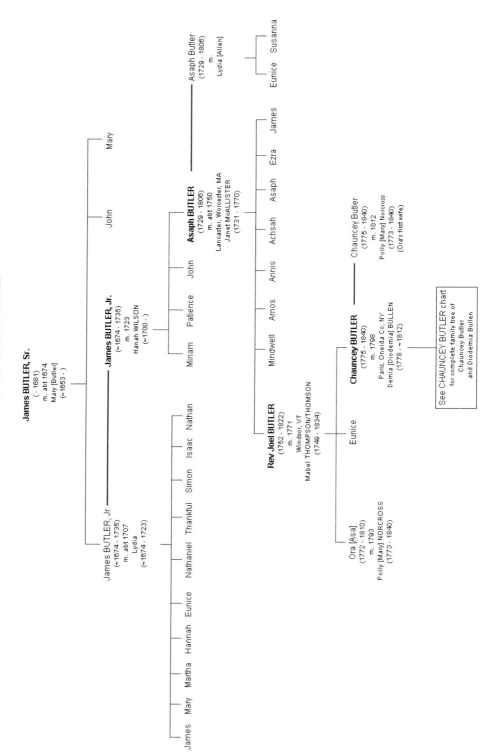

DESCENDANTS of JAMES and MARY BUTLER

James BUTLER, Sr.
(- 1681)
m. abt 1674
Mary [Butler]
(~1653 -)

James BUTLER, Jr.
(~1674 - 1735)
m. abt 1707
Lydia
(~1674 - 1723)

James   Mary   Martha   Hannah   Eunice   Nathaniel   Thankful   Simon   Isaac   Nathan

James BUTLER, Jr.
(~1674 - 1735)
m. 1723
Hanah WILSON
(~1700 -)

John   Mary

Rev Joel BUTLER
(1752 - 1822)
m. 1771
Windsor, VT
Mabel THOMPSON/THOMSON
(1749 - 1834)

Miriam   Patience   John

Asaph BUTLER
(1729 - 1806)
m. abt 1750
Lancaster, Worcester, MA
Janet McALLISTER
(1731 - 1770)

Eunice

Mindwell   Amos   Annis   Achsah   Asaph   Ezra   James

Asaph Butler
(1729 - 1806)
m.
Lydia [Allen]

Eunice   Susanna

Ora [Asa]
(1772 - 1810)
m. 1793
Polly [Mary] NORCROSS
(1773 - 1840)

Chauncey BUTLER
(1775 - 1840)
m. 1798
Paris, Oneida Co, NY
Demia [Diodemia] BULLEN
(1778 - ~1812)

Chauncey Butler
(1775 - 1840)
m. 1812
Polly [Mary] Norcross
(1773 - 1840)
(Ora's first wife)

See CHAUNCEY BUTLER chart
for complete family tree of
Chauncey Butler
and Diodemia Bullen

DESCENDANTS of CHAUNCEY and DIODEMA (BULLEN) BUTLER

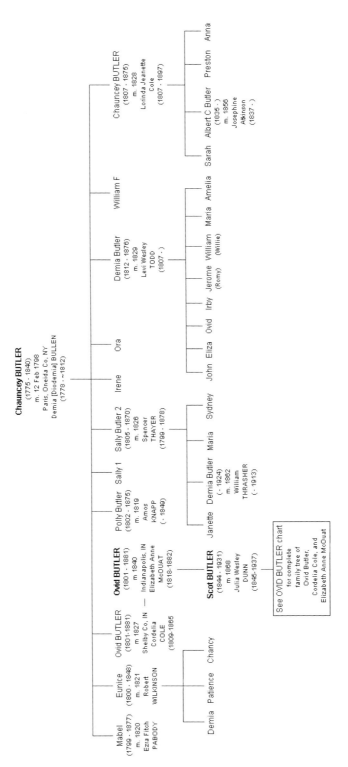

Chauncey BUTLER
(1775 - 1840)
m. 12 Feb 1798
Paris, Oneida Co, NY
Demia [Diodemia] BULLEN
(1778 - ~1812)

Mabel
(1799 - 1877)
m. 1820
Ezra Fitch
PABODY

Eunice
(1800 - 1848)
m. 1821
Robert
WILKINSON

Ovid BUTLER
(1801-1881)
m. 1827
Shelby Co, IN
Cordelia
COLE
(1809-1865)

Ovid BUTLER
(1801 - 1881)
m 1840
Indianapolis, IN
Elizabeth Anne
McOUAT
(1818-1882)

Polly Butler
(1802 - 1875)
m. 1819
Amos
KNAPP
(- 1849)

Sally 1

Sally Butler 2
(1805 - 1870)
m. 1826
Spencer
THAYER
(1799 - 1878)

Irene

Ora

Demia Butler
(1812 - 1876)
m. 1829
Levi Wesley
TODD
(1807 -)

William F

Chauncey BUTLER
(1807 - 1875)
m. 1828
Lorinda Jeanette
Cole
(1807 - 1897)

Sarah

Albert C Butler
(1835 -)
m. 1856
Josephine
Atkinson
(1837 -)

Preston

Anna

Demia   Patience   Chancy

Janette   Demia Butler   Maria
             (- 1924)
             m. 1862
             William
             THRASHER
             (- 1913)

Sydney

John   Eliza   Ovid   Irby   Jerome   William   Maria   Amelia
                                  (Romy)   (Willie)

Scot BUTLER
(1844 - 1931)
m 1868
Julia Wesley
DUNN
(1845-1937)

See OVID BUTLER chart
for complete
family tree of
Ovid Butler,
Cordelia Cole, and
Elizabeth Anne McOuat

DESCENDANTS of OVID BUTLER

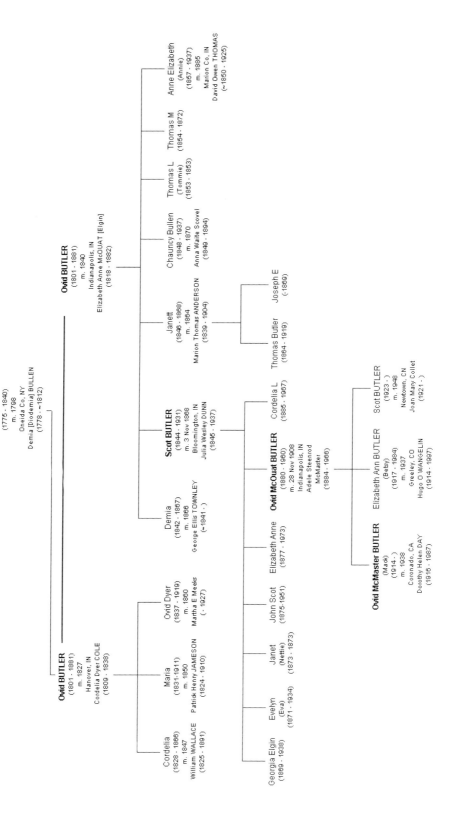

Chauncey BUTLER
(1775 - 1840)
m. 1798
Oneida Co, NY
Demia [Diodemia] BULLEN
(1778 - ~1812)

Ovid BUTLER
(1801 - 1881)
m. 1827
Hanover, IN
Cordelia Dyer COLE
(1809 - 1838)

Ovid BUTLER
(1801 - 1881)
m. 1840
Indianapolis, IN
Elizabeth Anne McOUAT [Elgin]
(1818 - 1882)

Cordelia
(1828 - 1866)
m. 1847
William WALLACE
(1825 - 1891)

Maria
(1831-1911)
m. 1850
Patrick Henry JAMESON
(1824 - 1910)

Ovid Dyer
(1837 - 1919)
m. 1860
Martha E Meeks
(- 1927)

Demia
(1842 - 1867)
m. 1866
George Ellis TOWNLEY
(~1841 -)

Scot BUTLER
(1844 - 1931)
m. 3 Nov 1868
Bloomington, IN
Julia Wesley DUNN
(1845 - 1937)

Janett
(1846 - 1868)
m. 1864
Marion Thomas ANDERSON
(1839 - 1904)

Chauncy Bullen
(1848 - 1937)
m. 1870
Anna Waite Scovel
(1849 - 1894)

Thomas L
(Tommie)
(1853 - 1853)

Thomas M
(1854 - 1872)

Anne Elizabeth
(Annie)
(1857 - 1937)
m. 1885
Marion Co, IN
David Owen THOMAS
(~1850 - 1925)

Georgia Elgin
(1869 - 1938)

Evelyn
(Eva)
(1871 - 1934)

Janet
(Nettie)
(1873 - 1873)

John Scot
(1875-1951)

Elizabeth Anne
(1877 - 1973)

Ovid McOuat BUTLER
(1880 - 1960)
m. 28 Nov 1908
Indianapolis, IN
Adele Steenrod
McMaster
(1884 - 1966)

Cordelia L
(1885 - 1967)

Thomas Butler
(1864 - 1919)

Joseph E
(-1869)

Ovid McMaster BUTLER
(Mack)
(1914 -)
m. 1938
Coronado, CA
Dorothy Helen DAY
(1916 - 1987)

Elizabeth Ann BUTLER
(Betsy)
(1917 - 1984)
m. 1937
Greeley, CO
Hugo D WANGELIN
(1914 - 1997)

Scot BUTLER
(1923 -)
Newtown, CN
Joan Mary Collet
(1921 -)

DESCENDANTS of DAVID and ELIZABETH (HARVIE) McOUAT

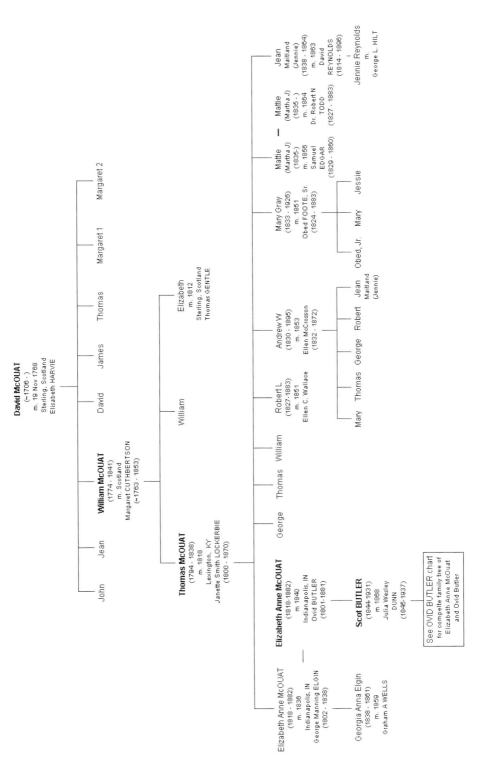

David McOUAT
(~1706 -)
m. 19 Nov 1768
Sterling, Scotland
Elisabeth HARVIE

John   Jean   **William McOUAT**   David   James   Thomas   Margaret 1   Margaret 2
(1774 - 1841)
m. Scotland
Margaret CUTHBERTSON
(~1763 - 1853)

Thomas McOUAT   William   Elizabeth
(1794 - 1838)   m. 1812
m. 1818   Sterling, Scotland
Lexington, KY   Thomas GENTLE
Janette Smith LOCKERBIE
(1800 - 1870)

George   Thomas   William   Robert L   Andrew W   Mary Gray   Mattie   Mattie   Jean
Elizabeth Anne McOUAT   (1827-1883) (1830 - 1895) (1833 - 1926) (Martha J) (Martha J) Maitland
(1818 - 1882)   m. 1851   m. 1853   m. 1851   (1835 -)   (1835 -)   (Jennie)
m. 1840   Ellen C. Wallace Ellen McCrosson Obed FOOTE, Sr. m. 1856 m. 1864 (1838 - 1864)
Indianapolis, IN   (1832 - 1872) (1824 - 1883) Samuel Dr. Robert N m. 1863
Ovid BUTLER   EDGAR TODD David
(1801-1881)   (1829 - 1860) (1827 - 1883) REYNOLDS
                                                                                                      (1814 - 1896)

Scot BUTLER   Mary   Thomas   George   Robert   Jean   Obed, Jr.   Mary   Jessie   Jennie Reynolds
(1844-1931)   Maitland   m.
m. 1868   (Jennie)   George L. HILT
Julia Wesley
DUNN
(1845-1937)

Elizabeth Anne McOUAT
(1818 - 1882)
m. 1836
Indianapolis, IN
George Manning ELGIN
(1802 - 1838)

Georgia Anna Elgin
(1838 - 1861)
m. 1859
Graham A WELLS

See OVID BUTLER chart
for compelte family tree of
Elizabeth Anne McOuat
and Ovid Butler

DESCENDANTS of WILLIAM and ELIZABETH (NEWALL) LOCKERBIE

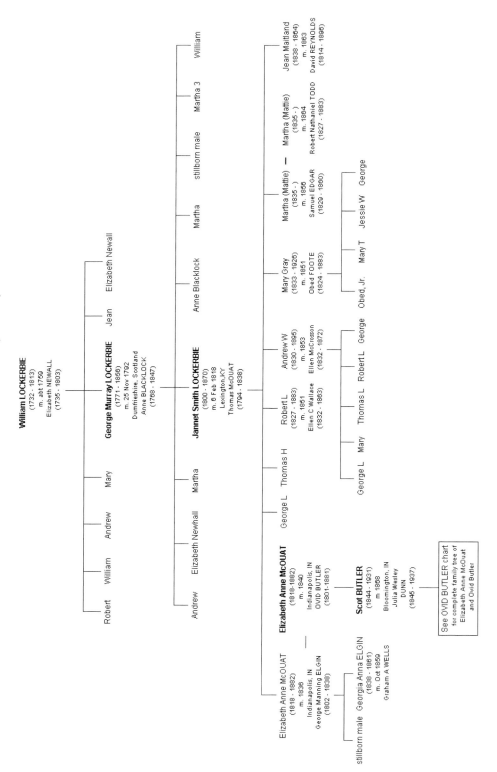

William LOCKERBIE
(1732 - 1813)
m. abt 1759
Elizabeth NEWALL
(1735 - 1803)

Robert William Andrew Mary **George Murray LOCKERBIE** Jean Elizabeth Newall
(1771 - 1856)
m. 25 Nov 1792
Dumfrieshire, Scotland
Anne BLACKLOCK
(1768 - 1847)

Andrew Elizabeth Newhall Martha **Jannet Smith LOCKERBIE** Anne Blacklock Martha stillborn male Martha 3 William
(1800 - 1870)
m. 6 Feb 1818
Lexington, KY
Thomas McOUAT
(1794 - 1838)

George L Thomas H Robert L Andrew W Mary Gray Martha (Mattie) Martha (Mattie) — Jean Maitland
(1827 - 1883) (1830 - 1895) (1833 - 1926) (1835 -) (1835 -) (1838 - 1864)
m. 1851 m. 1853 m. 1851 m. 1856 m. 1864
Ellen C Wallace Ellen McCrosson Obed FOOTE Samuel EDGAR Robert Nathaniel TODD David REYNOLDS
(1832 - 1863) (1832 - 1872) (1824 - 1883) (1829 - 1860) (1827 - 1883) (1814 - 1896)

Elizabeth Anne McOUAT
(1818 - 1882)
m. 1840
Indianapolis, IN
OVID BUTLER
(1801-1881)

George L Mary Thomas L Robert L George Obed, Jr. Mary T Jessie W George

Elizabeth Anne McOUAT
(1818 - 1882)
m. 1836
Indianapolis, IN
George Manning ELGIN
(1802 - 1838)

Scot BUTLER
(1844 - 1931)
m 1868
Bloomington, IN
Julia Wesley
DUNN
(1845 - 1937)

stillborn male Georgia Anna ELGIN
(1838 - 1861)
m. Oct 1859
Graham A WELLS

See OVID BUTLER chart
for complete family tree of
Elizabeth Anne McOUAT
and Ovid Butler

Index

Abolitionists, 7

Adams Express, 67, 70, 75

American Knights, 10

American Revolution, 152

Anderson, Miss _____ (sister of Marion Thomas Anderson), 95

Anderson, Janett /Net/Nettie (Butler), 27, 28n3, 34, 35, 36, 38, 47, 57, 60, 61, 62, 64–65, 67, 68, 69, 78, 79, 85, 86, 94, 95, 96, 97, 98, 99, 103, 107, 112, 121, 122, 126, 128, 134, 136, 137, 141, 142, 143n1, 145, 148n1, 161, 163, 164, 167, 172; letters from, 44–46; marriage, 64–65, 66, 67, 69; birth of son, 131–32, 135; illus., 17

Anderson, Joseph E., 163

Anderson, Marion Thomas, 28n5, 62, 64, 68, 70, 71, 75, 76, 79, 81, 86, 88, 92, 95, 97, 103, 112, 121, 122, 126, 128, 133, 135, 136, 142, 143n1, 163, 164, 172; marriage, 64–65, 66, 67, 69; and birth of son, 131–32; wounded, 136–37, 141, 182; escapes from Libby Prison, 175, 181; illus., 17

Anderson, Thomas Butler, 131–32, 134, 135, 136, 142, 143n1, 163, 164; illus., 18

Andersonville Prison, 37n3, 133, 163, 175

Annan, Dumfriesshire (Scotland), 155

Antietam (Md.), 168

Applegate, Berg, 125, 126n1, 127, 164

Applegate, Mary J. (Beaty), 28n4, 34, 35n7, 118, 122, 124, 125, 127, 132, 164

Arlington National Cemetery (Washington, D.C.), 179

Army of Tennessee, 168

Army of the Cumberland, 4, 9, 28n9, 29, 31, 43, 169, 179

Army of the Ohio, 166, 170

Army of the Potomac, 28n6, 83, 166

Army of the Republic, 37n4

Atkinson, Alonzo/Lon M., 36, 37n2, 59, 65, 67, 68, 70, 71, 75, 164, 165

Atkinson, Nancy Elizabeth (Burns), 37n2, 71, 165

Atlanta (Ga.), 82, 84, 104, 105, 107n2, 123, 126, 129, 168, 169, 179; campaign, 4, 173, 174; siege of, 78n1

Augusta (N.Y.), 152

AWOL (Absent without Leave), 73n4. *See also* French furlough

Bachtell, Samuel, 6

Baltimore (Md.), 60, 100, 101

Bannaels, Orlando, 119

Barbour, "Pet," 127

Bassett, Marcia Melissa. *See* Goodwin, Marcia Melissa (Bassett)

Beaty, Davey/Davy, 35n7, 88, 164

Beaty, John, 35n7, 40, 124, 125, 132

Beaty, Mary. *See* Applegate, Mary J. (Beaty)

Beaty, Ned, 125

Bence, Mrs. _____, 90, 164

Bence, Anna A. *See* Hobbs, Anna A. (Bence)

Bence, Mary E. *See* Fletcher, Mary E. (Bence)

Ben-Hur: A Tale of the Christ, 184

Benton, Allen R., 47, 165

Bethany College (Va.), 4

Billerica (Mass.), 151

Bingham, Joseph J., 128, 130, 165

Blacklock, Anne. *See* Lockerbie, Anne (Blacklock)
Bloomington, 170, 171
Boaz, William T., 124, 164
Bolton (Mass.), 152
Bragg, Braxton, 9, 30, 31, 41, 58, 165, 168
Brandenburg (Ky.), 9
Brewer, U. C., 102, 165
Bridgeport (Ky.), 58, 59n2, 93, 126, 165
Brown, Dr._____, 95
Brown, George, 63, 72, 165
Brown, Leonidas (Lidi) E., 49, 59, 165
Brown, Mary, 97, 165
Brown, Mate/Matti/Mati, 40, 102, 109, 165
Brown, Phil, 59, 97, 165
Brown, Ryland Thomas, 165
Brown, Thomas A., 63, 165
Brown, Tom, 72; death, 95, 97; funeral, 102
Brown, William, 72
Bullock, Avery, 154
Burford, Eugenia Frances. *See* McOuat, Eugenia Frances (Burford)
Burns, Mrs._____, 36, 49
Burns, Nancy Elizabeth. *See* Atkinson, Nancy Elizabeth (Burns)
Burnside, Ambrose Everett, 36, 37n4, 59, 163, 165
Butler, Dr._____, 133
Butler, Amos, 152
Butler, Amos (Asaph), 151
Butler, Anna Waite (Scovel), 38, 39n1, 55n1, 78, 111, 143, 145, 179; illus., 19
Butler, Anne Elizabeth/Annie. *See* Thomas, Anne Elizabeth/Annie (Butler)
Butler, Asaph, 152
Butler, Chauncey (Scot's grandfather), 151, 152, 153, 154, 167, 174, 183
Butler, Chauncey (Scot's uncle), 42, 59, 62, 79, 92, 103, 107, 108, 109, 113, 115, 116, 117, 118, 119, 133, 145, 166, 170, 173; illness, 55, 57, 61, 106; illus., 19
Butler, Chauncey (Scot's brother), 42, 63n9, 78, 79, 81, 83, 84, 87, 88, 90n1, 92, 93, 94, 95, 97, 98, 101, 105, 108,

110, 111, 113, 114, 115, 121, 125, 127, 132, 138, 145, 161, 165, 167, 172, 179, 183; marriage, 39n2; letters from, 72; and enlistment, 73n4
Butler, Cordelia (Delia) (Scot's half sister). *See* Wallace, Cordelia (Delia) (Butler)
Butler, Cordelia (Scot's daughter), 146
Butler, Cordelia Dyer (Cole), 32n2, 63n4, 80n5, 112n1, 155, 160, 166, 167, 169, 170, 174, 184
Butler, Demia (Scot's aunt). *See* Todd, Demia (Butler)
Butler, Demia (Scot's sister). *See* Townley, Demia (Butler)
Butler, Deodemia (Bullen) (Scot's grandmother), 152, 167
Butler, Elizabeth Anne (Scot's daughter), 146
Butler, Elizabeth Anne (McOuat) Elgin (Scot's mother), 1, 2, 46n5, 116, 125, 130, 134, 136, 140, 145, 148n1, 155, 157, 158, 159, 160, 161, 166, 167, 169, 171, 172, 175, 176, 178, 182, 183, 184; fears enlistment will be son's moral undoing, 3; writes of Morgan's raid, 9; and topics of letters from, 11; marriage, 32n2; letters from, 32–34, 35–37, 39–40, 49–51, 51–53, 55–57, 58–59, 60–61, 61–63, 63–65, 68–69, 73–74, 78–80, 80–82, 82–83, 84–85, 85–87, 89–90, 93–94, 94–96, 98–100, 101–2, 103–4, 107–8, 109–10, 110–12, 113–14, 114–15, 117, 118–19, 119–20, 120–21, 121–22, 122–23, 123–24, 126–27, 128–29, 131–32, 133–34, 136–38, 139–40, 142–43; illness, 141, 142; illus., 16, 23
Butler, Eunice. *See* Wilkinson, Eunice (Butler)
Butler, Evelyn Mitchell, 146
Butler, Ezra, 152
Butler, Georgia Elgin. *See* Clifford, Georgia Elgin (Butler)
Butler, Hannah Wilson, 152
Butler, Ira, 153
Butler, James, 152
Butler, James I, 151
Butler, James II, 151, 152

Butler, Jane McAllister, 152

Butler, Janet (Nettie) (Scot's daughter), 146, 171

Butler, Janett/Net/Nettie (Scot's sister). *See* Anderson, Janett/Net/Nettie (Butler)

Butler, Joel, 151, 152, 153, 154

Butler, John Scot (Scot's son), 146, 171

Butler, Julia Wesley (Dunn), 28n1, 33, 38, 45, 57n3, 59, 97, 104, 107, 121, 145, 146, 170, 174; letters to, 26–28, 77–78; has school in Greencastle, 45; illus., 17

Butler, Lorinda Janette (Cole), 79, 117, 133, 166, 169, 170; marriage, 80n5

Butler, Lydia, 152

Butler, Lydia Allen, 152

Butler, Mabel. *See* Pabody, Mabel (Butler)

Butler, Mabel (Thompson), 152, 153, 154

Butler, Maria (Scot's half sister). *See* Jameson, Maria (Butler)

Butler, Maria (Scot's niece), 63n5

Butler, Maria (Scot's cousin), 167

Butler, Martha (Meeks), 63n5, 167

Butler, Mary, 151

Butler, Ora (Asa), 152, 153

Butler, Ovid (Scot's father), 1, 35n6, 109, 111, 112n2, 113, 114, 115, 117, 118, 119, 120, 121, 125, 128, 145, 151, 152, 153, 154, 156, 160, 161, 166, 167, 169, 170, 171, 174, 177, 178, 183, 184; opposes slavery, 1, 2, 3, 8; and agreement to Scot's enlistment, 3; founds university, 3–4; breaks relationship with Alexander Campbell, 5n4; political activity of, 7, 8; and ownership of the *Journal,* 8, 13n1, 175, 181; and attitude toward Sons of Liberty, 11; letters from, 29–32, 41–42, 43–44, 53–55, 65–67, 69–71, 75–76, 91–92, 105–7, 116, 129–31, 134–36, 140–41, 148; marriage, 32n2; and farm at Keithsburg, 107, 175; illness, 121, 139, 141, 142; and hopes for sons, 138; university named for, 146; law career, 154–55, 173; illus., 16, 23

Butler, Ovid (Scot's son), 146

Butler, Ovid Dyer (Scot's half brother), 58, 59n1, 62, 63nn4–5, 99, 100n5, 104, 109, 117, 123, 136, 155, 167, 169

Butler, Polly (Norcross), 153

Butler, Sally. *See* Thayer, Sally (Butler)

Butler, Scot, 161, 164, 166, 168; enlistment, 1; writes recollections of war, 1, 5, 147; and experiences in Lexington (Ky.), 2–3; ill health stops first enlistment attempt, 3; physical description of, 3; joins U.S. Signal Corps, 4; letters from, 11, 26–28, 77–78; receives *Journal,* 12; academic career, 145, 146, 147, 148, 171; and extracurricular societies, 180; illus., frontispiece, 17, 24

Butler, Thomas Lockerbie, 148n1, 161

Butler, Thomas McOuat (Mack/Mackie), 95, 97, 102, 103, 107, 109, 111, 113, 116, 117, 121, 148, 161, 168; illus., 21

Butler, William E., 168

Butler College. *See* Butler University

Butler University, 4, 33, 35nn4–5, 37n2, 42, 45, 47, 48, 55, 64, 69n1, 78n2, 88, 91, 102n4, 104, 111, 119, 121, 145, 146, 147, 148, 164, 165, 166, 170, 171, 172, 174, 178, 179; board of trustees, 71n1; graduation, 93

Butler's Grove, 37n1, 101, 105, 111, 113, 114, 115, 116, 119, 133, 168, 175

Butternuts, 27, 28n8, 33, 47

Cain, Capt. ____, 132

Cain, Mrs. ____, 132

Camp Burnside (Indianapolis), 86

Camp Carrington (Indianapolis), 81

Camp Morton (Indianapolis), 51, 84, 174

Campbell, Alexander, 4, 5n2, 5n4

Campbell, Thomas, 5n1

Canasaraga (N.Y.), 153

Carrington, Gen. ____, 112

Carter, ____, 71

Cartersville (Ga.), 103

Cassville (Ga.), battle of, 173

Catterson, George Norwood, 80n3, 168

Catterson, Jean Maitland (McOuat), 168

Catterson, Robert Francis, 123, 168; marriage, 79, 80n3, 97

Catterson, Sarah E. (Norwood), 168; marriage, 79, 80n3

Cedar Bluff (Ga.), battle of, 172

Challer, Thurston, 129

Chattanooga, 54, 56, 58, 59, 60, 61, 62, 64, 65, 66, 67, 68, 70, 75, 79, 92, 110, 111, 112, 126, 128, 129, 131, 134, 135, 136, 138, 140, 168, 179; battle of, 4
Chicago, 36, 113, 119
Chickamauga (Ga.), 41, 42n1, 43, 46n4, 170; battle of, 4, 168
Christ Church (Indianapolis), 158
Christian Chapel (Indianapolis), 41n1, 79; festival, 86
Christian Church (Disciples of Christ), 1, 3–4, 5n1, 5n4, 145, 151, 166
Cincinnati, 83, 122, 139; defense of, 184
Cincinnati Gazette, 41, 60, 112
Cincinnati Herald and Philanthropist, 7
"City Greys," 83
City Hospital (Indianapolis), 86, 87, 90
City Regiment, 99, 101
Clark, George Rogers, 178
Clarksburg, 163
Cleburn, Patrick, 179
Cleveland, 36
Clifford, Georgia Elgin (Butler), 146
Clifford, Perry Hall, 146
Clifford, Scot Butler, 146
Coburn, Augustus, 39
Coburn, Caroline (Test), 41n2, 68, 72, 73n2, 86, 90, 169, 182
Coburn, John, 3, 4, 31, 32, 33, 36, 38, 40, 52, 54, 57, 67, 68, 73n2, 74, 121, 123, 132, 169, 170
Cole, Abel, 155
Cole, Albert, 109, 111, 112n1, 113, 116, 117, 169, 170
Cole, Anne. *See* Mathers, Anne (Cole)
Cole, Barton/Bart, 98, 169, 170
Cole, Cordelia Dyer. *See* Butler, Cordelia Dyer (Cole)
Cole, Josephine, 109, 112n1, 113, 169
Cole, Lorinda Janette. *See* Butler, Lorinda Janette (Cole)
Cole, Scot, 98, 169, 170
Cole, Viola, 95, 98, 169
Congressional Medal of Honor, 28n5
Connersville, 38, 61n1, 170
Copperheads, 8, 10, 11, 29, 32n3, 112, 113
Corydon, 9

Cotton, W. A., 91
Council Bluffs (Iowa), 95
Crab Orchard (Ky.), battle of, 4
Crawfish Spring (Chickamauga, Ga.), 41
Crawfordsville, 184
Crittenden, G. B., 170
Crittenden, Thomas Leonidas, 45, 46n4, 170
Crook, William, 175
Crown Hill Cemetery (Indianapolis), 95, 145, 148, 176, 178
Culver, _____, 93

Danville, 102n4
Darling (boat), 139
Davage, Charley. *See* Davidge, Charley
Davenport (Ill.), 119, 175
Davidge, Charley, 38, 39n4, 132, 170
Davis, Jefferson, 112
De Pauw University, 173
Demia Butler Society, 146, 180
Democratic party, 10, 132, 157, 158, 172, 180; Southern sympathies of, 2, 8; support of slavery causes members to leave, 7
Department of Missouri, 179
Department of the Cumberland, 3, 6n12, 73n4, 182
Dille, Israel C., 33, 34n1
Dodd, Harrison H., 10
"Dough faces," 2, 8
Draft, 11; riots, 131n1
Duke, Basil W., 9
Dumfries (Scotland), 176
Dumont, Gen. _____, 110
Duncan, Mrs. _____, 132
Duncan, John, 47, 64, 83
Duncan, Mary Ella (Sharpe) Moore, 49, 179
Duncan, Robert P., 34, 35n10, 46, 47, 49n3, 95, 170, 179
Dunn, Evelina (Mitchell), 28n1
Dunn, George G., 171
Dunn, John E., 57, 59, 60, 97, 170; mustered out, 93
Dunn, John Wesley, 28n1
Dunn, Julia Wesley. *See* Butler, Julia Wesley (Dunn)

Dunn, Moses F., 171
Dunn, Samuel, 171

Earlham College, 178
Early, Jubal, 184
Eaton, A. C., 91
Edgar, James, 62
Edgar, Martha/Mattie Jeanette (McOuat).
    See Todd, Martha/Mattie Jeanette
    (McOuat) Edgar
Edgar, Samuel A., 62, 63n6, 158, 171,
    182; illness, 79; marriage, 80n2
Eighth Regiment, 84
Eleventh Regiment, 184
Elgin, Elizabeth Anne (McOuat). *See*
    Butler, Elizabeth Anne (McOuat) Elgin
Elgin, George Manning, 5n5, 32n2, 39n3,
    158, 159, 160, 171, 184
Elgin, Georgia Anna. *See* Wells, Georgia
    Anna (Elgin)
Elgin, Margaret/Mollie. *See* Prescott,
    Margaret/Mollie (Elgin)
Elliott, Charles W., 146

Fairview (Rush Co.), 93
Fairview Academy, 165
Farlington, Capt. ____, 92
Fifty-first Regiment, 28n5, 45, 46n6, 66,
    69, 92, 163, 172, 181
Fifty-second Regiment, 139
Finley, ____, 62, 63, 68
First Methodist Church of Indiana
    (Greencastle), 173
First Presbyterian Church (Indianapolis),
    158
Fitz Walter, Theobald, 161n1
Fletcher, Allen, 164
Fletcher, Calvin, 73n1, 80n1, 155, 171
Fletcher, Ingram, 72, 73n1, 83, 95, 171;
    ill, 90, 93
Fletcher, Mary E. (Bence), 90n2, 164
Fletcher, Stephen Keyes, 72, 73n1, 127, 171
Fletcher, Stoughton, 80n1
Fletcher Place (Indianapolis subdivision),
    80n1
Fletcher's Trade Place, 78, 80n1, 88, 172
Flook, Henry R., 31, 32n4, 44, 86, 90,
    172; ill, 48, 49; wounded, 84

Foote, Mary/Mattie Gray (McOuat), 79,
    157, 158, 172; marriage, 80n4; illus., 16
Foote, Obed (Scot's uncle), 56, 57n2, 79,
    172; marriage, 80n4
Foote, Obed Butler (Obe) (Scot's cousin),
    95, 98, 100n3, 107, 108n3, 158, 172
Foote, Shelby, 175
Forest, Nathan, 67n1, 95
Forest Home (Indianapolis), 29, 32n1, 61,
    107, 109, 110, 117, 120, 121, 122,
    123, 125, 126, 128, 129, 131, 133,
    134, 139, 140, 142, 145, 166, 169,
    174, 178, 184; illus., 15
Fort Donelson (Tenn.), 184
Fort Negly (Tenn.), 54
Fort Sumter (S.C.), 177
Fourteenth Regiment, 168
Frankfort (Ky.), 59n2
Franklin (Ind.), 61, 62, 64, 86, 90, 172,
    173
Franklin (Tenn.), 26, 27, 28n2, 37, 39n1,
    169; battle of, 4
Franklin College, 48
Fredericksburg (Va.), 27, 28n7; battle of,
    166
Free Democracy, 7
Free Soil Banner, 7
Free Soil party, 7, 8
French furlough, 72, 73n4. *See also* AWOL
Frenyear, George J., 172; death, 45, 46n6
Frenyer, George J. *See* Frenyear, George J.
Frybarger, Margaret/Molly, 60, 61n1, 172
Fryberger, Col. ____, 31

Galt House (Louisville), 139
Gardner, Serg. John E., 45
Garfield, James A., 177, 179
General Hanna (steamer), 157
Geneva, 152, 154, 183. *See also* Vernon
Georgetown (Ky.), 160
German immigrants, 80n1
Germantown (Pa.), 155
Gettysburg (Pa.), 29
Gilmore, James Roberts (pseud. Edmund
    Kirke), 112n4
Gist, George Washington, 64, 65n3, 83,
    84, 173
Goddard, Col. ____, 64

Goodwin, Elijah, 95, 96n2, 172
Goodwin, Marcia Melissa (Bassett), 173
Granger, Maj. Gen. _____, 28, 54
Grant, Ulysses S., 36, 52, 59, 83, 124,
    166, 174, 184
Gray, William H., 175
Greencastle, 45, 93, 97, 173
Greensburg, 127, 154
Greenville (Tenn.), 177
Griffin, Harry, 127
Grooms, Ollie. *See* Tilford, Ollie (Grooms)
Grubbs, _____, 122
Gunther, Charles, 175
Guy's Gap (Tenn.), 33, 34n1, 37, 39n1,
    173

Hall, ___, 172
Hamrick, Sed, 68
Hannah Thurston (novel), 65n1, 71
Hanover, 36, 55, 61, 62, 88, 92
Hanover College, 173
Harison, _____, 125, 126
Harrison, Benjamin, 44, 52, 53n2, 54, 68,
    173
Helena (Ark.), 29
Henderson County (Ill.), 105, 113, 116
Hendricks, Thomas Andrews, 33, 35n6,
    173–74
Hillis, David, 88, 91
Hillis, Lottie, 127
Hilt, George L., 158, 178
Hilt, Jennie (Reynolds), 158, 178
Hobbs, Anna A. (Bence), 90n2, 164
Hobbs, Walter C., 164
Hoffman, John T., 130, 131n1
Holloway, William R., 181
Hood, John Bell, 105, 107n2, 130, 135,
    136
Hooker, Joseph, 27, 28nn6–7, 91, 105,
    107n2, 166, 179
Hoshour, Samuel K., 78, 174
Hoss, George Washington, 46n1, 93, 95,
    104, 107, 122, 174
Hoss, Mrs. George Washington, 45, 46n1
Hoss, Julia, 93
Hoss, Nellie, 93
Hovey, Alvin Peterson, 92, 133, 134n1,
    174

Howard, Gen. _____, 68
Hunt, A. L., 98

Indiana: constitution (1816), 2; Southern
    sympathies in, 7, 8, 10, 11; formation of
    Republican party in, 8; Morgan's raid in,
    9, 10; Democrats take control of
    legislature, 10; secret societies in, 10,
    180; treason trials in, 10–11; aid
    societies in, 12–13
Indiana Free Soil Democrat, 7
Indiana General Assembly, 4, 8, 10
Indiana Home Guard, 9
Indiana Institution for the Deaf and
    Dumb, 174
Indiana Journal, 13n1, 181
Indiana Legion, 8, 9
Indiana Sanitary Commission, 12, 13, 52,
    57, 179
Indiana State Journal, 8, 13n1, 60, 64, 65,
    76, 81, 89, 90, 93, 99, 100, 109, 123,
    129n1, 132, 165, 175
Indiana University (Bloomington), 145,
    171, 174
Indianapolis, 1, 33, 117, 155, 156, 157,
    160, 172; troops mustered in at, 9;
    sanitary fair, 12, 123; soldiers' homes
    established in, 13
Indianapolis Journal. See *Indiana State
    Journal*
Indianapolis Printing and Publishing
    House, 182
Indianapolis Sentinel, 8, 111, 128, 165,
    179
Invalid Corps, 86
Irish immigrants, 80n1
Irvington, 146, 147, 171, 178, 182

Jackson, _____, 127
Jackson, John T., 33, 34, 35n4
Jackson County, 154
Jacques, Col. _____, 112
James, Henry, 146
Jameson, Booth, 156
Jameson, Donald Ovid, 156
Jameson, Maria (Butler), 62, 63n3, 86, 90,
    136, 154, 155, 169, 174; illus., 18
Jameson, Mary Booth (Tarkington), 156

Jameson, Ovid Butler, 156
Jameson, Patrick Henry/P.H. (Doct.), 38,
    39n5, 62, 63n3, 122, 132, 174; illus., 18
Jeffersonville, 83, 137
Jennings, Jonathan, 174
Jennings County, 154, 155, 174
Johnston, Joseph E., 30, 105, 107n2

Kankakee River, 124
Keithsburg (Ill.), 35, 37n1, 38, 88, 96,
    103, 108, 109, 112n1, 113, 117, 119,
    124, 129, 133, 134, 145, 169, 175
Kennesaw Mountain (Ga.), battle of, 173
Kentucky: and undeclared support of
    either North or South, 7; turmoil in, 8
Kentucky Gazette, 160
Kentucky Raiders, 176
Kingston (Ga.), 90
Kirke, Edmund. *See* Gilmore, James
    Roberts
Knights of the Golden Circle, 10, 180
Knightstown, 13, 62, 175
Knoxville (Tenn.), 66, 166
Kokomo, 65, 66, 67, 86, 141, 142

Ladies National Covenant, 81
Ladies' Home, 13
Laing, Sam. *See* Loring, Sam
Lake Superior, 39
Lala Rhook (poem), 62, 71
Lancaster (Mass.), 151, 152
Lane, Henry S., 14n3, 177
Lasselle v State, 2
Lee, Robert E., 28nn6–7, 29, 30, 81
Les Miserables (novel), 52
Lexington (Ky.), 2, 59n2, 155, 156, 158
Libby Prison (Richmond, Va.), 36, 37n3,
    60, 62, 66, 69, 163, 169, 175, 181
Libby Prison War Memorial Museum, 175
Libertarians, 7
Lincoln, Abraham, 7, 70, 112n4, 113,
    128, 130, 166, 175, 177, 179, 180, 184
Lincoln County (Ky.), 158
Lockerbie (Scotland), 155
Lockerbie, Anne (Blacklock), 155, 175,
    176
Lockerbie, George Murray, 2, 155, 156,
    158, 159, 175, 176; illus., 22

Lockerbie, Janette Smith. *See* McOuat,
    Janette Smith (Lockerbie)
Loing, Sam. *See* Loring, Sam
Long, Henry, 57
Longstreet, James, 179
Loring, Sam, 93, 124
Lost Mountain (Ga.), battle of, 173
Louisville (Ky.), 6n13, 33, 52, 54, 59n2,
    137, 139, 156

Madison, 154
The Magnificent Ambersons (novel), 156
Marietta (Ga.), 97; battle of, 173
Marion County Seminary, 157
Martin, Dr. _____, 139
Masonic Hall (Indianapolis), 81, 181
Massachusetts Bay Company, 151
Mathers, Mr. _____, 117, 170
Mathers, Anne (Cole), 117, 169, 170
Mathesian Society, 78, 80
Mathus, Anne, 107
May, A. P., 93
May, John, 158
McClellan, George B., 132, 177
McCrosson, Ellen Morton. *See* McOuat,
    Ellen Morton (McCrosson)
McOuat, Andrew W., 157, 158, 176;
    illus., 20
McOuat, Elizabeth Anne. *See* Butler,
    Elizabeth Anne (McOuat) Elgin
McOuat, Ellen C. (Wallace), 46n5, 158,
    176; illness, 42, 56; death, 44, 45; illus.,
    19
McOuat, Ellen Morton (McCrosson), 157,
    158, 176; illus., 20
McOuat, Eugenia Frances (Burford), 176
McOuat, Foote & Company, 157
McOuat, George Lockerbie, 157; illus., 21
McOuat, Janette Smith (Lockerbie), 2,
    35n8, 115, 128, 155, 156, 157, 158,
    167, 172, 175, 176, 178, 182; illness,
    138; illus., 22
McOuat, Jean Maitland. *See* Catterson,
    Jean Maitland (McOuat)
McOuat, Jean/Jennie Maitland. *See*
    Reynolds, Jean/Jennie Maitland
    (McOuat)
McOuat, Mack Butler, 158

McOuat, Martha/Mattie Jeanette. *See*
    Todd, Martha/Mattie Jeanette (McOuat)
    Edgar
McOuat, Mary/Mattie Gray. *See* Foote,
    Mary/Mattie Gray (McOuat)
McOuat, Robert Lockerbie, 42, 44, 45,
    46n5, 79, 100n2, 158, 176; injured, 99;
    and California gold rush, 157; illus., 19
McOuat, Thomas (Scot's grandfather),
    155, 156–57, 158, 159, 160, 167, 172,
    175, 176, 182; buys land in
    Indianapolis, 2; illus., 22
McOuat, Thomas Harvey, 157, 160
McOuat, William, 157
McOuat & May, 158
McOuat family: Southern sympathies of,
    3, 115, 129, 158, 171, 172, 176; and
    construction of St. Paul Episcopal
    Church, 181
Meeks, Martha. *See* Butler, Martha
    (Meeks)
Memphis (Tenn.), 139
Mercer County (Ill.), 37n1
Merrill, Jesse, 6n13, 42n1, 65n2, 168
Mexican War, 184
Minneapolis (Minn.), 133, 178
Minnesota, 38, 88, 100
Missionary Ridge (Tenn.), 136
Mississippi, 39n1
Missouri Compromise, 8
Missouri River, 51
Mitchell, Evelina. *See* Dunn, Evelina
    (Mitchell)
Moore, Joe, 179; marriage, 49
Moore, Mary Ella (Sharpe). *See* Duncan,
    Mary Ella (Sharpe) Moore
Moore, Thomas, 63n7, 71
Moores, Mr. _____ (of Merrill's Bookstore),
    86
Morgan, George W., 4, 6n12
Morgan, John Hunt, 9–10, 29, 30, 31, 33,
    34, 163, 166, 176–77
Morgan's Raiders, 9–10, 176
Morris, Thomas Armstrong, 86, 87n2, 88,
    93, 177
Morris, Tom, 93; ill, 88, 95
Morrison, Alec, 95
Morrison, Charley, 95

Morrison, Jim, 95
Morrison, Lizzie, 95
Morrison, Sam, 95
Morton, Oliver Perry, 3, 31, 38, 70, 72,
    74, 83, 109, 173, 174, 177–78, 180,
    181, 184; becomes governor, 8; calls for
    troops, 9; and opposition from the
    Democratic party in the legislature, 10;
    and organization of aid societies, 12, 13
Mullins, Henrietta, 61, 62, 68
Murfreesboro (Tenn.), 37, 39n1, 75, 173;
    battle of, 4
Myer, A. J., 6n13

Nashville (Tenn.), 37, 38, 39n1, 40, 47,
    51, 52, 54, 55, 56, 58, 59, 60, 62, 63,
    64, 67, 68, 70, 73n4, 75, 84, 86, 108,
    109, 110, 114, 131, 133, 134, 135,
    136, 137, 139, 140, 142, 163, 169;
    battle of, 4, 28n5, 173, 182
New Albany, 31
New Hope Church (Ga.), battle of, 173
New Mexico Territory, 184
New York (ship), 155
New York Medical Association, 183
New York Tribune, 181
Newcomb, Eliza (Pabody), 100n7, 178
Newcomb, Horatio C., 100, 178
Niagara (N.Y.), 36
Ninety-seventh Regiment, 168
Noblesville, 68, 94, 96, 117
North Western Christian College. *See*
    Butler University
North Western Christian University. *See*
    Butler University
Northwestern Confederacy, 10
Norwood, Sarah E. *See* Catterson, Sarah E.
    (Norwood)

Ohio River, 64
One Hundred Ninth Regiment, 170
One Hundred Seventh Regiment, 82n1,
    164, 167, 170, 182
One Hundred Thirty-second Regiment,
    63n9, 65n3, 69n1, 73n4, 89, 90n1, 92,
    95, 105, 165, 171, 172, 183
One Hundred Twenty-second Regiment, 72
One Hundredth Regiment, 60

Ontanogan (Mich.), 39
Order of Treason, 10, 180

Pabody, Eliza. *See* Newcomb, Eliza
    (Pabody)
Pabody, Ezra Fitch, 178
Pabody, Mabel (Butler), 88, 89, 178; ill,
    83
Paducah (Ky.), 139
Parish, _____, 122
Patriotic Women of Indiana, 12
Peace Democrats, 8, 180
Peachtree Creek (Ga.), battle of, 107n2,
    173
Penrod (novel), 156
People's party, 7
Philadelphia, 34, 155, 176
Pickerell, _____, 119
Pittsburg (Ind.), 8
Pittsburgh (Pa.), 154
Pope, Joe, 133, 134n1
Port Hudson (La.), 29
Portland (Maine), 170
Porton, Mr. _____, 81
Post, Col. _____, 137
Presbyterian Churches: Fourth
    (Indianapolis), 39
Prescott, Margaret/Mollie (Elgin), 38,
    39n3, 45, 58, 171
Progressive Citizens Education Society, 174
Pythonian Society, 180

Rappahannock River, 28n6
"Recollections," 1, 5, 147
Red River Expedition, 95
Redondo (Calif.), 179
Reeves, Mr. _____, 93
Republican National Convention (1864),
    100n6
Republican party, 3, 7, 8, 10, 13n1
Resaca (Ga.), 90; battle of, 173
Reynolds, David, 178; illus., 20
Reynolds, Jean/Jennie Maitland (McOuat),
    58, 59n3, 79, 157, 158, 178; illus., 16,
    20
Reynolds, Jennie. *See* Hilt, Jennie (Reynolds)
Richmond (Ind.), 107, 108n1, 178
Richmond (Ky.), 164

Richmond (Va.), 28, 37n3, 57, 112, 163,
    175
Riley, James Whitcomb, 156
Ringgold (Ga.), 77, 78n1
Ringgold Gap (Ga.), battle of, 78n1, 179
Robert Moore (boat), 139
Rochester (N.Y.), 178
Rock Island (Ill.), 113, 114
Rome (Ga.), 33, 66
Rosecrans, William Starke, 27, 33, 41, 42,
    48, 64, 168, 176, 179
Rubicon River, 27, 28n6
Rush County, 93

Sailors' and Soldiers' Homes Society, 12,
    13
Salem, 9
Sanders, Henry, 63
Sanders, Mrs. _____, 63
Savannah (Ga.), 136
Scipio, 154
Scott County (Ky.), 9, 158, 171
Scovel, Anna Waite. *See* Butler, Anna
    Waite (Scovel)
Scovel, H. G., 54, 55n1, 67, 70, 75, 96,
    137, 143
Scovel, Mrs. H. G., 96, 97, 137
Scovel, Mary, 62, 63, 69, 86, 88, 94, 96,
    111, 139, 143, 179; attends Butler
    University, 54, 55n1
Seaton, Capt. _____, 63
Sedgwick, John, 28n7
Seminary on University Square
    (Indianapolis), 169
Seventh Minnesota Regiment, 50, 185
Seventieth Regiment, 52, 93, 99, 173
Sharpe, Mary Ella. *See* Duncan, Mary Ella
    (Sharpe) Moore
Shaw, Edward, 70, 71n1, 75, 179–80
Shaw's Carriage Company, 179
Shelby, Isaac, 180
Shelby County (Ind.), 95, 155, 180
Shelbyville (Ind.), 35n6, 154, 173
Shelbyville (Ky.), 154
Shenandoah (Va.), 168
Sheridan, Philip H., 121, 124
Sherman, William T., 4, 78n1, 79, 82, 85,
    86, 90, 91, 97, 126, 129, 134, 136, 169

Shiloh (Tenn.), 34n1, 39n1, 170, 173, 174, 184
Short, Lydia, 181
Sigourney, Lydia, 35n5
Sigournean Casket, 33, 34
Sigournean Literary Society, 35n5, 180
Sixteenth Regiment, 164
Slavery, 1, 2, 3, 4, 5n4, 7, 8, 141, 156
Smith, Miss _____, 122
Smithfield (N.Y.), 152
Smithland (Ky.), 139
Soldiers Home, 84
Soldiers' Aid Society, 13
Sons of Liberty, 10, 112, 128, 130, 132, 180
Southport, 79
Springfield (Ill.), 62
Spurior, George, 36
St. Louis, 35, 50, 51
St. Paul (Minn.), 35, 36
St. Paul Episcopal Church (Indianapolis), 100n4, 176, 181
Stanton, Edwin M., 183
Stevenson (Ala.), 73n4, 86, 92, 93
Stirlingshire (Scotland), 156
Stone, Barton W., 5n1
Stone-Campbell movement, 1, 2
Stone's River (Tenn.), 170
Streight, Abel D., 28n5, 81, 112, 128–29, 137, 163, 172, 181; capture, 66, 67n1
Stringfellow, Horace, Jr., 99, 100n4, 181
Stuart, J. E. B., 9
Sulgrove, Berry R., 13n1, 100, 175, 181
Sullivan (N.Y.), 153
Sunbeam (steamer), 39

Tammany Hall (N.Y.), 131n1
Tarkington, Booth, 156
Tarkington, Mary Booth. See Jameson, Mary Booth (Tarkington)
Taylor, Bayard, 64, 65n1, 71, 181–82
Teacher's College (Indianapolis), 147
Test, Thaddeus, 182; death, 39, 41n2
Thayer, Demia. See Thrasher, Demia (Thayer)
Thayer, Sally (Butler), 182
Thayer, Spencer, 182
Third Division, Fourth Corps, 135

Third Regiment, Minnesota Volunteer Infantry, 185
Thirty-first Regiment, 72, 74
Thirty-third Regiment, 1, 3, 28n9, 31, 34n1, 52, 53n1, 56, 57n1, 70, 72, 73, 86, 93, 169, 172, 184
Thomas, _____ (sanitary agent for Indiana), 70, 71
Thomas, Anne Elizabeth/Annie (Butler), 36, 37n5, 40, 102, 103, 109, 111, 113, 116, 117, 121, 129, 161, 166; illus., 21
Thomas, David Owen, 166
Thomas, Henry, 135, 136n1, 182
Thompson's Station (Tenn.), 169; battle of, 28n2
Thrasher, Demia (Thayer), 107, 108n2, 182
Thrasher, William M., 107, 108n2, 182
Tilford, J. M., 78n4, 182
Tilford, Julia, 78
Tilford, Ollie (Grooms), 118, 124, 127
Tilford, Samuel E., 78n4, 81, 82n2, 118, 127, 182
Todd, Demia (Butler), 102n3, 182
Todd, Irby Smith, 62, 63n2, 72, 92, 103, 182; ill, 88; injured, 94; in hospital in Knoxville, 101, 102n3
Todd, Jerome Jillete (Romy), 62, 63n2, 69, 72, 73n5, 78, 83, 88, 95, 102n3, 183
Todd, Levi W., 101, 102n3, 182
Todd, Martha/Mattie Jeanette (McOuat) Edgar, 62, 63n6, 73n5, 157, 158, 171, 182, 183; marriage, 78, 79, 80n2, 85; illus., 16, 21
Todd, Ovid, 62, 63n2, 72, 73n5, 88, 92, 182
Todd, Robert Nathaniel, 73n5, 158, 182; marriage, 79, 80n2, 85
Todd, William P. (Willie), 63n2, 72, 73n5, 78, 88, 94, 102n3, 182
Townley, Demia (Butler), 27, 28n4, 29, 33, 34, 35n4, 36, 37, 44, 45, 61, 62, 64, 68, 74, 78, 84, 86, 94, 95, 98, 99, 101, 103, 108, 109, 115, 127, 132, 133, 145, 148n1, 161, 164, 167; letters from, 37–38, 46–47, 48–49, 87–88, 96–97, 125–26; teaches at Franklin College, 48; returns from Nashville,

107; illness, 119, 120, 121, 122, 123, 124, 126, 128, 134, 142; illus., 18
Townley, George Ellis, 167
Townsend, Dr. _____, 62
Tullahoma (Tenn.), 170; campaign, 179
Tweed, William "Boss," 131n1
Twelfth Regiment, 108n2, 182
Twenty-fourth Regiment, 174
Typhoid fever, 95

Union Clubs, 10
Union Depot (Indianapolis), 177
Union Leagues, 10
United States Sanitary Commission, 14n13, 60, 183
United States Signal Corps, 4–5, 6n13, 27, 28n9, 32, 38, 41, 54, 64, 65n2, 66, 69, 70, 120, 168, 171, 172
University of Chicago, 147
University of Heidelberg (Ger.), 145, 171

Van Dyke, Henry, 146
Vance, Samuel C., 89, 90n1, 98, 108, 183
Vawter, _____, 90
Vawter, Eliza (Scot's cousin), 62, 90
Vawter family, 183
Vernon, 61, 62, 64, 86, 88, 89, 92, 101, 103, 154, 172, 174, 178, 183; Morgan's raid in, 10, 176. *See also* Geneva
Vernon Seminary, 154
Vicksburg (Miss.), 29, 36

Wabash College, 169
Wainwright, Maria, 98, 100n2
Wainwright, Samuel, 100n2
Wallace, _____ (with Chauncey Butler), 81, 83
Wallace, Dr. _____, 64
Wallace, Andrew, 80n1
Wallace, Cordelia (Delia) (Butler), 38, 39n6, 40, 62, 86, 101, 108, 110, 111, 132, 136, 143, 155, 169, 184

Wallace, David, 32n5, 102n2, 184
Wallace, Ellen C. *See* McOuat, Ellen C. (Wallace)
Wallace, Ester, 132
Wallace, Jim, 34
Wallace, Jimmy, 101; illness, 79
Wallace, Lew, 32n5, 101, 102n2, 169, 174, 182, 184
Wallace, W. J., special agent of Gov. Morton, 70, 71
Wallace, William, 31, 32n5, 38, 40, 41n3, 93, 99, 101, 102n1, 108, 111, 137, 169, 173, 182, 184; marriage, 39n6; illus., 22
Wallingford, Estis, 56, 57n1, 184
Washington, D.C., 81, 184
Waterbury (Vt.), 152
Webb, _____, 122
Wells, Doct. *See* Wells, Graham A./H.
Wells, Georgia Anna (Elgin), 148n1, 160, 171, 184
Wells, Graham A./H., 122, 138, 184
Whig party, 7, 8, 13n1, 175
White County, 39
White River, 156, 157
Wild Cat (Ky.), 169
Wiley, W. H., 91
Wilkinson, Chancy, 50, 51n1, 185
Wilkinson, Eunice (Butler), 51n1, 152, 185
Wilkinson, Robert, 51n1, 185
Wilson, Woodrow, 146
Woburn (Mass.), 151
Women's rights, 4
Woollen, W. W., 154

Yankton (S.Dak.), 185
Yeats, William Butler, 146
Young Ladies' Literary Society, 35n5

Zollicoffer, Felix, 169